MONEY AND THE MATURE WOMAN

How to Hold On to Your Income, Keep Your Home, Plan Your Estate

FRANCES LEONARD

ADDISON-WESLEY PUBLISHING COMPANY

Reading, Massachusetts   Menlo Park, California   New York
Don Mills, Ontario   Wokingham, England   Amsterdam   Bonn
Sydney   Singapore   Tokyo   Madrid   San Juan
Paris   Seoul   Milan   Mexico City   Taipei

To Richard, my husband and best friend

Library of Congress Cataloging-in-Publication Data

Leonard, Frances, 1939–
    Money and the mature woman : how to hold on to your income, keep
your home, plan your estate / Frances Leonard.
      p.   cm.
    Includes index.
    ISBN 0-201-60897-9
    ISBN 0-201-62700-0 (pbk.)
    1. Aged women—Finance, Personal. 2. Retirement income.
3. Estate planning.   I. Title.
HG179.L4417 1993   92-34822
332.024′042—dc20   CIP

Jacket design by One Plus One Studio
Jacket photography by Ron Busselen
Text design by Anna George
Set in 10.5-point Garamond by CopyRight, Inc.

1 2 3 4 5 6 7 8 9-ARM-97969594
First printing, January 1993
First paperback printing, February 1994

Contents

Introduction:
Your Sex, Your Age, and Your Money

The world of money is different for you and me. We're women. And that can make a lot of difference when it comes to strategies for survival — especially investment strategies, estate planning, and managing medical costs in our post-fifty-five years:

- With more years ahead of her, a female investor is "younger" than a male investor of the same age. Her investment portfolio might handle more risk.
- A man is better off taking Social Security at sixty-two than is a woman.
- Social Security and Medicare favor women; pensions favor men.
- Women must plan for two deaths; men, just one.
- The average man's estate will provide for his wife; hers will not include him at all.

This book is about these differences, and many more. In the discussions that follow, we'll talk about these issues and how awareness of them can give you the edge in the great money game. The goal is to get you up and running and in control of your own financial future so that the choices you make will be the very best possible for your very best future.

The first step is to acknowledge that men and women arrive at maturity from different places — and proceed through it to different futures. Let's call this gender awareness. Both men and women can use gender awareness to their advantage in developing their investment and financial programs. Knowing whether a particular option favors the average man or disfavors the average woman can give you the boost you're looking for as you plan for the final third of your life.

Men are welcome here, certainly — gender-aware strategies will work for everyone. But what follows tilts toward women by using (fictional) illustrations drawn from our own lives to explore the many investment and planning options available.

Gender-aware financial planning is not difficult to master. It's all a matter of keeping in mind a few things we all know anyway and thinking through how they'll affect a particular course of action. These commonly known differences between (average) women and men are:

- Women start retirement with less money than do men.
- Women live longer than men.
- Most women die single; most men die married.

Women drag with them into retirement the financial effects of years of discrimination in the work force, their biological and social roles of caregiving and birth, and gender biases in important economic laws such as Social Security and pensions. We begin our retirement years poorer than men by about 40 percent; then, to compound our problems, we live one-third longer after the age of sixty-five, thus exposing our fixed incomes to relentless erosion from inflation. Women live longer but die poorer.

Finally, as a consequence of longevity and the tradition of women marrying somewhat older men, the average woman can expect about fifteen years of widowhood; the average man, none.

We'll see how each of these factors makes critical differences in investment and planning strategies — from applying for Social Security to writing your will. With gender awareness, we can go a long way toward closing the gap with men. We women must plot a different course to arrive at the same place.

First, let's take a look at you. You were lucky enough to have been born into the twentieth century. In 1850, the life expectancy of the average American was only forty. But in 1993, if you were born a female sixty years ago, you can expect thirty-one more years of life if you're in good health and have good habits and good genes. You're expected to live to ninety-one!

Chances are, you feel pretty good about yourself, too. Thirty years ago, researchers found that women's mental health peaked at twenty, declined steadily until forty, then sharply declined compared to men. The same studies, repeated fifteen years later, found that this was no longer true. Mills College, a women's college, recently polled its alumnae and learned that the peak of self-satisfaction came after age fifty.

You are lucky as well to be a decade or so older than the baby boom. In 1900, only 4 percent of the population was over sixty-five. As oddities, these few folks could do little to combat harmful stereotypes of helpless old biddies and geezers. Today, nearly one in eight Americans is over sixty-five — and in twenty years, it will be one in five. And this will be a female generation (more about this later, but never underestimate the significance of this fact). And of course, soon to enter their sixth decade, the baby boomers are changing the face of aging. The more positive media image will benefit everyone older as well.

Your generation is wealthier than the boomers can expect to be at the same age — and any American generation now foreseeable. Despite the problems you have with pensions and health benefits, younger generations will probably have it worse. Pensions and health benefits are eroding in the workplace, especially among younger workers of both genders. Real wages for boomers are significantly lower than for you — their parents — with costs of housing, college tuitions, taxes, and medical care significantly higher. Your golden years will gleam like no other in history *and* in the foreseeable future.

Of course, this upbeat picture ignores the gap between the income and assets of males and females over fifty-five. Your generation is stamped with decades of economic discrimination against women so pervasive that scarcely any aspect of life escaped it. And this economic gap is not expected to end soon: experts predict that by the time today's thirty-five-year-old retires, poverty for retired people will be restricted to *women* living alone. Our job here is to recognize these traps and develop strategies to avoid them.

Each generation has its own style, forged in the heat of its common experiences. You will not become today's "old lady" stereotype. That was another generation's way of aging. Each generation writes a new book, adopts a new look — and you will, too. Born in the 1920s, 1930s, or 1940s? You are shaped by depression, war, boom times, frozen food, TV, movies, paperback books — and a technical explosion like none other in history.

And now you can expect that one-third of your life remains to live and plan for — and planning is what we'll do in the pages that follow. We'll keep an eye out for common gender-blind strategies that don't work for us the same way they work for men — and that thus exacerbate our unfavorable economic circumstances and confusion.

One example: Financial advisers typically suggest that retirement income be 60 to 80 percent of preretirement income. Fine for many men with good pensions, lots of Social Security, investments, a higher base to start from — and one-third fewer years to plan for. Women should plan to replace at least 100 percent of their preretirement income, and even then will still fall short of the average retired man's income.

In addition, women need to plan for this unavoidable reality: chances are overwhelming that we will die single. Eighty-five percent of us do, while 85 percent of men die married. This difference in marital status at the end of our lives augurs far more than a lonely road ahead. *Marital status deter-*

mines wealth. At all ages, but especially in later years, if you draw a line between the American haves and have-nots, the single most reliable predictor of wealth is not race or gender, but marital status. If you put the marrieds on one side of the line and the unmarrieds on the other, you will divide the poor from the rich.

Most of us women will find ourselves on the unfortunate side of the line in our last years; most men will not. To prepare for this eventuality takes different planning from that for married life. And in these pages we will work it through.

The female proportion of the population increases with every passing year. And here you lucked out again. Coming up fast, friends, is the biggest bunch of old folks this country has ever seen. And since old folks are mostly womenfolk, within a decade the national agenda could be set by women. Over the next twenty years, as the boomers enter retirement, women will become the majority in the largest (and "voting-est") population segment in the land. Women's concerns will finally be fully attainable through the ballot. We can elect women into office and fund education, child care, and health. And you can expect to live to see this day — the first time in American history when women will control the political agenda.

You are already an extraordinarily lucky woman.

Now let's get to work on improving your fortune.

1
Every Woman for Herself
Finance 101

The Big Three sources of retirement income are traditionally seen as investment income, Social Security, and pensions. All three carry subtle, but important, gender biases, which mean planning differences for women and men. In addition, and out of necessity, today's mature woman is adding fourth and fifth income sources: a paid job and home equity. The traditional three retirement standbys have proved just too fragile for many women — so as men retire earlier and earlier on their pensions, women do so later and later. At the same time, many women are living on the equity in their homes.

So a man's retirement income stool stands on three legs:

- Social Security
- pension
- investment income

And a woman's stands on five:

- Social Security
- pension
- investment income

- employment
- home equity

In the chapters that follow, we'll learn how women can build all five legs; then hold on to their gains against con artists and medical catastrophe; and finally, how to construct an estate plan of which any woman would be proud.

We'll start with investment income, since it is the safety net for weaknesses in the other four: weaknesses that affect the futures of the vast majority of women in America.

I am a firm believer in every woman for herself. By this I mean controlling your own investment programs. No one, no matter how responsible and qualified, has your interests at heart as keenly as you do. You are quite capable of learning enough about the common investment vehicles around to make your own decisions about their role, if any, in your portfolio.

In fact, you already know much more than you think. Stocks, bonds, and other securities are sold in a marketplace — and you already know heaps about markets. When you buy more cans of soup when prices are low than when they are high, you end up with a cupboard full of savings. The financial community would say you are "dollar-cost averaging your portfolio of equities." When you get a raincheck on an advertised special, you're locking in today's price for a future purchase. Financiers would talk about the "futures market" and call your raincheck an "option."

The principle is the same whether it be soup or securities. In this chapter we will learn about common investment vehicles, translating the financier's jargon into our own. You'll find that the principles that guide sound investing are the same ones that rule your weekly budget. "High finance" sounds intimidating — but for a woman with decades of marketing behind her, it is just buying and selling, and we women know a lot about that.

Because we are so dependent on our investments, we women are very vulnerable to the intimidation factor. We're so afraid of doing the wrong thing that we are much too likely to do it anyway by putting all our eggs in the one basket we understand: insured bank or savings deposits. Or we go the other way, abdicating all responsibility and turning our affairs over to a broker or money manager. Worse yet, in our desperation and ignorance, we fall victim to scams and swindles that can wipe us out.

In this chapter we will describe common investment devices suitable for most women's portfolios, along with their advantages and disadvantages. We'll explain how they work, using plain English and illustrations drawn from our own everyday experiences. Then, after we've become comfortable with what's out there, in the next chapter we'll discuss investment strategies.

The purpose of this chapter is to remove the mystery surrounding esoterica such as zero-coupon bonds, mutual funds, treasuries, Ginnie Maes, tax-exempt bond funds, and so forth — and to make you as comfortable with them as you are with your passbook savings. The goal is to enhance your own ability to decide for yourself how your funds will be managed, and what degree of professional advice is appropriate for you.

For perspective, remember that virtually all investments are one of two things: equity (you own something) or debt (you loaned someone money). As you read about the types of investments that follow, keep in mind that they are all variations on this two-note theme: debt and equity, equity and debt. We'll talk more about debt and equity as we go along; it's enough for now to know that the financial universe is a limited one — quite manageable, in fact, for you and me.

We'll begin with some of the more common devices appropriate for an ordinary woman's investment portfolio. *Portfolio*, by the way, is just a fancy way of describing your collection of investments. Think of it as your kitchen cupboard — full of purchases made at different times, at different prices, and for various purposes.

But before we start, here's an old law-school trick. It will work for you, too, in the discussions that follow.

If you feel a little lost after reading through a section or chapter, *read it again*. You'll be surprised how much clearer something is the second time around.

The Costs of Plain Vanilla:
Checking and Savings Accounts

Here is an old friend you're probably already overfamiliar with. In the old days, your bank gave you two choices: a *passbook savings account* paying 5.25 percent, and a *checking account* paying no interest.

No longer. Now you need a master's degree in math to sort your way through the variations available for checking and saving — and that's before you even get to certificates of deposit (CDs). Most checking accounts pay interest now. Often, the more you keep in your account, the higher the rate of interest the bank will pay. If you maintain a sufficient minimum balance (often earning no interest), many banks will lower or eliminate the monthly service charge. Obviously, the price you pay for this feature is what you could earn by placing the minimum balance in a higher-paying savings account or CD.

You and your calculator can easily learn whether this is a good deal. If a $5,000 balance (earning no interest) frees you from a $9 per month service charge, then $9 × 12 months equals $108, or 2 percent per year on $5,000 (you find the percentage by dividing 108 by 5,000 — thank God for calculators!). In other words, you are better off putting the $5,000 into anything earning more than 2 percent, and paying your $9 service charge.

But this is nickel-and-dime stuff. You shouldn't keep any more than a couple of months' budget in your checking account anyway. Your checking account, even if interest bearing, should never be regarded as an investment. It is a convenience, no more. Its virtue is its *liquidity* — which simply means you can convert it to cash in your hand fast.

You might want to keep another four months' budget in your bank savings account — the kind you can withdraw from at any time. You want ease of transfer between your checking and savings accounts. They are insured to a total of $100,000 if your institution belongs to the Federal Deposit Insurance Corporation (FDIC — the government agency that insures bank accounts) or the Savings Association Insurance Fund (SAIF — the successor to the FSLIC that insures savings and loans), but you definitely don't want to keep anything near that amount in checking and ordinary savings combined.

Your bank and savings-and-loan (S&L) deposits, by the way, are *debt* instruments — you have loaned the bank your money at a rate of interest. You are the creditor, the bank the debtor.

A Little Sauce on Your Vanilla: Certificates of Deposit

Of course, your bank or S&L (or stockbroker) would be delighted to sell you a *certificate of deposit*. These differ from ordinary savings and checking by their time requirement (in other words, they are less liquid). For a period of time, your money will not be available to you in a CD without penalty. One month, three months — four years, or more. The longer the term — usually — the higher the rate of interest. If you are investing during a period of historic low interest rates, think very carefully before you lock your money up for years with an interest rate you may come to regret. However, if rates are high, but falling, you would do best to lock in the higher rate for the longer term.

Banks and S&Ls in trouble frequently advertise CD rates well above the going rate, in the hope of attracting enough funds to keep them afloat. Stockbrokers scour the country for such offers and will be happy to get one for you for a price — but only through a bank the brokerage does business with. You may well do better for yourself by contacting the institution directly. Large newspapers' financial pages usually offer a chart showing the highest paying in the country every week or month. You can call the institution yourself, even if it is three thousand miles away, and set up an account without sharing the interest with a broker.

> **You can usually contact any financial institution in the country by calling an 800 number. If you know the name of the company — for example, Bank of America — simply call the 800 information operator, (800) 555-1212, and ask.**

If you decide to chase high interest rates in this way, be aware that the institution may fail. If it is insured through the government (never do business with a bank or S&L that isn't), your principal and interest will be safe up to $100,000 per institution (including all branches). If you have several accounts at one institution, they will be combined for the $100,000 limit, unless you hold them in different legal capacities — for example, as custodian of your granddaughter's college savings or executor of your sister's estate.

Be careful. Because of the 1980s savings-and-loan debacle, Congress continues to search for a way to prevent overreaching by the institutions. Various methods have been proposed, including a $100,000 limit per depositor regardless of how many institutions and accounts are involved. Before you do business with a shaky or an extra-high-paying institution, verify its government-insured status and ask your broker, lawyer, or CPA if any changes in depositor protection are in the offing.

> **Your nice fat interest rate on your ten-year CD may not be as secure as you think. If the institution fails, the government agency or new owner can reduce the interest to current market levels. This is one reason to buy your CDs only from healthy institutions.**

The advantages of CDs are many: They are easy to understand, they are safe up to their insured limit, they are predict-
able. Some CDs pay interest to you periodically, others pay you
nothing until maturity. If you die before the term is up, your
executor can cash out the CD early with no penalty. Otherwise,
you can get your money out early, but — unless you have an
emergency clause — only by paying a penalty.

Most CDs count as a "fixed-rate" investment because during their term they pay a stated rate of interest. Long-term fixed-
rate income, because of its vulnerability to mounting inflation,
is generally a bigger problem for women than for men — a
pension paying a fixed rate of $500 per month will buy less
at the end of a woman's life in fifteen years than at the end
of her husband's in ten, for example. But CDs don't pay for
life — just a stated period of time. Therefore, the gender bias
inherent in fixed-rate lifetime income is not such a problem
with CDs. And of course a CD, like any other bank deposit,
is a debt instrument.

Bank and S&L deposits have their place — a small one —
in your portfolio. Safety and liquidity are their strong points,
as well as the comfort of a local office and staff you get to know
personally. But before you decide to commit all your assets
to CDs and savings accounts, you owe it to yourself to become
familiar with alternatives that may well serve you better.

When You Own the Ice Cream Store: Stocks

A stock (or share) is a piece of a company. The owner of
the stock is called a *shareholder.* Big publicly traded companies,
such as IBM or GM, issue millions of shares of stock. When
you buy stock, you become one of the owners of the company.
You own *equity* in the company, just as you have equity in your
home (so stocks are also called *equities*). Your shares can make
(or *lose*) money for you in two ways:

- The share goes up in price (growth, or capital gain [or
  loss]).

- The company distributes some profits (dividends, or income).

The process works like this:

Imagine, for a moment, that you operate a catering business from your home. It is very successful, and now it is time to expand. You need $100,000 to buy cooking equipment, a delivery van, the deposit on a one-year lease, salary and fringes on one employee, legal fees, and insurance. Your local banker lends you $50,000, and your mother lends you $10,000.

Your brother and some friends of yours are willing to back you, too, but they prefer to have an equity interest in your business, rather than a debt interest (such as the bank and your mother). You, your brother, and two friends each put up $10,000 in return for a one-quarter ownership (equity) interest in the company.

Everything goes well, and at the end of three years, your business is profitable. You pay back your banker and your mother (you *retire the debt*), and divide the profits of $4,000 among the four owners (you pay *dividends*). These profits are separate from the business's *capital worth*. A company with no profits can still increase in value (*capital gain*), a common situation with young companies.

Then your brother sells his share to a friend for $15,000. His original $10,000 investment appreciated by 50 percent ($5,000) (a capital gain). Your mother, a creditor, made $2,400 on her loan to you of $10,000 (8 percent simple interest for three years). Your brother and mother each put up $10,000 — but his return was much more, because in addition to his $1,000 dividend, he made $5,000 appreciation (gain). A financier would categorize his dividend as earnings from income, and his capital gain as earnings from growth. Your mom's debt income of $2,400 pales beside his equity return of $6,000. In this case, $10,000 invested in equities outpaced $10,000 invested in debt by $3,600, because of the one-two punch of dividends *and* capital gain.

Does this mean that it is always better to hold equity rather that debt? No. Let's say your catering business just broke even. You were able to pay the rent, service the debt, and meet the payroll — but nothing was left over to divide among the four shareholders (profits, distributed as dividends). Because businesses that don't show a profit are not always the most popular investments, your brother could get only $8,000 for the stock he sold. He never was paid a dividend, and lost on his investment (a *capital loss*). Your mother still made $2,400 interest on her loan because the business was able to pay its debts, but your brother made less than nothing. Her $10,000 investment made her $2,400 richer; his $10,000 investment *cost* him $2,000.

But things can get worse. Imagine that your business went under. The money coming in did not equal the money going out. You owed the bank and your mother more than the business was worth if you sold all its assets (*negative net worth*). In bankruptcy, all the assets were sold (the cooking equipment, the flour and sugar, the delivery van, the office computer, and so on). Let's say there was $50,000 after the sale. The catering business's debts totaled $75,000, plus $25,000 in payroll, income, and sales and other taxes. Obviously, $50,000 isn't enough to pay obligations of $100,000. Taxes are paid in full first, leaving $25,000 to divide among the creditors, who are paid next, so your mother received thirty cents on the dollar for the money she lent you. You, your brother, and friends lost everything.

Another example: Your son, Dennis, needs your help in buying his first home. You can afford to put up $30,000 for the down payment, but you can't make it a gift. As with most investments, you can help Dennis in either of two ways: through debt or equity. With the first, you loan Dennis $30,000, probably with a first or second mortgage backing your loan (a *secured* debt — which means that if Dennis defaults on your loan, you can sell [*foreclose*] his house and get your money back). At the end of the agreed term, say fifteen years, Dennis pays you back, and you earned the 8 percent interest you agreed on during the fifteen years. If you take the equity route, however, your $30,000 would represent your *ownership* share in the house, probably as a tenant-in-common (more about these in Chapter 6). Your name would be on the deed with Dennis. You would not be paid interest, but when the house sells, you would share in the appreciation — however spectacular or woeful that may be. Your upside opportunity in an equity transaction can multiply your investment by the hundreds. Your downside risk is equally compelling: you can lose every nickel. Only you can decide how to structure your deal with Dennis. Either way, be sure you understand the alternatives.

Debt and equity. Two ways to finance something, two ways for you to make money.

Equity offers the opportunity for growth. Debt, in its pure form, does not. Your debt instrument pays interest only (income), whereas your equity share can increase in value (growth) *and* pay dividends (income). Equities, or stocks, are inherently risky. They go up, they go down, they stay flat. Over the long term (longer, say, than five years), however, money invested in the stock market generally earns more than money invested in debt (bonds, notes, bank deposits).

How much risk should *you* take? That's a very personal decision, touching on health, wealth, and personality. We'll talk about that when we discuss investment strategies in the next chapter.

When You Are the Lender: Bonds, Mortgages, and Notes

A note, mortgage, or bond (the financial world calls these *debt instruments*) is no more than an IOU. The company (or government, or individual) borrows money from you and promises to pay it back with interest by a certain date. As with your catering company, the note- or bondholders (the banker and your mother) do not share in the business's success or failure in the same way shareholders do. No matter how fabulously well the company does, the debtholder will get only his or her interest and principal back. But if things go wrong, the creditors are paid everything owed to them before even one penny is paid to the shareholders.

Generally, this makes bonds and notes a more conservative investment than equities, provided you hold the debt until maturity. You can still lose everything if the business can't even pay its debts, but at least you stand ahead of the shareholders in bankruptcy court.

Corporate bonds are usually *unsecured* (unlike mortgages, which are a lien on property). The mortgage holder will get her money out of the failing company before the corporate bondholder, because the mortgage holder can foreclose.

You can sell your bond or note before it matures. If you buy a $1,000 bond from XYZ Corporation earning 5 percent for ten years, if all goes well XYZ will send you your interest payments periodically (usually twice a year), and at the end of ten years, you will get your $1,000 back. But you can sell your 5 percent XYZ bond before the ten years are up, and how much you get for the bond will depend on the state of the *bond market* at the time you wish to sell. You could get more than your $1,000, or you could get less. Because of this, some risk is added.

Let's talk about the catering business again. You decide to expand again, and this time your sister Carol buys a twenty-year corporate bond issued by your company. This means that Carol loans the corporation $10,000 for twenty years at 7 percent interest, the prevailing rate at the time. For the next twenty years, your business expects to pay Carol interest, and after twenty years, the full $10,000 will be returned. Five years later, Carol needs the money, so she sells the bond to her friend, Kirby, who then "owns" the right to receive 7 percent interest from your catering company for the remaining fifteen years. But because prevailing interest rates at the time are 9 percent, Carol must sell her bond for less than she paid for it (her bond is *discounted*) — Kirby isn't going to pay $10,000 for the right to receive 7 percent when she could get 9 percent on a bank

CD. So Kirby pays Carol $7,700, and Carol loses $2,300 of her $10,000 (the *principal*). By dividing 7 percent by 7,700, you'll see that Kirby effectively is getting slightly more than 9 percent on her investment, even though the stated interest rate remains at 7 percent (remember, Kirby will get $10,000 back from the catering company in fifteen years, even though she paid Carol only $7,700). Of course, if Carol had held the bond until it matured after twenty years, her $10,000 principal (assuming the company remained sound) would be safe.

It could work the other way as well. If, after five years, interest rates had fallen to 4 percent, Kirby would pay Carol *more* than $10,000 for her 7 percent bond. Carol would make money — in addition to the interest.

But falling rates pose a danger of their own: Bond prices rise, yes, when interest rates fall. Always. But you, as CEO (*chief executive officer* — the boss) of your catering business, do not want to pay Carol or anyone else 7 percent in a 4 percent market. So you decide to refinance your debt by *calling* the bond. That means you pay the creditor back early. Carol, who thought she had locked in 7 percent for twenty years, finds herself paid back after only ten years and forced to reinvest her $10,000 somewhere else at only 4 percent. Investors call this *interest-rate risk*. If Carol has been living on the 7 percent, her standard of living drops sharply.

> **On any debt instrument, know if it is callable when you buy it. Corporate bonds usually are, real estate mortgages usually can be refinanced, and government securities are sometimes callable as well. A promissory note may or may not be, according to its written terms.**

Government bonds have a mixed track record. United States Treasury bonds (and bills and notes) are as safe as you can get, because the United States has the power to print money or raise taxes to retire its obligations. Other government units, such as states and municipalities, aren't always so highly regarded. U.S. Treasuries can be purchased from your broker or bank, for a price, or directly from the Federal Reserve bank at no cost.

> **You don't have to go in person to a Federal Reserve bank branch to do this. You can establish a "Treasury Direct" account at your local bank, which will receive the interest payments from the bonds directly. Ask your bank, or call the nearest branch of the Federal Reserve bank. They can send you forms to set up the account and tell you how to buy the security directly from the Reserve bank — which will save you money.**

The lowly U.S. Series EE savings bond is now deserving of respect. It won't make you rich, but its interest rate is adjusted every six months after you've held it five years, and it has a floor to protect you if rates drop. Interest is exempt from state and local and deferred on federal taxes until the bond is redeemed. Taxes can be waived if the bond is used for college tuition and the holder meets certain income tests. EE bonds range from $50 to $10,000, and cost half the face value — a nice way of making a large gift for a small sum. For example, $250 will buy a $500 bond (its *face value*). You can cash in your EE bond anytime after six months, but it won't pay its full face value until it matures. You can trade your EEs for HH bonds, which pay interest semiannually (unlike EE bonds, which don't pay until redemption) and start at $500. Your banker or broker will be happy to sell you savings bonds.

State and local bonds do not have the pristine record of U.S. Treasury instruments, but neither is it necessarily suicidal to include some in your portfolio. State and local governments have limited taxing ability and cannot print money, so sometimes they default. Municipals (as both state and local bonds are called) are important in your tax strategy and are discussed in the next chapter. There are rating services you can check if you are buying individual issues rather than through a mutual fund. Ask your librarian for bond-rating services.

U.S. zero-coupon bonds are backed by Uncle Sam, very safe, and a nice addition to the fixed-income side of your portfolio when interest rates are high. Ordinary U.S. bonds pay interest (or *coupons*) on a regular basis. Zeros pay no periodic interest, thus the name zero coupon, or "strips" because the coupons have been stripped from the security. Instead of paying periodic interest, zeros are sold at a discount. Like the Series EE savings bond, you pay a fraction of the face value and receive full face value at maturity. The nice thing about zeros for planning purposes is that you can buy them to mature on any day from five to thirty years after purchase. Do you want to give your newborn grandson a nice gift? Buy a zero that matures on his eighteenth birthday. Or your own sixty-fifth birthday. Or your fiftieth wedding anniversary. If you hold it to maturity, your bond will be paid in full, guaranteed by Uncle Sam. Should you want to sell it early, however, like any other bond, you will get more if interest rates have fallen since your purchase, less if they've risen. Corporations offer zeros, too — but of course they aren't backed by the U.S. government. You can buy zeros from brokers or mutual fund families.

Ginnie Maes (GNMAs) are U.S. government-backed mortgages from the Government National Mortgage Association. You don't directly lend your money to the homeowner — a bank has already done that. When you buy a GNMA, you are a *secondary* buyer. Just as Kirby bought Carol's note in the catering example given earlier, with a GNMA (and similar government-backed securities) you buy a mortgage that has already been negotiated between the home buyer and the bank. To help certain people qualify for mortgages, the United States guarantees the mortgage. Your principal is safe, because if the borrower defaults, the government will pay the loan. Your broker can sell you GNMAs, or you can buy into a mutual fund of GNMAs. The latter is more convenient, because many funds offer check-writing privileges, you can add to and withdraw from the fund, and your initial investment will probably be lower than buying a GNMA directly. Be aware, however, that your share price in a GNMA fund will fluctuate like all fixed-income securities (we discuss all kinds of mutual funds below). When interest rates rise, your share value will fall. Also, the high interest paid by the fund when you begin may fall as interest rates fall, because the borrowers pay off their mortgages and refinance at a lower rate.

Collateralized mortgage obligations (CMOs) are a complex security involving government-sponsored mortgages, which, unlike GNMAs, have the implied (but not guaranteed) U.S. government backing. There is a slight risk of default, as well as an interest-rate risk, so many financial advisers do not recommend CMOs for the average small investor.

Promissory notes are often issued by individuals. You can buy blank promissory notes at many stationery stores. They may or may not be secured by *collateral*. Collateral is what the debtor puts up to *secure* the debt (thus the term *securities*). When you finance your new car through the dealer, the collateral is the car itself. If you don't pay (*default*), the dealer will repossess your nice car. A mortgage is secured by the underlying real estate. You default, and the bank *forecloses*. Obviously, a note is only as secure as the collateral and the good faith and solvency of the debtor. You can sue the debtor in court if he or she defaults on your unsecured note. Although a note between family members can seem useful, it is risky in that it can be terrible for family relations. Stick with corporations and the government for your investments.

> **If you must make a loan on a personal note, get good collateral and have a business lawyer register your secured interest with the proper local authorities, so that if your borrower attempts to sell the collateral, you'll have recourse against the buyer. The Uniform Commercial Code sets forth a registration procedure for all states, and the attorney's fee for this simple job should be quite affordable. Be sure to negotiate the attorney's and filing fees with your borrower, or you could end up with a very low net return for your money.**

Financiers are creative, so the pure forms of common stock and bonds have been augmented by many hybrid creatures that share characteristics of both. You can convert some bonds to stock (*convertible* bonds), and you can buy stock that has priority over common stock in a bankruptcy (*preferred* stock). Of course, as you move away from the pure forms of debt and equity, you begin to compromise on risk and return. So long as you understand that every financial instrument holds a combination of risk and return in varying proportions, you can gain a basic understanding of every investment vehicle available.

Owning Without Controlling: Limited Partnerships

An investment adviser or broker may try to interest you in joining a *limited partnership*. But you should think through the idea carefully before buying into one. A limited partnership and a corporation confer very different rights on their owner/investors.

When you own stock in a corporation, you and the other owners vote for a board of directors, which, through hired management (executives), runs the company. If enough shareholders are unhappy, they can vote the directors out. If you aren't happy, but your other shareholders refuse to vote a change, you can sell your shares instantly through a broker, assuming the corporation is publicly traded (on the New York or American stock exchange, for example). In other words, if you are unhappy with how the company is doing, as a corporate shareholder you have two remedies: vote out the directors, or sell your shares.

In a limited partnership, you don't have the right to change management, and selling out can be quite difficult. The *general partner* controls the enterprise, and the *limited partners* have no power to oust him or her. The limited partners only finance the deal. If the limited partners become unhappy with the general partner, there is little they can do but try to sell their partnership share to someone else. This can be difficult if the enterprise is in trouble, to say the least.

A limited partnership can be compared to a family enterprise. Let's say you, your husband, and your two grown children own a restaurant. Although you and your husband invested money, you are really silent partners, in that your son and his wife manage the operation. You put in no time at all but expect to share in the profits, should that day arrive. Suppose your husband becomes very ill and you need your money back. You try to sell your interest in the restaurant, but find no ready buyers because no one really likes your son's management style, his personality, or the food. At this point you discover the real cost of illiquidity, because to get any of your money out, you must sell your interests for one-fourth what you put in.

Limited partnerships run the same risks, only it's worse because you are dealing with strangers. The limited partners usually have no say in the management of the enterprise — it is the general partner's show. If all goes badly, as it surely can, you can do very little to change the situation, or convince someone else to buy you out. Some traders will buy "used" shares in limited partnerships, but they might offer less than twenty-five cents on the dollar. Limited partnerships have a poor reputation of late, and I don't recommend your including them in your portfolio under ordinary circumstances.

Brokerage Accounts

Stocks and corporate bonds are publicly traded on the New York Stock Exchange, the American Stock Exchange, and several others — including exchanges overseas. You buy them through *stockbrokers*. It is easy to open a brokerage account. Just look in the yellow pages, and call any large house, such as Dean Witter or Merrill Lynch. The stockbroker either will buy and sell for your account according to what he or she recommends, or will respond to your own direction. The broker makes money by charging a commission every time you buy *or* sell a security. Few financial advisers today would recommend that the average investor is best off with substantially all his or her assets in individual stocks. Because of the commission on purchases and sales, some brokers are inclined to buy and sell rather more than you might like. If this is done excessively, it is called *churning* your account, and the Securities and Exchange Commission (SEC), the government agency that regulates securities and the markets, should be notified. Unfortunately, women are especially vulnerable to churning, since too many of us place too much faith in our professional advisers.

> **You can receive damages if it is determined that your account was churned. Start by complaining to the SEC and perhaps consulting with an attorney specializing in securities law. Your contract with your broker no doubt requires that you take your disputes to arbitration, rather than to court. The United States Supreme Court has approved of this requirement. You should still see an attorney to evaluate your complaint and, if necessary, represent you before the arbitration panel. Of course, an attorney may well see damages you don't recognize. Your $6,000 claim might be worth thousands more because of punitive damages and other remedies.**

Of course, brokers buy and sell more than stocks and bonds. You can get government securities through your broker (costing you more than if you purchased the security directly from the federal reserve bank), you can buy bank CDs from anywhere in the country, and you can buy (and sell) much, much more.

If you decide such an account is for you, give careful consideration to using a *discount broker*. They are listed in your yellow pages, and their commissions are much lower than regular brokers. Discount brokers only execute your buy and sell orders. They do not research companies and recommend buying and selling them. Some financial advisers are not impressed with the track records of "full-service" brokerage houses and recommend discount brokers all the way, assuming you want a brokerage account at all.

One of the problems with a brokerage account is the lack of *diversity*. Diversity in your portfolio is all-important for the ordinary investor. The fewer companies you own, the more vulnerable you are to a market slide. A broadly diversified portfolio means that when one segment of the market slips (say, auto stocks), your account is stabilized by the rise in another segment (your computer stocks). The more your holdings are diversified, the more stable your portfolio will be over time. There is a way for small investors to diversify their holdings mightily. See the mutual fund discussion below.

Once you've gained experience and confidence, a brokerage account may well fit into your program. Brokers can introduce you to the world of options trading and futures contracts, margin accounts, short-selling, and puts and calls. For the average investor, these speculative devices are not appropriate. But if you, like some, want to commit, say, 3 percent of your portfolio to high-risk speculation (and you can afford to lose *all* of it), a brokerage account is probably in your future.

Never get talked into something you don't understand. Make a parallel in your own experience, if you can. Let's say your broker has suggested you sell "call" options on some of your stocks. You ask her to explain, and then you think it over. You remember that at Thanksgiving when the store advertised turkeys at thirty-nine cents per pound but ran out, it gave you a raincheck. For your summer barbecue, you turned in your raincheck when turkeys were eighty-nine cents per pound, and "made" $10 on your twenty-pound bird. However, if turkey prices fell to twenty-nine cents right after Thanksgiving and never recovered, you'd have thrown your raincheck away. Why buy turkey at thirty-nine cents when it's available at twenty-nine cents? When the store gave you the raincheck, it issued a *call option*. You had the right to purchase the bird at the stated price *at your option*, even when prices changed. You did not have to exercise your option if the market in turkeys fell.

When your broker suggests you sell call options, she means this: You own three hundred shares of Widget Company, now trading at $45 per share. Someone offers to pay you $1 per share for the option to buy your shares at $50 per share within three months. You sell the option, and pocket the $300 (you still own the shares). Very nice, you think. How can you lose? If the price goes to $55, the buyer buys your stock at $50 (*exercises the option*), and you're ahead both the $300 option price *and* the 11 percent increase in value of your $45 stock, which you sold for $50.

But notice what you've done — by selling the option you have eliminated yourself from the upside potential of your stock. No matter how high it rises, you won't get more than the option price ($50) for it. Of course, if the stock doesn't go above $50 within the three-month period, the buyer doesn't exercise the option to buy and you *do* end up $300 ahead (the price paid for the unexercised option). You still have your stock, and you made money selling the (now expired) option — which you can now sell to another speculator. With calls, you win your bet if the option isn't exercised. You lose (by limiting your gain) if it is. The broker is delighted to sell calls, because your portfolio turns over faster — and she makes as much of a commission on the sale of your stock as she does on the purchase.

Futures contracts are another speculative toy offered by brokers. As with the option, you are buying the right to purchase a commodity at a future time at a price determined today. Pretend, for a moment, that you are the organizer of a kids' club cookie sale. It is now February, and the sale will be in July. The club has not set the price for the cookies yet, but it needs $100 right now to go on a field trip. Last year the cookies sold for $2.50 per box. One of the mothers says she will give the club the $100 it needs now, in exchange for the right to buy all the cookies at $2.60 per box in July. The club agrees. In July, the mother buys the cookies at the agreed price, and sells all two hundred boxes for $3.50 per box. On her *futures contract* the mom makes $180, or $80 profit ($3.50 minus $2.60 times 200 less $100). You think this is a nifty idea, so the next year, *you* buy the contract, again for $100, agreeing on a price of $3.25. But it's a bad year for cookies, and they sell for only $2.75. Unlike the option contract, you do not have the option *not* to buy the cookies. You must buy them at $3.25, and therefore lose money when you sell them at $2.75. You feel like a chump.

You've probably heard someone tell of making a fortune on *selling short*. "Shorting" the market is a concept that confuses many — but not you, because you've done it many times yourself in your everyday affairs. You just called it "borrowing." Let's say you borrowed a dozen eggs from your neighbor on Monday and promised to return them to her on Friday. The Sunnyside Jumbo eggs you borrowed (and used) on Monday cost $1.82 that day. On Thursday, you bought the replacement Sunnyside Jumbos — but you only had to pay $1.68, because egg prices had dropped. You returned the eggs to your neighbor on Friday, never realizing that you had profited by $0.14 by using $1.82 eggs and returning $1.68 eggs. If the replacement eggs had cost you $2.18, you would have gulped and paid it anyway, because you were obligated to replace the eggs on Friday, no matter the cost.

Short-sellers play the same game. The short-seller makes a bet that the price of a particular stock will fall. The speculator (selling short is always speculation — a very bad idea for beginners) borrows a particular stock from the broker — say, 100 shares of Anything Common on Monday — with an agreement to replace the stock on Friday. He or she sells it immediately for its current value, $50 per share, or $5,000. On Wednesday, the price falls to $48, so the short-seller buys another 100 shares for $4,800. On Friday, the broker gets back the 100 shares the speculator bought at $48, and the short-seller has made $200 (less commission to the broker). Of course, if prices rise, the short-seller loses the bet.

Your broker will lend you money to buy more securities (and charge you interest on the loan, plus the commissions on the purchases). This is called buying on *margin*, and probably is not for you under ordinary circumstances. Margin buyers are usually speculators, not investors. They borrow the money to buy the securities expecting the market to rise — after which they'll repay the brokerage. But if the market falls, the customer gets a *margin call* from the broker requiring he or she sell securities so that the broker's loan is covered. (The broker doesn't want to ride the market all the way down with you — brokers aren't stupid.) If the market continues to fall, the speculator's entire holdings can be liquidated to repay the broker.

Brokers (who, by the way, may be called "account executives" or "financial advisers" where you do business, but they're all stockbrokers nevertheless) have been known to oversell speculative services. Sandra wanted to take her children to Italy to see her father, who was not expected to live through the year. Sandra had $10,000 in various stocks and bonds and needed $12,000. She asked her broker's advice and explained her objective — she wanted an investment that would safely earn 20 percent in six months (40 percent per annum) so that her father could see his grandchildren one last time. Instead of telling Sandra that this would be impossible to do safely, her broker talked her into opening a margin account and buying pork belly futures — a contract to buy the commodity at a future date for an agreed price. If the price of bacon rises, Sandra's in good shape; she pays the agreed price, then turns around and sells the commodity for much more. But if the price falls, Sandra pays the hog farmer more than Sandra can get for the bacon, so she takes a loss when she sells it. Futures are a risky business. The broker told Sandra that she would triple her money in six weeks, but after three margin calls, Sandra was wiped out.

> **Sandra had a remedy. She hired a lawyer, who made a claim under the "know your client" rule. The broker is liable for damages if, knowing the client's objectives and ability to withstand loss, the broker recommends unreasonably risky investments. Sandra settled for $12,000 and made the trip.**

New brokers build their clientele through a practice called *cold-calling*. You'll get a phone call out of the blue from someone encouraging you to open a brokerage account. Don't do it. Women are susceptible to this approach, because so many of us are alone and managing our affairs for the first time. A promise of professional guidance can be very tempting. If a brokerage account is for you, you need to do your homework before signing on with a green broker just starting out. Ask your friends, your lawyer, or your CPA for recommendations.

If you have a brokerage account that has done well by you over time, by all means stick with it. You want to be sure your investments have done at least as well as the Standard and Poor's 500 over the same period. The S&P 500, like the Dow Jones and other *market indexes*, is just a market basket of particular stocks tracked by the indexer on a continuous basis. If the S&P 500 rose 19 percent over a three-year period, and your stocks were up only 6 percent, your broker owes you an explanation. Your account has *underperformed* the market.

But for most average investors, there is a much better way to invest in securities. Mutual funds have come into their own in the last decade and are the investment vehicle of choice for most investors who want to take overall charge of their investing program, without the risk of tracking individual stocks and bonds.

Investing in Thousands of Businesses: Mutual Funds

A mutual fund is nothing more than a bunch of people getting together to buy their investments in a group. They hire someone to manage the fund, and trust the manager to buy and sell securities on behalf of the group. For this service, they pay the manager a fee (usually, with administration expenses, this may cost you about 1 percent of your investment per year). The manager does not earn a commission on purchases and sales, so there is no incentive to churn. Furthermore, because millions (or billions) of dollars are managed by the fund, hundreds or even thousands of companies will make up the portfolio. Now *that's* diversity.

Over thirty million Americans have invested more than $1 trillion in mutual funds. You have a choice of over two thousand funds, each with its own investment objective and strategy. Some funds offer aggressive growth (high risk), others pay income only (low risk). A *growth* fund focuses on stocks that are expected to increase in value. If the fund manager bought Widget common stock at $35 per share, he or she hopes to sell it at, say, $40, thus realizing a $5 (or 14 percent — divide 5 by 35 to get the percentage) capital gain. The profit is in the gain. The manager of an *income* fund, on the other hand, concentrates on securities that pay interest or dividends. These aren't expected to change much in price, so they are less volatile and less risky, but their potential for gain is lower, because the interest/dividend mix will pay something near the market rate, no more. Many funds promise growth and income, a compromise of risk and return. Some are bond funds, some stocks, some both; some hold government securities, some mortgages, some money market instruments (usually corporate IOUs).

Mutual funds offer diversity, professional management, and liquidity. They are easy to get into and out of. But they do not guarantee your return, nor are they insured by the government in the sense that bank deposits are.

Some funds are sold through brokerages, financial planners, or sales agents; others you buy directly from the fund itself. The first, because the salesperson makes a commission when he or she sells the fund to you, are called *load* funds. The load is the commission you pay when you buy it (a front-end load) or, in some cases, sell it (a back-end load). The load can cost you up to 8 percent of your investment — a high price. *No-load* funds are sold directly by the company over the phone or by mail. A true or pure no-load fund charges you nothing when you sign on, nothing when you sign off, and nothing to advertise the fund (12b-1 charges). Both loads and no-loads charge a management fee, which differs from fund to fund. Whether a fund is load or no-load has nothing to do with its investment strategy or track record. Load funds cost you more, that's all.

Hundreds of mutual funds today are organized into *families of funds*. Vanguard, Benham, T. Rowe Price, Franklin, Fidelity, Janus — the list seems endless. Each family offers a smorgasbord of funds, and usually you can switch your money between the funds in the family with a phone call, with some limits. You can even write checks off many funds. As with other financial institutions, you can arrange to have the earnings mailed to you periodically or reinvested in the fund. Remember, to reach virtually any financial institution in the country, call the 800 information operator: (800) 555-1212.

Your library is a good place to start learning about funds. *Kiplinger's*, *Smart Money*, and *Money* magazines; *Forbes*, *Lipper Analytical Services* — your librarian can direct you to these and more. You don't need to subscribe to expensive investment newsletters to gain a fundamental understanding of the funds, but you might find the affordable cost of one of the consumer-oriented money magazines well worthwhile, since they track funds and other investments for you.

Several leading no-load fund families cooperate in putting out very useful material for the novice investor. The Mutual Fund Education Alliance offers *The Investor's Guide to Low-Cost Mutual Funds*, as well as a kit featuring video and written educational materials to teach you all you need to know about this type of investment. Although sponsored by the industry, the material is excellent for the beginning investor and includes easy-to-understand instructions on how to tailor your own portfolio. Call the Mutual Fund Education Alliance at (816) 471-1454, or write 1900 Erie Street, Suite 120, Kansas City, Missouri 64116, for the alliance's current materials and prices. This is an excellent place to get started.

There are zillions of kinds of funds. Here are a few:

- *Tax-exempt* bond funds invest in state and municipal bonds, the income from which is not taxable by the Internal Revenue Service (IRS). These bonds pay higher interest rates than U.S. bonds, because they are riskier. Still, a well-put-together bond fund can minimize the risk by insuring part of the portfolio and investing only in the highest-rated issues. A double tax-exempt fund will avoid taxes on both your federal and state returns. This is a good idea *only* if you are in a high tax bracket, because generally other investments pay higher returns, after tax, if your bracket is low. For example, a tax-exempt bond earning 6 percent effectively yields 7.68 percent to a 28 percent taxpayer but only 6.9 percent to one in the 15 percent bracket (multiply the interest rate by your tax bracket, then add the result to the interest rate — use your handy calculator — $6 \times .28 = 1.68$ — added to 6 percent = 7.68 percent). A double tax-exempt, because it also avoids state income tax, yields more. Although the income from tax-exempts is free of federal income tax, it *is* included in your total income when determining whether or not you're "rich" enough to owe tax on your Social Security. More about this later when we discuss Social Security.

- *Index* funds seek to duplicate the numerous stock indexes. An index, such as the Dow Jones industrials, or Standard & Poor's 500, is just a way of measuring the performance of the stock market. The indexer selects certain stocks for the index, then tracks their performance. When the Dow Jones rises, it means only that on average, the thirty stocks on the Dow Jones index rose; among the thirty are such familiar giants as Coca-Cola, Disney, McDonalds, Philip Morris, and Sears. A broader index, such as the five hundred stocks on the S&P's index, might actually fall when the Dow rises. Some indexes track several thousand stocks. Most advisers consider the S&P 500 to be a good, midlevel measure of market performance.

  When you invest, for example, in an S&P 500 index fund, you are expecting to do as well as the market as a whole, as exemplified in the five hundred stocks picked by S&P. In down times, you'll go down; in up times, up. You are not attempting to beat the market, as you are in growth funds. But because over the long term — over five years, say — the S&P 500 has returned between 8 and 9 percent annually, you're hoping your funds will duplicate that record. No guarantees.

- *Growth* funds, usually invested in equities, emphasize capital gain over income. A growth stock might be a newer company, which isn't mature enough to pay profits (dividends) to its shareholders, because it is plowing its profits back into the company — expansion, research and development, securing patents. An investor in such a stock doesn't expect much in the way of dividends; rather, he or she looks for an increase in the price of the stock as the financial community begins to recognize and value the young company. Some funds seek *aggressive* growth; these carry more risk for their objective of more return. Among these are *small capital* funds, which invest in smaller and newer companies rather than in *blue chips* (large, well-established companies such as IBM and AT&T). More conservative growth funds limit themselves to blue chips. Because blue chips have reached their potential, investors expect them to pay dividends and have a more stable stock price. A blue chip fund would expect lower returns, but also less volatility, than aggressively managed funds.

- *Bond* funds may be government only, or high-grade corporate bonds, or even junk bonds (the fund will probably call the junk bond fund the *high-yield* bond fund). Junk bonds are high-paying bonds issued by troubled companies and government agencies. Some investors have done very well in junk; for others, they've been a disaster.

- *Growth and income* funds, because of their stability and income, tempered with an opportunity for capital gain, are often preferred by retirees. They're a compromise, of course. Don't expect the highest income, or the highest gain.

- *Sector* funds are limited to one sector of the economy — perhaps toys, pharmaceuticals, aerospace — you name it. Many people have done extremely well in the right sector fund. Some financial advisers feel sector funds defeat the very purpose of a mutual fund by limiting diversity and tying the manager's hands. Sector funds are more speculative (that means riskier) than broader-based funds.
- *Money market* funds are for your cash. They'll pay a little more than your bank savings, are virtually as liquid, and have a safe track record, but are not insured by the government. Tax-exempt money market funds are riskier than their taxable counterparts. Don't expect growth here — after accounting for taxes and inflation, money funds don't offer growth. As interest rates rise and fall, so do the money market rates. Your bank or S&L offers money market checking accounts, which of course, are insured by the government to $100,000. But the interest you can earn in a money market mutual fund may be a little higher, and although not insured or guaranteed, these (taxable) funds have a sound track record. If you're buying into a family of funds, you probably should participate in their money market fund so you have a place to park your cash when you switch out of one fund and don't yet know what you want to replace it with.

Margaret could see no reason to pay a salesperson a commission to sell her what she could buy for herself with a phone call. She studied the Mutual Fund Education Alliance's list of funds and selected three no-load families. She phoned them, asked for applications and *prospectuses* (which give information required by the SEC), and in the unhurried privacy of her home selected four to invest in. Each required an initial deposit of $1,000 to $3,000 (some funds require more, some less). She chose a short-term government bond fund for safety, a Standard and Poor's 500 stock index fund for moderate growth and risk, an aggressive equities fund for growth, and a money market fund to hold cash. When Margaret could no longer live with the market swings in the aggressive growth fund, she called the family and switched out of that fund and into the fund family's money market fund. There she held her money until she decided to invest overseas. She called the fund family and opened a fund that invested only in Southeast Asia, an area she thought would continue to grow. Little by little, as Margaret grew accustomed to mutual fund investing and learned her own comfort level with risk, she added funds of a broader variety. Soon her "kitchen cabinet" of funds held more than soup, flour, and sugar. She added cumin, tarragon, and cayenne in small amounts as accents. And she began to have fun.

INSURANCE

Of course, Margaret doesn't have to dance with only one partner. Stocks, bonds, and the mutual funds that hold them are just a few of the financial options available in this capitalist economy of ours. Insurance companies offer a variety of products designed to pay death benefits and retirement income — in addition to disaster protection such as auto, fire, liability, and health. Life insurance products, including annuities, are often marketed to the consumer as worthwhile investments competitive with securities or other purely financial vehicles. Most objective financial advisers will tell you to place your investment dollars elsewhere; nevertheless, life insurance products do have some characteristics that make them extremely useful under the right circumstances and therefore an appropriate part of some retirement portfolios.

In Chapters 5 and 6, we'll talk about life insurance and annuities used as will substitutes and in charitable gift planning. In this section we'll talk about

- term and whole life insurance
- credit life
- disability insurance
- guaranteed investment contracts
- annuities

The Good and the Bad About Life Insurance

Traditionally, men carried life insurance to insure their family's future. As the family matured and the children left home, the insurance would be either dropped or, more likely, diminished over time.

Any insurance on the wife would be secondary and seen primarily as a way to pay funeral costs and housekeeping services for a limited time. With the entry of women into the paid labor market, and with female heads-of-household on the rise, the insurance industry had a marketing epiphany: perhaps women represented an untapped gold mine. And the campaign was on.

Think through your insurance strategy carefully. For people past middle age, premiums escalate rapidly. You and your husband have different needs, and if you're unmarried, insurance may not be a necessary part of your portfolio at all.

Husbands first. Unless you are quite certain that your circumstances will be very comfortable after his death, be cautious about dropping his policy just because the kids are grown. Get written estimates from Social Security and the pension administrator for *your survivor's benefit* after his death (explained in Chapter 3). It is distressing how many unpleasant surprises lurk out there for surviving spouses (read *widows*) in the form of greatly diminished (or even absent) spousal benefits.

Life insurance provides one thing well: a death benefit. When insurers add investment income (*cash value*) to this, they have historically done very poorly. Life insurance that pays only a death benefit is called *term* insurance. If you drop it, you get nothing back. You cannot take a loan out against it. It is simply and purely a death benefit. *Whole* — or *universal* — life insurance, in contrast, builds cash values. Part of your premium is invested for you and builds up over the lifetime of the policy. Whole life, or cash value, policies are the darlings of insurance salespersons because the premiums are large and therefore so are the commissions. The salesperson will have charts that dazzle you with the mounting cash value of your policy. You may be told that when you are sixty, you will have a $60,000 cash value with your whole life policy — available if you cash it in, or as collateral for a loan — and no accrued value in a term policy.

Don't listen to them. Buy the term policy and invest the difference in premiums in a mutual fund. By the time you're sixty, you'll probably have more than the $60,000 the whole life policy promises, and you'll still have the term death benefit, to boot! The salesperson doesn't want you to recognize that with whole life, if you die, the death benefit is paid and the cash value disappears. If you had bought a term policy and invested the difference in premiums separately, you'd still have your term death benefit *and* your investment as well.

Lately, some life policies offer *accelerated death benefits* (ADBs). In such a policy, you can take your death benefits before death, provided your doctor certifies that you are terminally ill and imminent death is expected, usually within six months. This can be an effective way to pay the high costs of illness, but shop very carefully if you want such a policy. Most companies charge a much larger premium for this coverage, but some do not. Do not confuse ADB coverage with long-term care insurance, discussed in Chapter 7. It does not substitute for it.

Credit Life Insurance: You Can Do Without It

Credit life insurance pays the balance on the underlying debt should you die. Your mortgage, for example, would be paid off by mortgage insurance. Credit life is usually more expensive than ordinary term life insurance. You're better off declining the credit policy and taking out ordinary term life to pay off your debts.

Death Isn't the Only Threat: Disability Insurance

If you're depending on earned income — either yours or your husband's — death isn't all that threatens it. Sometimes a job-ending disability can go on for years — and, of course, the life insurance is no help at all. Disability insurance will pay cash benefits, usually monthly, during the period of the disability — up to the limits of the policy. Disability insurance is mandatory in most states for salaried workers (by payroll tax), but the self-employed often forget to protect themselves. Workers can apply for Social Security disability at any age, but it is for long-term disabilities. Disability insurance for short-term disabilities is worth considering *if* you would be seriously compromised by such. Consider the premiums against your need; look at your emergency reserves; then decide if you can afford to go without disability protection. Generally, disability premiums are far costlier for women than for men.

GICs: Insurer's Answer to CDs

A *guaranteed investment contract* (GIC) is similar to a bank CD, except that it is issued by an insurance company and is not insured by the government. GICs usually pay slightly higher interest than CDs because of the risk that the company might fail — as has happened.

All fifty states have insurance guaranty funds designed to protect policy and annuity holders of collapsed insurers — but only up to a limit (usually $100,000). Check with your agent or insurance department for particulars.

Annuities: No Friend of Women

Generally speaking, an annuity is a life insurance product that doesn't require your death for the payout. You pay a life insurance company a premium (one or more), and they pay you back over time (perhaps monthly) or a lump sum. Your annuity can pay you for life or for an agreed period of time, perhaps ten years. It can start (or end) on a stated event, such as the remarriage of a widow.

Many people purchase annuities as a substitute for a pension. Pensions, in fact, are nothing more than annuities that were earned on the job as a form of deferred compensation. Folks without adequate pensions often feel an annuity is the appropriate way to supplement their Social Security. After all, annuities can be set up to pay monthly, quarterly — or at just about any other interval. With a steady, regular payout, the annuitant has a stable cash flow with the virtue of predictability. If you like this idea, keep in mind that the convenience comes with a price. You'll probably get more bang for your buck in another type of investment. A mutual fund, for example, can be set up to pay you monthly or periodically — interest only, or interest and capital gain, or even income plus some of your principal. CDs can be arranged to do the same, and most government and corporate bonds pay interest semi-annually while the bond is maturing. Annuities can also contain hidden costs. For example, frequently you are penalized for surrendering the annuity within the first several years.

Many (objective) financial advisers counsel against annuities as ordinary investments, because many other instruments do so much better. For special purposes, however, annuities are a useful tool. Tax planning is one of them, because the earnings are taxed when paid — in the future. We discuss the use of annuities in estate planning in Chapter 5.

If you do purchase an annuity, make sure the insurance company will be there when the payoff is due. Natasha was a very careful investor. When she decided on an annuity to secure her old age, she didn't take the agent's word for it about the strength of the insurance company. After all, she would be depending on the annuity to pay her monthly for the rest of her life. Since the annuity was the cornerstone of her retirement income, naturally she was wary. She went to the library and asked for insurance ratings services. The librarian gave her the publication produced by A. M. Best, a well-known, old-line insurance ratings firm. She found that the insurer she was investigating had the highest rating Best offered, but she didn't stop there. She phoned Best just to make sure the rating was current. After she bought the annuity, she called Best twice a year just to make sure (and paid a small fee each time). One month before the insurer filed for bankruptcy, Best was still giving it the highest rating. Best explained that it didn't want to cause a run on a troubled company, but later it changed its system after heavy criticism.

Had Natasha checked the other ratings services in her library she would have been alerted to some real problems. In the end, Natasha lost 20 percent of her retirement money — and was grateful that it wasn't more. The GIC holders in the company lost much more. Natasha is a fictional representative of the real victims of major life insurance companies that collapsed in the early 1990s despite the highest A. M. Best ratings less than a month prior to going under.

You can hedge your bets by doing business with insurance companies that have the highest ratings from at least two of the following four insurance raters — and no lower than the fourth level from any one rater (call them for their ratings levels):

- **A. M. Best: (908) 439-2200**
- **Duff and Phelps: (312) 368-3157**
- **Moody's: (212) 553-0377**
- **Standard & Poor's: (212) 208-1527**

Many annuities contain a costly gender bias. Because of the longer statistical life expectancy of women, the insurance company selling an annuity payable for life will either charge women a higher premium or lower the payout. The dollar difference can be significant. Generally, women are given an eight-year handicap in gender-based annuities, meaning that a woman of sixty will pay the same (or higher) premium as a man of fifty-two. Your insurer will tell you this is fair, because women have a longer life expectancy to stretch the payments over. However, neither you nor your insurer knows whether you, individually, will have a long life. Only 20 percent of women outlive the male life expectancy. For this reason, gender-based annuity tables are illegal sex discrimination for employment-based pensions.

For life insurance, where gender-based tables should work to women's advantage (since women, as a group, live longer, the insurer has longer to invest the premium before having to pay the death benefit), women are generally given only a three-year advantage. The very same insurance company will commonly give an eight-year penalty for a woman annuity customer, but only a three-year life insurance advantage to her. This is one reason that women's groups have been severely critical of insurance as an investment vehicle for women.

Okay — so insurers have their strategies, and you are entitled to yours. One of them should be to avoid gender-based annuities like the plague.

REAL ESTATE

This section will look at *investment* real estate. Your home is certainly valuable in all sorts of ways, including financial. We'll talk about that in Chapter 4.

Investment advisers are all over the map when it comes to real estate investing. Some feel that real estate has no place in the ordinary investor's portfolio (other than as a residence); others think realty should represent up to 30 percent of your net worth.

My feeling is that real estate investing is not for beginners or the average investor who wants to live hassle-free. The three characteristics of every investment apply to real estate just as well: risk, return, and liquidity. Give real estate a D on liquidity, a C on risk, and from A to F on the return.

Rental property comes with the responsibility of being a landlord or the cost of hiring a manager. Raw land may be hard to liquidate and pose unknown future returns. The value of property does not depend simply on demand. Zoning changes can affect values; so can disasters.

But for the individual who is familiar with these problems, real estate can be a real money-maker. Many people stake their retirement on the income from a duplex, a condo, or even a second home.

One way to become a real estate investor without the problems of hands-on management is through a *real estate investment trust* (REIT). A REIT is real estate's answer to mutual funds. A group of investors pool their funds to buy real estate (usually commercial, such as apartments, offices, or shopping malls). While stocks were booming, however, REITs were plunging. You shouldn't go into a REIT unless you know exactly what you're doing and where the real estate market is going. No guarantees, of course. The collapse of real estate in the early 1990s brought many REITs down as well.

GOLD, ANTIQUES, ART, AND OTHER TANGIBLES

The average investor's portfolio is quite complete without involving tangibles such as precious metals, art, and antiques. Yes, these items are properly counted as part of your net worth; and yes, people have made money on the right choices. There is a popular assumption that tangibles provide a hedge against inflation, but this is far from certain. Much more than inflation affects the art and antique market — fads, foreign interest, the influence of an important collection. Tangibles have to be insured and stored — costly considerations — yet they do not earn income.

The sensible thing, of course, is to buy wisely when you decorate or furnish your home. If you enjoy antiques and fine art — by all means, go for it. But for heaven's sake, don't let anyone tell you your portfolio "should" be 10 percent in precious metals, collectibles, purebred animals, antique autos — or any other tangible — just as a matter of investment philos-

ophy. Your cupboard is quite complete without escargot —
unless, of course, you love escargot.

So these, in a nutshell, are your ordinary investment
choices. No one puts everything into a portfolio, any more than
you put everything in your cupboard. Neither do you fill your
cupboard with one thing only. You pick and choose according
to your own needs, arriving at a balance that's just right for
you. How to do that is the subject of the next chapter.

CHECKING YOUR INVESTMENT IQ

1. Would you call your bank savings debt or equity?
2. How much interest do you earn on your checking
    account?
3. Do you know the true cost of keeping a minimum
    balance?
4. Can you live nine months to a year on your emergency
    cash?
5. Could you, if necessary, get $1,000 cash in your hands
    today?
6. Have you deducted tax and inflation from your CD inter-
    est rate?
7. Do you have more than $100,000 in any one bank or S&L?
8. Are you happy with your portfolio ratio of growth and
    income?
9. Have you handed over your affairs to a professional?
10. Do you have any investment you don't completely
    understand?
11. Is your portfolio well diversified?
12. Will you spend an hour per week studying the market?
13. Do you know you can sue your broker (agent, lawyer,
    CPA)?
14. Do you understand the difference between growth and
    income?

15. Does your husband have life insurance? How much?
16. Do you understand the advantages of term life over whole life?
17. Have you thought through your insurance package?
18. Do you understand the gender bias in many annuities?
19. Have you calculated your net worth?

2
Playing the Woman's Card
Investment Strategies

Remember Dr. Spock's comforting words about baby care? "You know more than you think you do."

They apply equally to money care. If you're new to money management, you'll want to get used to new words for old concepts. The old concepts are as familiar to you as a trip to your corner store — but all dressed up in technical jargon, they take on the mystique of the unknowable. Experts report that women are one-third more likely than men to say they are not confident about making financial decisions. *There is no need for this!*

It's all about the Wizard of Oz, and once unmasked, no-load mutual funds and zero-coupon bonds and tax-exempt municipals are as tame as that old guy pulling the levers behind the screen. When the smoke clears — as any economist will tell you — it all boils down to this:

> *Money makes money;*
> *and the money that money makes*
> *makes more money.*

In this chapter we'll look at some money strategies tailor-made for women.

Our first task is to recognize that women enter retirement differently from men.

- First, we're poorer. Because our retirement income is only 60 percent of men's, the poverty rate of women older than sixty-five is double that of men.
- Next, we live longer. Although Social Security and government pensions are adjusted for inflation, most other retirement income sources such as pensions and investment income are not. Wages, at least potentially, keep up with inflation. But we women have one-third more "postwage" years than men (the years after sixty-five), and this makes for some tough planning.
- Finally, we are likely to live our last years alone, unlike the vast majority of men. It costs more to be single than married.

We have to plan differently — and plan hard — to surmount these economic realities. And we can do it.

Your investment portfolio, like your kitchen cupboard, should be a balance of things, each with its own job to do. Depending on your needs and means, the contents of your cupboard will fluctuate from time to time. You have staples, such as flour and rice, that are always in your cupboard. You don't expect miracles from them, but they're dependable and do their job. Solid mutual funds, U.S Treasuries, high-rated bonds — a CD or two — might be the staples of your portfolio. Your neighbor's cupboard, like yours, contains a mix — a somewhat different mix, to be sure, but very likely with similar staples. Perhaps you buy different brands — her soup is Campbell's, yours is Andersen's — but you both buy soup. Her growth and income mutual fund might be with one family of funds, yours with another — but you both feel that well-managed mutual funds are basics.

As we work through these strategies, keep your cupboard in mind. Understand that when you balance your portfolio (as when you fill your cupboard), you will not duplicate your neighbor's. There is no "one true path" to filling your portfolio. Don't panic if others are rushing to one fund. Don't wake up in agony wondering if you should buy gold bullion. Save your angst. Take your time, make your decisions. Your portfolio is just for you.

Don't be intimidated by the sheer numbers of choices. There are thousands and thousands of investment opportunities. If you're new to investing, you'll feel overwhelmed. But remember this: although there are more than four thousand mutual funds, there are *nine thousand* different products in your supermarket. Your market doesn't overwhelm you, though, because you approach it with a plan. You determine your needs, make your list, and proceed to the products you want, ignoring all others. From time to time you'll miss the best buys; from time to time your neighbor will get in on a good deal that you won't. Do you lose sleep? Of course not. It's a big market out there, and so long as your cupboard choices serve you, you don't sweat the peaks and valleys. When you were new to shopping, you stuck to a few familiar brands. As you gained experience, you branched out. Some new products worked for you, others you dumped.

Approach your investment program the same way. Begin with some tried-and-trues — CDs, government securities, a Standard and Poor's stock index fund, a money market mutual fund. After several months, add a little something more exciting. Don't commit much money to it at first. Give it time to prove itself. Over the course of a year or two, you will build a fine portfolio, just for you.

Before we go any further, make a ballpark estimate of your annual budget (before taxes) after retirement. Make this your sensible, target budget, without respect to present income. Is it $30,000 per year? If you're average, $10,000 of that will have to come from investment income. And at 5 percent, taking taxes into consideration, you'll need to invest around $250,000 to earn $10,000 per year plus the tax.

Building the savings leg of your five-legged stool is the business of this chapter. We will apply what we learned in the last chapter about investment vehicles. There are some pretty neat strategies out there — of course, they'll work as well for men as for women — but *we* need to pay more attention, because the savings leg of our retirement stool is wobbling like crazy. At the same time, that leg is our main opportunity to even the playing field with the men we know and love.

We'll learn how to balance our portfolios, how to evaluate our tolerance for risk, how to plan for inflation, and how to structure our investments. We will learn that we can *make more money by not spending it than by saving it*.

A Word About Professionals

There is a proper role for professionals in your financial life, but keep firmly in mind the distinction between an adviser and a salesperson. Someone calling him- or herself a "financial planner" or "investment adviser" can be anyone who wants to sell you insurance, securities, trusts, or realty. Certified Financial Planners have undergone training but still may be selling a product, such as insurance or mutual funds. That's okay, so long as you recognize the conflict inherent in the arrangement. Salespeople's advice can never be *entirely* for you, because of their own financial involvement — they are working for both of you. Some investment or financial counselors sell nothing but their time — by the hour, usually.

Good financial planners have many helpful tricks up their sleeves. Seek counsel if you want — especially as you're gaining experience — but make it your goal to be a savvy, knowledgeable investor. The true professionals in your life will appreciate it, too.

There are some professionals you'll always want and use. The professionals who manage mutual funds are the very reasons you want those funds. You may consult tax advisers, lawyers, bankers, or brokers. When you want to buy insurance, you'll find it easiest to buy through an agent. When you want to buy stock, you'll use a brokerage, because you can't do it directly. There's a big difference between consulting with experts and turning your affairs over to them. The aim here is to make sure that you're the boss and orchestrator.

You should check the bona fides of anyone who will advise you. For attorneys, call the state bar association to learn if they've been disciplined. Check with the National Association of Securities Dealers (NASD) for brokers or other financial advisers; their number is (800) 289-9999.

Investing Versus Speculation

This book is not about speculation. For that, spend the day at the races. You'll have more fun and probably lose less. One reason investing is so intimidating to many is that stories abound about "highfliers," "losing one's shirt," "playing" the market, and so forth. If you like to gamble, the financial markets afford plenty of opportunity — *but know when you cross the line from investing to speculating.*

Just as you'll lose money when you speculate, so, too, will you lose it by being overly conservative. You can keep your cash in your safe-deposit box and watch it lose value daily to inflation. A bank savings account may keep you even with inflation, but it will probably not grow. Trustees, who are under a fiduciary duty to "prudently invest," are prohibited from keeping trust funds in nonearning (even if completely safe) accounts. So the legal definition of a prudent investor precludes both ends of the investing scale. It is imprudent to speculate; it is imprudent to stand still. The key is moderation — a prudent mix of risk, safety, stability, and liquidity.

Here, we mature women have an advantage. We've managed our households for decades. We've been the principal buyers of a variety of commodities — from soup to nuts, and furniture to sheets. We know in our bones the principle of moderation. It's no wonder that investment clubs formed by women across the country have track records exceeding two-thirds of those made up only of men.

Some, not too kindly, tell us that women were born to shop. Okay, then — let's go shopping!

Become Money-Wise for Free

To make wise choices, you must first get acquainted with the universe of investment opportunities.

The countless investment letters can cost you hundreds of dollars per year. You can obtain help sorting them out by asking your librarian or bookstore for guides to financial newsletters. Investment newsletters are expensive and vary widely in their track record.

But you really don't need this expense. You can do well for yourself for free. Your local library has many books on investing — mutual funds, pensions, everything. You might want to start with back copies of *Kiplinger's*, *Smart Money*, and *Money* magazines. Go back about a year and read them front to back. Get in the habit of reading your local paper's business section. Most papers carry syndicated columnists, such as Jane Bryant Quinn and Scott Burns, who specialize in investor-friendly advice. Bob Brinker's ''Money Talk'' on weekend radio and Rick DuPuis's PBS TV show ''Inside Money'' are very down-to-earth, and there are many others as well.

These advisers are free, free, free — but remember that, virtually without exception, they will not be focusing on the special considerations women investors need to keep in mind — longevity and long single years chief among them. You will have to do that for yourself. Don't resent the hour or so per week you'll spend keeping your portfolio up-to-date — you spend that much time and more shopping for groceries.

Structuring Your Portfolio

Managing your own money is all very simple, really. In general, you need to know only three things about any type of investment:

- the risk (how easy is it to lose everything)
- the return (how much you get after taxes and inflation)
- the liquidity (how easily can you cash out)

All investments are a combination of risk, return, and liquidity. Generally, the higher the risk and the lower the liquidity, the higher the return.

How tolerant should you be of risk in your own portfolio? That varies considerably. The older you are, most financial advisers will agree, the less risk you should take. You don't have time left to start over if all goes wrong. Many advisers recommend a mix of conservative and aggressive (read "risky") investments that becomes more conservative with age.

One rule of thumb is to subtract your age from 100 and allocate at least that percentage to stocks. But we're gender aware around here, so we know that, for women, 104 is the magic number, and 96 for men (allocating the eight-year life expectancy differential between the genders). A 64-year-old woman, then, would allocate 40 percent of her portfolio to equities; a man of the same age, 32 percent.

Some advisers would structure a low-risk portfolio thus:

- 30 percent in cash
- 20 percent in blue-chip stocks
- 20 percent in high-grade bonds
- 10 percent each in foreign, aggressive growth, and income stocks

A medium-risk portfolio might be allocated this way:

- 25 percent in blue-chip stocks
- 20 percent each in cash and high-grade bonds
- 15 percent in foreign stock
- 10 percent each in aggressive growth and income stocks

And a high-risk allocation might be like this:

- 25 percent each in blue-chip, aggressive growth, and foreign stocks
- 10 percent each in cash and high-grade bonds
- 5 percent in income stocks

Of course, advisers vary considerably in the proportion they recommend — according to the biases of the adviser and his or her comfort level with risk. And you have to bring your own circumstances to bear on this rough rule. If you know that your chronic health condition makes a long life unlikely, adjust your ratio accordingly. If you have substantial financial needs coming up over the short term, you don't want to fund them with aggressive (and therefore volatile) growth stocks, because they may plunge just as you need the money. Many professionals feel that money you will need in five years or less should be held conservatively — market swings that are tolerable in long-term investments could catch you down in the short term.

Finally, the risk character of an investment can change from time to time. The international climate makes foreign stocks risky at some times, prudent at others, for example. A prudent allocation to certificates of deposit when interest rates are 5 percent higher than the rate of inflation would be not so handsome if rates on treasuries are 3 percent higher than inflation and the CDs are running only 1.5 percent higher than that.

So look over your holdings, and determine by dollar amount what percentage of your investment pie is almost risk-free and what proportion is definitely not. Some advisers feel 25 percent equities would be the lowest proportion acceptable even in an eighty-year-old's portfolio, but you have to decide for yourself your personal comfort with risk.

Women, with our longer lives but lower incomes, must tailor these proportions a little differently from men. On the one hand, a woman of sixty is a "younger" investor than a man of the same age (she has one-third more time to recover her losses). This could mean she can tolerate more risk. On the other hand, if her net worth is low, then her risk tolerance could be quite low as well — at the same time, her need for growth would be high.

Counting On Inflation and Taxes

Your nice corporate bond, promising 8 percent for the next ten years, is not so nice when you subtract, *as you must*, inflation and taxes. When you're working out your future budgets, you absolutely must be realistic about these somber facts.

Amy retired early, expecting that the $16,000 per year she would earn on her 8 percent long-term bonds would be just enough to supplement her pension and Social Security. She forgot taxes in her projections, so the actual amount available to her was less than $11,000. Each year her $11,000 declined further by the rate of inflation (4 percent), so after five years, it "bought" only $8,970. Amy had to go back to work.

Many respected financial advisers believe that interest-bearing investments *at best* hold their own. They are little better than the proverbial mattress (which loses to inflation but isn't taxed). Anyone investing for growth must look elsewhere, and growth-oriented mutual funds remain most advisers' favorites for the average investor.

However, if, like most retirees, you expect interest-bearing securities to play an important role in your portfolio, you can use the inflation rate to judge the degree of risk each opportunity poses.

How do you know when too high is too risky? Historically, the inflation rate plus three percentage points has been a reasonable return on a near risk-free investment such as U.S. Treasuries. So if inflation is 3 percent, 6 percent on a thirty-year Treasury bond would be quite acceptable. As the return goes up, so does your risk. At ten points above inflation, your risk is quite high. The company that has to pay interest substantially above market rates to entice someone to lend it money has a reason — and you may not like it.

Inflation and taxes are critical factors in your own investing strategies. Never underestimate their substantial effect on your bottom line. Always know the current inflation rate (the financial pages of your newspaper will list it, or you can call any financial institution or your reference librarian), and always subtract it from any quoted return. If the investment offers 15 percent, and inflation is 11 percent, your true return is 4 percent. If the rate offered is 7 percent, and inflation is 3 percent, you are making the same 4 percent.

Then knock off a third (or whatever your rate is, remembering to include your state tax too) for taxes, and you can see your fat returns trim down in a hurry. Keep this in mind as interest rates rise and fall. Until you account for inflation and taxes, you don't know what the *real* rate is — your real income may be staying about the same despite the fluctuations.

To calculate the rate of inflation over a period of years, you need to know the consumer price index (CPI) for the beginning and the end of that period. Ask your librarian for the figure, or look it up yourself in the *Statistical Abstract of the United States* at your library. Let's say you invested $10,000 in August 1986, and five years later its value was $13,000. The CPI in August 1986 was 109.6, and in August 1991 it was 136.6 (what cost $109.60 to buy in 1986 cost $136.60 in 1991). Over the period, then, inflation was 24 percent. Your 1986 $10,000 needs to be $12,400 in 1991 just to stay even. Your real gain was only $600 (although you'll owe tax on the full $3,000 as a capital gain, but life — and the IRS — are not fair).

Women's extra years are welcome ones, of course — but they are *very* expensive. Fixed incomes (your bonds, for example, and your pension) grow steadily smaller every day in terms of purchasing power. You know very well what hamburger cost when you were a bride and what you pay for it now. Your 1932 dollar buys very little today. Likewise, your 1992 dollar will shrink by 2002. How much? In recent times inflation has fluctuated widely — from less than 3 percent to more than 10 percent.

Over the long haul, though, an average inflation rate of 5 percent is a fair rule of thumb. If you receive $10,000 per year in fixed income in 1992, diminish it by 5 percent per year ($10,000 × .05 = $500) for ten years to learn what it might buy in 2002 ($10,000 less $500 leaves you with $9,500 after year one; $9,500

less \$475 (.05 × 9,500) yields \$9,025 after year two; and so forth.) Your income loses half its value in fifteen years if inflation is 5 percent.

After you've figured out inflation's annual effect on your fixed income, you must develop a strategy to replace it somehow. Spending 5 percent less is one way; working at odd jobs might be another. Without some way of combating inflation, women especially, with our longevity, become poorer and poorer with each passing year.

As a general rule, debt instruments (bonds, notes) are more vulnerable to inflation than equity (stocks, real estate). This is because you receive a fixed amount over a period of time with a debt instrument. As time goes by, your \$2,000 every six months begins to look puny. Equities have traditionally been considered a hedge against inflation, because the value of the company expands with inflation. Of course, businesses can collapse. But in balancing your own portfolio, keep in mind that women are more exposed to inflation than are men because of longevity, so equities may play a greater role in a woman's portfolio than in a man's.

There *is* an (ironic) silver lining. Because women, as a group, have far less pension and investment income than men, the strongest leg of our retirement income stool is Social Security. That means that Social Security forms a greater proportion of retired women's income than retired men's. And Social Security is adjusted for inflation. The result? An average retired woman is more likely to have a greater proportion of her retirement income shielded from inflation than the average retired man. Of course, we have to be poorer than men to pull this off — but any port in a storm.

Never ignore inflation and taxes.

Inflation is inevitable, but you can do something about taxes. If you are in a high bracket (remember, add your state bracket to the federal), you might consider deferring tax on your investments. If you have wage income, put everything you can afford into 401(k) or 403(b) plans at work, as well as your fully funded IRA (more about these things in Chapter 3). You don't have to begin to withdraw the funds until you are age seventy and a half, so until then your funds earn much more tax-deferred. Think of the IRA, 401(k), and so on as a color you paint your investment. Your tax-deferred accounts are pink, let's say, and the rest are blue. You can use the same types of things — stock funds, bonds, CDs — with your tax-deferred funds. It's just that the color is different — the IRS doesn't take taxes from your pink accounts until you withdraw the funds — your blue accounts are taxed every year. If you don't work for pay, you can't contribute to IRAs and the like — a true gender bias against the hardworking homemaker. You *can* buy an annuity, which is tax-deferred, or buy tax-free (municipal) bonds or funds. However, be sure that you understand the good and the bad about annuities, as explained in Chapter 1.

A Penny Saved Is Much More Than a Penny Earned

There are more ways than one to skin the retirement income cat. Savings strategies — yes — but *budgeting* wisely is money in the bank, too. Real money. But you already knew that. When you frugally clipped grocery coupons, you were way ahead of the guys who make their money advising folks like you.

> **By the way, one of the great American bargains is available only to people over fifty. Membership in the American Association of Retired Persons (AARP), now thirty-two million members strong and growing by thousands every day, costs only $8 per year. For this you get discount prescriptions, insurance (life, health, auto, and home), the bimonthly *Modern Maturity* magazine, and discounted hotel and motel rates everywhere in the country. Your first night in a motel will probably pay for your dues and then some — you can easily make a profit on your AARP membership. Write**

to 601 E Street NW, Washington, D.C. 20049. Their telephone number is (202) 434-2277.

The way the money boys translate small savings into big bucks is worth noting — especially on those days when the tedium of saving a penny here and a penny there makes you question the value of your effort.

Here's how your little savings go big time: When Suzanne decided it was time to retire, she added up her Social Security, pension, and investment income and came up short. She calculated she would need about $50,000 more invested at 5 percent to meet her annual budget, when she included her tax obligations. She wasn't willing to delay retirement for the ten years it would take her to save the money, so she cut her budget by $2,000 per year — the equivalent of $50,000 invested at 5 percent less taxes. Suzanne retired when she wanted, with very little sacrifice, by understanding that a penny saved is *not* a penny earned — because of taxes and inflation, it is a good deal more.

It costs you about $1.24 in pretax dollars to buy something worth $1 (assuming a 15 percent federal income tax bracket and 5 percent state tax). You can put $25 in a 5 percent savings account to earn the $1.24, or you can choose not to spend the dollar. Either works out the same for you financially. So your $1 not spent — in effect — saves you $25! And if you're in a higher tax bracket, or you pay higher state sales and income taxes, your dollar saved is worth even more than $1.24. Think of it this way: you get a 24 percent return when you save that dollar — totally risk-free. Can you match that in the market? If you can save 10 percent per week on a family food budget of $100 by using coupons, it's the same as having $10,000 invested at 5.25 percent — and that's before taxes. Feel better already? A $10,000 windfall courtesy of your daily newspaper.

Get rid of your credit card debt. At 18 percent, a $2,000 balance costs $360 per year. I can handle that, you say. But to earn that $360, you need to invest

$8,000 at 4.5 percent — more, if you pay taxes. Eight thousand dollars is a lot to tie up just for the privilege of paying the bank.

Go over your budget with a fine-tooth comb. Get rid of obsolete expenditures. Start with insurance. Can you get by with one car (and one car insurance)? Can you drop some life policies? Do you have overlapping Medicare supplement policies, or cancer or accidental-death policies? Add up the expenses you can forgo, then translate them into bucks in the bank. You'll impress yourself!

The federal government publishes scads of useful penny-saving pamphlets. Here are just a few:

- *How to File a Claim for Your* [pension] *Benefits* **(free)**
- *New Car Buying Guide* **($.50)**
- *Nine Ways to Lower Your Auto Insurance Costs* **(free)**
- *What You Should Know About the Pension Law* **($.50)**
- *How to Buy a Manufactured (Mobile) Home* **($.50)**
- *Résumés, Cover Letters, and Interviews* **($1)**

You can find these and many more listed in a free booklet. Write for the *Consumer Information Catalog*, Consumer Information Center, Dept. 92, Pueblo, Colorado 81009.

Your Emergency Cash Account

You want to set aside emergency funds in a safe, liquid account. For many, this will be a passbook savings account. Others will prefer the somewhat higher interest offered by a mutual fund money market account. Both are safe and liquid, but only the bank account is insured by the government. The traditional advice is to keep six months' wages in your emergency fund. If all your income is from wages, this is good advice — for men. Women, as a class, stay unemployed longer than men, so better put aside enough to last at least ten months, and a year or more if you are over fifty.

If most of your income is from Social Security, pensions, annuities, or other "unearned" entitlements, job loss is not your worry. Your emergency fund should reflect a different concern — namely, catastrophic medical expenses. Keep enough safe and accessible to pay the deductibles and copayments your health insurance and Medicare won't pay, keeping in mind that you're virtually on your own for long-term care — Medicare and the ordinary policies that supplement it don't cover it. We'll learn more about financing long-term care in Chapter 7, but for emergency purposes, $10,000 in your passbook or money market account should be a sensible target.

Correcting Your Seasonings: Asset Allocation

You already know how to achieve an exquisite balance — you pride yourself on just the right mix of ingredients for your meatloaf. You've even adjusted the recipe at different times of your life. One time you lightened up on the salt; another, the fat. Your personal portfolio should be just like that. As your needs change, so will your "recipe." Spicier when younger, perhaps; toned down a little as you mature.

Once you've set aside your emergency cash, it is time to balance your portfolio. The concept is easy: you're going to balance income with growth — that is, safety with risk. As stated earlier, your tolerance for risk is partly personal, and partly reliant on your circumstances. The older you are, the less you should seek growth — but remember, as a woman you are "younger" than a man of the same chronological age, because you have more years to go. More risk may be tolerable in your portfolio than in your twin brother's.

Assume you are fifty-five, and have $100,000 to invest. Draw a circle and label it "$100,000." You decide to divide your circle into thirds, and label one sector "income." The other two-thirds (or $67,000) will be invested for growth. You arrived at this allocation after your library stint, where you noted that advisers recommended ratios ranging from 50/50 to 75/25 (equities to income) for a fifty-year-old. You consulted your own comfort level and found that a two-thirds/one-third ratio seemed reasonable to you.

Now things begin to fall into place. You begin by thinking through your $33,000 allocated to income. You know your choices range from stable, safe, low-paying CDs to volatile but higher-paying, long-term bonds. You draw another circle. Label this one "income investments." Another three-way split seems reasonable to you, so you divide the $33,000 income section of your pie among conservative, moderate, and riskier devices. You turn your attention to your growth funds, make another pie, label it "growth," and divide this $67,000 pie into sectors representing low, moderate, and high risk. If you like to speculate, many advisers have no problem with keeping 3 to 10 percent of your growth funds in highly speculative funds. Just be sure you can afford to lose it.

And that's all there is to it. You've now got a handle on your assets, and you've balanced your portfolio. Of course, picking *which* funds and devices out of the thousands available is another story. But it is certainly feasible, even for the average investor. Persevere at your self-education program at the library and radio. Slowly, certain funds will begin to surface again and again as reliable performers. Keep to the no-load funds, be measured in your approach by neither developing "brand loyalty" to your fund nor excessively chasing the last quarter percent. Be more conservative during your learning phase than you'll want to be later — and you'll do fine.

Dollar-Cost Averaging:
Tailor-Made for Women

One way to reduce the risk inherent in the growth side of your portfolio is to *dollar-cost average* your way into the fund. By investing a set amount every month into your stock fund, you even out the inevitable ups and downs of the market.

Think of purchasing coffee. If you buy $25 worth of coffee month in and month out, you will get more cans of coffee in some months than in others. When prices are high, your $25 might buy eight cans; low prices get you ten cans. As your cupboard fills, more cans will be low-priced ones, inevitably, because low-priced cans are accumulating faster than high-priced ones. In time, the average price on your inventory of cans will get lower, as the cheaper cans overtake the more expensive ones. From an investor's point of view, this is perfect! At some point you may want to sell your cans, and you can sell them all at the high price, even though their average price was low.

Dollar-cost averaging is terrific for women, since usually we don't have large bundles of cash to invest all at once. The slow, disciplined approach — perhaps $200 per month into the stock fund — is often our only option. It's nice to know it's a money-maker as well — *even in a flat market*.

Bonnie received a $40,000 inheritance from her mom. She wanted to invest the entire amount for growth, but instead of writing a $40,000 check to her growth fund, she put it in her money market fund within the same family of funds and instructed the manager to transfer $3,300 on the same day every month from the money fund to the stock fund. Her first transfer bought 120 shares, because the stock market was at an all-time high. The next month, stocks had fallen, so her $3,300 bought 175 shares. The following bought 160 shares, and her final purchase, because the market broke all records, was for only 115 shares. By dollar-cost averaging, Bonnie acquired more shares when the market was down, less when it was high.

Ellen and Dave each received $500 at Christmas. They each owned shares in the same growth (stock) fund. Dave put his entire $500 in on January 1, when the share price was $12.50 (he got forty shares). Ellen put $100 in on January 1 (eight shares), $100 on February 1 (nine shares), $100 on March 1 (ten shares), $100 on April 1 (nine shares), and $100 on May 1 (eight shares). Each has invested $500, yet Dave has forty shares worth $12.50 per share, and Ellen has *forty-four* shares also worth $12.50 per share. Ellen has a $50 profit, *plus* the interest earned on the portions of her $500 left in the money market fund while she was dollar-cost averaging her gift into the stock fund. Dave has no profit and no interest. This strategy works whether the market is rising or falling. Over time, by sheer mathematical necessity, a higher proportion of Ellen's shares were bought "low" rather than "high" — the goal of every investor!

Handling Your Windfall

Everyone dreams of it — a bunch of money comes out of nowhere to solve all our problems. And it happens in real life, too: inheritances; lump sums from employment, and divorce and lawsuit settlements; even the lottery. The first priority for most women should be to put the money into a tax-deferred retirement account forthwith. No new car, no cruise, no remodeled bath. We need our retirement savings more than men.

Of course, reality enters. Even if your dream is a fully funded 401(k) or IRA, competing interests, such as emergency funds, intervene. After all, unless you put the $35,000 from your 401(k) that you received when your company downsized into a qualified retirement account, you will be taxed and penalized on it. But if you do, you can't get at it until you're age fifty-nine and a half. What if you need it for medical emergencies before then, or to pay living expenses if you don't find a job? The best advice is to put it in an IRA rollover set up for this purpose (the usual $2,000 annual contribution limit is waived for rollovers). Then, if and when you need it, withdraw the money a little at a time. You will be taxed on the withdrawals, and penalized 10 percent of the amount withdrawn. But that's better than being taxed and penalized on the whole $35,000 for failing to roll it over within the sixty-day time limit.

Building a Ladder

Let's say you have $50,000 to invest — you want U.S. Treasuries because of their safety, but you are in a quandary. Short-term bills and notes don't pay as much as longer-term instruments, but they turn over in as little as three months. You don't want your money tied up for years at a time. You want long-term rates, with short-term accessibility.

There is a way to get the benefits of both. In 1983, Clare put $10,000 (each) into two-year, four-year, six-year, eight-year, and ten-year Treasuries. In 1985, her two-year note matured, and she replaced it with a ten-year note. As each security matured, she replaced it with a ten-year note. By 1993, all of Clare's $50,000 investment will be in ten-year notes, maturing every two years thereafter. Clare will enjoy longer-term returns with short-term access.

Paying Off Debt

How would you like to earn 18 percent risk-free? In the investment marketplace, an 18 percent investment would be highly risky. But if you pay off your credit card debt, you are in effect earning 18 percent (or higher, even) absolutely risk-free. The same is true of all your debts. Pay them off and pay yourself a handsome return. After you have set aside your emergency funds, line your debts up with your investments and compare the rates. Use your lowest yielding investments to pay off your highest-costing debts.

Some things really are too good to be true. Some investors get a little too clever by half, and end up in the unfriendly arms of the taxman. When mortgage rates hit bottom, some hotshots borrowed against their paid-up homes at 8 percent, then put the proceeds into a tax-exempt bond fund paying 6 percent. Because the home loan was tax-deductible, the effective rate was 5.04 percent after 37 percent state and federal taxes. Borrowing at 5 percent and lending at 6 percent tax-free — these were happy campers! Until they learned, to their horror, that mortgage monies are not tax-deductible if their proceeds go into a tax-exempt fund. Paying 8 percent against earnings of 6 percent — not so nice.

Perhaps you are working now and can afford to save but want to own your home free and clear on the day you turn sixty and retire — but your mortgage won't be paid off until you are 68. Ask your bank to calculate how much will be due on your sixtieth birthday, assuming you pay it all off on that date. You buy a zero-coupon bond in that amount, to mature on that date. You buy the zero today at a discount, and use it later to pay off your home. Buy Treasury zeros if they'll be in a tax-exempt account. Otherwise buy tax-exempt zeros.

Only home mortgage interest is tax-deductible these days. Your department store, credit card, and car loan interest no longer is subsidized by the taxpayer. Some people feel that taking out a home-equity loan and repaying all other debt is a wise move, since this strategy essentially converts nondeductible consumer interest into deductible mortgage interest.

Be very careful. This is a sound strategy if you can easily pay your debts. If you default on your car loan, they'll repossess only your car. But if you default on your equity line, they'll take your house.

Living on the Earnings

Everyone dreams of perpetual money.

Example: If you invested $100,000 in one well-known fund in 1976, and drew out $10,000 per year, you'd end up with $292,980 in 1991. Of course, the high-flying 1980s with their torrid interest rates and stock advances had something to do with this, but the example does illustrate what an investment in a strong mutual fund can do for you.

> **Need a rule of thumb for quick calculations? The *rule of 72* tells you how long it will be before your investment will double. Divide the rate of return (say 7 percent) into 72, and you've got your answer — 10 years. If your rate is 8 percent, then 72 divided by 8 equals 9 years. The rule of 72 assumes your funds are tax-deferred and earning compound interest.**

When the Interest Isn't Enough

We mothers cherish the idea of leaving a nice nest egg for our children. We'll live on the interest of our $300,000 plus Social Security, and when we die, the three kids will each have $100,000. Nice thought, but too many of us oversacrifice to make this happen.

At some point, it may be time to have a talk with yourself about priorities. If you just can't make it on the interest anymore, it isn't a sin to invade the principal. Of course, if your funds run out before you do, you'll have to face other alternatives — such as taking a job, or cashing out your house (see Chapter 4), or at the very worst, using Supplemental Security Income (SSI — welfare), discussed in Chapter 3.

You want to be a well-informed money manager — since your client is so special — so realize that *amortizing* your funds can be a systematic part of your financial planning *if all else fails*. It is a last line of defense. In any case, if you find you *must* spend principal, it's much better to do so according to a plan rather than willy-nilly because you are denying the reality of your situation.

First, tap your taxable investments before you draw your tax-deferred ones. Taxable money is more expensive to keep around than tax-deferred. Then work up a bare-bones budget and withdraw only what you need by the month, so that the remainder keeps earning interest. How might $100,000 be drawn down systematically? Earning 7 percent compound interest, you could draw $1,160 per month for ten years, or $772 for twenty years, after which the fund would be exhausted. You would base your strategy on your life expectancy. You could withdraw $590 indefinitely, because you would be withdrawing interest only.

A Hidden Trap for the Creditworthy

When Jane was turned down for a mortgage, she was aghast. Her credit was impeccable — she had never missed a payment on her several credit cards, nor was she ever even late. The banks continually flooded her with preapproved cards with large credit lines. But she certainly didn't abuse the cards. In fact, combining the unused credit lines, she had $25,000 unused credit. How could her record be in question?

Jane's problem was that she had too much of a good thing. In evaluating her mortgage application, the bank noted the unused credit available to her for the asking, and decided that although she could afford the mortgage, if she ran her cards up to the available limit, she would be in trouble. They chose not to take that chance.

The lesson here is to be practical about your cards. One Visa and one MasterCard, both low or no fee and low interest, is all you need. When the companies automatically raise your credit limit, decline it in writing. Five thousand dollars of credit per card should be enough to cover your occasional large credit purchase. You really don't want to be carrying $10,000 in debt at the exorbitant rates charged, so large limits are not necessary. And although large limits speak to your good credit record, ironically, they can work against you, as Jane learned.

Banks are leery of large unused credit lines because they calculate your ability to repay their loan by applying a percentage of debt against your income. If your actual debt repayment is only 10 percent of your monthly income, the bank will find you creditworthy. But creditors worry if they see the potential for a 30 percent debt, for example, in unused credit lines. How do they know you won't run those lines to the limit and get in trouble? You should worry, too, if your monthly debt payments exceed 20 percent of your net income. Keep it below that — well below, if possible.

While we're talking credit, let's not forget the credit bureaus. Three large firms dominate the industry — a giant industry that has been heavily criticized lately for ruining lives. In a recent year, the Federal Trade Commission's consumer office listed credit-reporting agencies as its single biggest source of complaints. The nonprofit Consumer's Union studied 161 credit reports and found *43 percent* of them in error.

> **You can check your credit file. Find the credit-reporting agencies operating in your area in your yellow pages. Your file will be free if the agency gave you a negative report recently that resulted in a credit refusal. Otherwise, the agency may charge a reasonable fee.**

Tax Strategies

When the money you sweated over to invest at 6 percent is taxed by the state and feds at 30 percent, it should get your attention. Of course, as a good citizen, you are willing to pay your share for the roads, schools, parks, and other things that are better for us to buy collectively rather than individually. But you probably don't like paying more than your share, so here are some of the ways ordinary investors can keep taxes to a minimum.

The most important thing to understand is that avoiding taxes (not *evading* — that's illegal) should *not* be your primary goal. The *bottom line* is your first consideration, and you can easily end up with less in your pocket with a "tax shelter" than without. Some exotic tax shelters have been brought to heel by the IRS — at great cost to their investors; others are legal but very risky. Ask Arabian horse breeders. As an average investor, you should never invest in something you don't fully understand. Obedience to that rule should keep you out of trouble most of the time.

But even sound tax shelters are not for everyone. Every worker can benefit from fully funding the tax-deferred vehicles available to him or her. But if you are not employed and not in the highest tax bracket, it's likely you will make more money by paying the tax and investing for a higher return.

Workers get a break with IRAs and the other tax-deductible or -deferred devices. Investors who don't have employment income (for simplicity we'll call these wages, although income from self-employment is also included) can defer taxes *only* by investing in special tax-favored devices such as municipal bonds, annuities, and U.S. savings bonds. Wages, up to a limit, can turn almost any regular investment into a tax-favored one simply by waving a magic wand called Individual Retirement Account (IRA); Keogh; deferred compensation plan (401(k), 403(b)); or Simplified Employee Pension (SEP-IRA). When the magic wand passes over your equities fund, or corporate bond fund, or CD — it's like icing a cake. A good thing becomes an even better thing. Nonwage income can't ice this cake. Nonwage income is limited to cookies — some are good, but cake is bigger and better.

You can establish and contribute to an IRA up to age seventy and a half. Thereafter you must begin withdrawing it — all at once, if you like — but at least in increments that will deplete the fund over your life expectancy. See your tax adviser about this, because IRA moneys withdrawn early (before age fifty-nine and a half) or too late are penalized in addition to the tax due on all IRA withdrawals. IRA contributions are limited to $2,000 per year ($2,250 for a single-earner couple).

IRAs, for all their usefulness, are gender biased. First, like all tax-favored vehicles, IRAs favor the higher paid. People in higher tax brackets get a proportionately higher return — $1 is worth more protected from high taxes than from low. Women, being lower paid, are disproportionately in the lower brackets. Also, people who don't earn as much can't afford to set aside savings, and women are usually in that group. Finally, if only one member of a working couple has a pension, both spouses will be disqualified from deducting the IRA from their taxable income (although they can both contribute to their tax-deferred IRAs, and should). This hits hardest at women, who are only half as likely as men to have a pension but are disqualified from deducting their IRA because their husbands have a pension. It is unrealistic to assume that all couples will remain together long enough to both benefit from the pension earned by only one of them.

> **If you are in this situation and are self-employed, set up an SEP-IRA for yourself (see Chapter 3). Call the IRS and ask for the form required to start one, or call the retirement division of any large mutual fund family, which will send you what you need. You will be able to deduct it from your taxes despite your husband's pension.**

Nevertheless, if you have wages, you want to fund your IRA to the maximum — especially after age fifty-nine and a half if you can, because then you can withdraw as much or as little as you like whenever you want. It makes no sense at all to keep $2,000 in ordinary savings when it can be in tax-deferred savings. At forty you may worry about locking up all your funds until you're almost sixty, but after fifty-nine and a half there is no reason to hesitate.

> **From time to time, Congress debates changes in IRA rules to allow for withdrawals for a variety of reasons such as first house purchase, college tuition, and medical emergency. Obtain up-to-date information before establishing your IRA.**

The *401(k)* and *403(b)* are great devices available only to paid workers. Through payroll deduction, your contributions are directed into whatever accounts your employer permits: mutual funds, insurance annuities — you name it. Unfortunately, many employers limit their programs to some pretty poor choices. High-load mutual funds are one example. Employee groups really should conduct their own investigations into appropriate 401(k) investment vehicles and enlighten their employer. A 401(k) (and its sister, 403(b), for nonprofit and public employees) is better than an IRA because you can put more into it, your employer can match (or even exceed) your contribution, and it is always tax-deductible *and* tax-deferred.

If you're not a paid worker, your choices are more limited. Your magic wand won't turn your taxable aggressive growth mutual fund into a tax-deferred one. You'll have to stick with investments that themselves are tax-favored, such as *municipal bonds*. All sorts of public bonds are called municipals whether or not a municipality stands behind them (for example, library districts, dam building projects, school districts, and public ballparks can all raise money by selling bonds — even though no city is involved). Because small districts find it hard to borrow money at fair rates, the feds help them out by declaring the interest to be exempt from federal income tax. This tax break will entice you to lend them money at 6 percent when you could otherwise get 7 percent, assuming you're in a high tax bracket. But some municipals have a problem. Although not catastrophic, defaults are hardly unknown. Your best bet, if municipals fit into your tax strategy, is to buy into a well-managed tax-exempt mutual fund. Some bonds and funds will also exempt you from state income taxes. Look for no-load funds invested in high-grade bonds, partially insured.

If you must purchase bonds directly, know the difference between *revenue* bonds and *general obligation* bonds. Wayne didn't, to his sorrow. He bought $5,000 in revenue bonds issued by his hometown to build a ballpark, in order to lure a major-league team to the area. The bondholders would be paid back by the revenue generated by the ballpark. A revenue bond is backed by nothing more than hope. Sometimes this is good enough; in Wayne's case it wasn't. The ballpark was built, no teams came to play, the entity went bankrupt — and Wayne was repaid ten cents on the dollar when the park was finally sold for far less than its construction cost. Colleen was smarter. When she bought bonds issued by her state to build prisons, she made sure they were general obligation bonds. That meant the taxpayers of the state stood behind the bonds — they would be repaid out of general revenues.

Maybe you have $1,000 to invest and you want to do it in a tax-favored way. Should you put it in an IRA? A 401(k) or 403(b)? How about tax-exempt bonds or mutual funds? Perhaps U.S. Treasuries? Here's a brief summary of each.

An IRA is

- always tax-deferred
- sometimes tax-deductible
- limited to $2,000 contributions per year
- unavailable before age 59½ without penalty
- for anyone with funds earned on the job or from alimony
- nearly unlimited in scope of investment vehicles
- not available to borrow from
- subject to the risk of the investment selected
- taxed when withdrawn

401(k)s and 403(b)s are

- always tax-deferred
- always tax-deductible
- often contributed to by employer
- only for wage-earners whose employer has set one up
- unavailable before age 59½
- often available to borrow from

- limited to the employer's authorized investments
- limited to a percentage of income
- subject to the risk of the investment selected
- taxed when withdrawn

Tax-exempt bonds and bond funds are

- available to anyone with any kind of income
- available in any amount
- liquid at any age
- limited to investments with no potential for growth
- limited to investments usually paying below market
- sometimes risky, depending on the issuing agency
- sometimes subject to state and local taxes
- not taxed when withdrawn

U.S. Treasuries are

- as safe as investments get if held to maturity
- subject to principal loss if sold before maturity
- available to anyone with any kind of income
- available in any amount
- not a growth investment
- not a particularly high-paying income investment
- subject to federal income taxes
- not taxed when withdrawn

If you are a worker with $2,000 to invest tax-deferred, always choose the IRA over a tax-exempt bond fund, for example. Why, since both are tax-deferred? Because in an IRA your funds can be invested virtually anywhere. They can earn the *market rate* (the same rate as fully taxable investments) and still be tax-deferred — while buying tax-exempt bonds limits you to the below-market rate tax-favored instruments pay. For example, $2,000 in a municipal bond fund might earn 4 percent, whereas the same amount in your IRA in a GNMA fund might earn 6 percent.

Some people like to buy *annuities* because they are not taxed until they pay out. This is one way someone in a very high bracket can throw earnings into his or her later years, when the tax bracket may be lower. Many investment advisers feel the returns earned by annuities do not, even when combined with their tax characteristics, justify the strategy. As you may remember from Chapter 1, many annuities pay women less or charge them more. The companies that justify this by pointing to women's (statistically) longer life span could just as well base their actuarial charts on race — they could pay African-Americans more (or charge them less) because of their shorter (average) lives. But do they? Not on your life.

Always keep the three factors (risk, return, and liquidity) in mind in evaluating any investment. Annuities carry the slight risk of a collapsing insurer, somewhat lower returns than comparable investments, and limits on liquidity. This doesn't mean they are never appropriate. For the right purposes — for example, to carry out provisions in a will or to provide a stream of income to a minor or spendthrift (see Chapter 5) — annuities are a handy tool. But like life insurance, which does one thing very well — pay a death benefit — annuities lose their luster when they try to move from being "niche" investments into the mainstream. As ordinary investment vehicles, they don't compete well with their competitors.

> **If you have an annuity, should you take a lump-sum payout, or annuitize it over your lifetime? Annuitization is a better value for most people — and that goes double for women with our longer life spans.**

So that's the story on the investment leg of your retirement income stool. Social Security and pensions, if you're fortunate, provide two more legs for that stool. In the next chapter we'll see how to make those legs as sturdy as they can be.

CHECKING ON YOUR STRATEGIES

1. Do you know how much Social Security you'll have?
2. Do you know how much pension income you'll have?

3. After accounting for these two, how much of your retirement budget is unmet?
4. Is mathphobia holding you back? Do you use a calculator?
5. Do you know how to figure 3 percent of 150? Do it, then see below.
6. If the yield is 8 percent, and taxes are 15 percent, what is the after-tax yield?
7. Do you feel you must have a financial adviser?
8. Does he or she get commissions from your purchases?
9. Where do *you* draw the line between investing and speculating?
10. Do you understand your own psychological tolerance for risk?
11. Do you understand that rigid aversion to risk is costly?
12. Have you looked over the financial magazines in your library?
13. Are you in the habit of reading your newspaper's financial pages daily?
14. What is the risk, return, and liquidity of each of your assets?
15. Do you figure in tax and inflation when figuring your yields?
16. Do you know your combined state and federal income tax rate?
17. What is the current inflation rate? Where can you find it?
18. Are you as debt-free as you can reasonably be?
19. Do you carry more than two credit cards?
20. Do you know how much interest and fees each card costs you?
21. Have you given thought to tax-protected investments?

Answers
Question 5: $.03 \times 150 = 4.5$
Question 6: $8 \times .15 = 1.2$, so 8 percent minus 1.2 = 6.8 percent, which is the after-tax yield.

3
Social Security Is for Women
(and Pensions Are for Men)

The chapter title may be a little far-reaching, but it's in the ballpark. Social Security's beneficiaries are predominantly women, pension beneficiaries are predominantly men. Both programs are suffused with gender bias — but as we'll see, these biases cut both ways and can present opportunities as well as hurdles.

For example, as a class, we women get more bang for our buck from Social Security than do men. Here's why:

- More of us can apply younger.
- More of us will draw longer.
- More of us qualify without a work record.
- More of us qualify for the higher wage/benefit ratio.

Of course, diamonds are known to have flaws. We apply younger because we are more likely to be the widowed. We draw longer because we live longer. We qualify for dependent's benefits because our own wage history is so low. And because we are the lower paid, our benefits will replace a higher percentage of our wages.

Still, Social Security is to be applauded for providing widow's and other dependent's benefits, and for weighting benefits to the lower paid. For women, these features are lifesavers.

We can, in many cases, apply gender awareness to the many options Social Security and pension programs offer, and thus greatly increase the odds against making expensive mistakes. Let's take a look at where we are and how to get where we want to be.

Despite the rich widow of popular belief, most women woefully trail men in retirement income. Only half as many women as men get pension income, and those who do get half as much. Women, as a group, have weaker ties to the paid labor market, and even those who work a lifetime for pay are more likely to work at jobs without fringe benefits and at lower wages. Because Social Security, pensions, and retirement savings are directly affected by your job history, it should be no surprise that retired women have only 60 percent of the income of retired men.

This makes for some fancy planning if we women are going to end up where we want to be. The challenges are quite surmountable — especially when you keep in mind our critical planning advantage: our extra retirement years in which to put forward our plans.

In this chapter we will keep in mind the profound differences between men's and women's incomes as they approach retirement — not only in amount, but in source as well. We'll formulate strategies to work around them, using quirks and gender biases in Social Security, pensions, and savings plans to even the playing field.

Analyzing your retirement income situation is actually pretty easy. Remember, there are really only three components to track on the traditional three-legged retirement income stool:

- Social Security
- pension
- retirement savings

For women, add the following:

- employment
- home equity

A well-funded retirement rests firmly on all legs. But a woman's stool is likely to wobble and tip, as shortened or missing legs can't carry their share.

In this chapter we'll keep an eye out for the gender biases inherent in the money world — including in helpful systems such as Social Security — and use them to our advantage. Gender awareness should be an important part of your financial strategies, because male/female differences in longevity, retirement income base, and marital status can turn a smart move for a woman into something not so smart for most men. So as we go along, we'll focus on ways to use gender awareness to manipulate your entitlements in ways that should work especially well for you as a woman. We'll start with Social Security, then move on to pensions.

SOCIAL SECURITY

Do not take Social Security lightly. It is likely to be the mainstay of your retirement. It would be politically impossible to junk the biggest social program in America, serving forty million older residents, so you can forget all the naysayers and predictors of doom. Social Security is a dynamic program — always was — so it will be adjusted from time to time as demographics change. But you can count on it being there for you until the day you die — and for those dependent on you even after that.

You can also forget those who propose making Social Security into a voluntary program — a sort of super-IRA. IRAs and other voluntary savings programs don't cut the mustard when it comes to providing the basics for the entire population, rich or poor. Tax-subsidized savings programs are popular with the rich, not so popular with the plain Janes and ordinary Joes of the land. Folks who posit that they could do better investing their funds on their own ignore these important features of Social Security, which are absolutely critical for women:

- Pensions are rarely adjusted for inflation — Social Security is adjusted annually.
- Social Security is not taxed for people with up to $25,000 ($32,000 for couples) per year (1994), and 50 to 85 percent is taxable after that.
- Investment income fluctuates according to market prices and interest; Social Security only rises.
- Neither your pension nor your savings will pay extra if you are married; Social Security will.
- If you become disabled before retirement, Social Security will come to your rescue with no reduction in your future benefits — unlike your investments.
- If you die young, Social Security will pay your minor children — try that with your pension.
- Social Security alone will pay benefits to a divorced spouse without a reduction in the primary beneficiary's benefit.
- The average Social Security benefit in 1994 is $674 per month, considerably more than the average pension. The maximum benefit is $1,147, which rises annually.
- Virtually every worker in America is covered by Social Security or a comparable government pension — including part-time teenagers at the fast-food counter. Fewer than half of all workers are covered by pensions in the private sector, and virtually no teenagers, part-timers, or minimum-wage earners.

Social Security is America's largest social program by far ($366 billion in the trust fund), and as such it is rightfully goaded and prodded to do its job even better. There is plenty of room for improvement in the system, as I will explain as we go along. But make no mistake about it: Social Security is the most important women's program in the United States by far. Women, whose pension and investment income lags far behind those of men, rely much more on Social Security as their retirement income base than do men; and women form the substantial majority of Social Security beneficiaries. It's true that the program, despite its neutral language, is suffuse with gender biases. But bias, don't forget, works both ways. We will explain the biases that work *for* women as well as against them, and how to plot the course that will work best for you.

First Things First

Most of your Social Security business can be taken care of by calling this one all-important toll-free number:

(800) 772-1213

Make a note of it in your phone file, because with that one number you can obtain a Social Security number, apply for benefits, inquire about a missing check, get free pamphlets, and talk to a real live person who will answer your Social Security questions.

Most important for planning purposes, by calling this number you can request the application for the Personal Employment and Benefits Statement (PEBS). This free service allows you to project your future earnings and retirement date, then receive back from Social Security an estimation of your future benefit.

> **Before you read any further, call Social Security at the toll-free number given above and ask for the PEBS application. Get one for your husband, too. Make a practice of getting a PEBS at least every three years until you begin drawing Social Security.**

When you receive the information, check the earnings record for accuracy. Because women commonly change their names during their working lifetimes, mix-ups in records can occur.

With your PEBS in hand, you are in a position to do some serious planning. One leg of your stool is taking shape. If you are some years away from retirement, you have the opportunity to build and manipulate that leg, as we'll soon see. If you are already drawing Social Security, your options are narrower, but not nonexistent. We'll talk about those, too.

> **We'll use the following terms in our discussions: *Spousal* benefits are paid to a man or woman who is married to the *worker* whose work record earned the benefits. A *divorced spouse* receives benefits from a worker's record if he or she was married to the worker for at least ten years. A *widow(er)* receives benefits from the record of a deceased worker, and a *divorced widow(er)* receives benefits from a former spouse's record, now deceased.**

The Early Retirement Option

The Social Security benefit structure is built on the assumption that "full" retirement occurs at age sixty-five (for people born between 1938 and 1960, the "full" age rises gradually to sixty-seven). At full retirement age, a worker receives 100 percent of his or her primary insurance amount (PIA). Keep this concept in mind, because as we work through these strategies, we will frequently refer to the PIA.

Social Security permits a worker to draw as early as age sixty-two, but his or her lifetime benefits will be only 80 percent of the PIA.

> **If you must retire early because of health, consider applying for Social Security disability. There is no reduction for receiving Social Security disability early, then switching to full retirement benefits at sixty-five. Social Security disability is not related to need — just to your ability to work.**

Obviously, your application date calls for a strategy. Obviously, too, if you have no other resource, you'll have no choice. But if an early withdrawal is optional with you, you have your first opportunity to turn a classic Social Security gender bias to your favor. Here's why:

Twins, Dorothy and Carl, each applied for benefits at age sixty-two. Each had the same three years between sixty-two and sixty-five to enjoy the early benefit. Carl died at sixty-eight, Dorothy at seventy-three. The ratio of "early years" to reduced later years for Carl was 3:3. In other words, Carl benefited for three years and paid for it with a penalty lasting three years. Dorothy's ratio was 3:8. Three years of benefit, eight years of penalty. Assuming their PIAs were $600, their reduced benefits were $480 per month. Each was ahead the thirty-six "early" months of $480 payments for a total of $17,280. Carl paid for this with a $120 monthly reduction over the next three years, or $4,320. His "profit," then, was $12,960 (the gain of $17,280 less the cost of $4,320). Dorothy, on the other hand, "paid" her $120 reduction for eight years, for a total of $11,520 — a net gain for Dorothy of $5,760. Carl "made" $7,200 more than Dorothy on the deal — but, of course, he had to die to do it. As a class, then, men, with their shorter lives, are more likely to have a higher ratio of benefit years to burden years than are women after taking early benefits. Still, note that Dorothy was better off taking early benefits than she would have been by waiting. If Dorothy had lived past seventy-seven, she would have been ahead by waiting until sixty-five to draw her benefits.

For yourself, consult your financial circumstances, your health, your genes — then formulate a strategy custom-made just for you.

When the new retirement age of sixty-seven is fully phased in, the reduction in PIA for withdrawal at age sixty-two will rise to 30 percent, but if you were born before 1938, you don't have to worry about that.

Some feel that taking early Social Security is a good strategy, no matter what your life expectancy. Roxie, for example, didn't need the income when she was sixty-two but decided to take the benefit anyway, despite its lifetime 20 percent reduction. She invested her $640 monthly check at 7.5 percent, and at sixty-five had a $25,748 nest egg. Then she withdrew the $160 per month interest (still at 7.5 percent), which, combined with her $640 reduced Social Security benefit, brought her to $800 per month, the same amount she would have drawn from Social Security had she waited until she was sixty-five — *and she has more than $25,000 in the bank to boot!*

For applicants between sixty-two and sixty-five, the 20 percent reduction is proportionately reduced — so you can employ this strategy any time before you are sixty-five. Widow(er)s and divorced widow(er)s can apply for reduced benefits as early as sixty.

You may be able to have it both ways — an early, reduced benefit, then at sixty-five a full PIA — by manipulating the *dual entitlement rule*, discussed next.

Be Sure You Understand the Dual Entitlement Rule

You could be eligible for Social Security in two, three, or even more ways, for example, through

- your own work record
- your husband's record
- your former husband's record

You won't get all three checks, but Social Security will compute your benefits and give you the highest one. Patty was eligible for $425 on her own work record, $550 on her husband Frank's, and $800 as her former husband's widow. Since she married Frank after she turned sixty, Patty was able to take her divorced widow's benefit of $800 rather than her spousal of $550 or her own worker's benefit of $425.

Widow(er)s and divorced widow(er)s remain eligible on their former spouse's records *only* if they remarry for the first time after the age of sixty. An earlier remarriage forfeits the benefit from the former marriage.

The dual entitlement rule can work nicely for women, in that widows and divorced widows (and widowers, of course — hereinafter, for simplicity's sake, consider both genders included in the term *widow*) who qualify both on their own work record and as widows can choose to take their own (reduced) benefit early, then switch to their full widow's benefit at sixty-five. This way the reduction for early retirement stops at sixty-five (when you discontinue receiving your own worker's benefit) instead of continuing for a lifetime. Sonya, for example, was dually entitled to $500 on her own work record, or a widow's benefit of $500 (assuming, for both, an application at age sixty-five). She applied for her own worker's benefit at age sixty-two, receiving 80 percent, or $400 per month. At sixty-five, she applied for her widow's benefit of $500, which she continued to receive, unreduced, for the rest of her lifetime.

Women are in a better position to play this game than men, because widow's benefits are usually paid to women, not men. Why? When a married couple gets Social Security, the worker gets 100 percent of the PIA, the spouse gets 50 percent — for a total of 150 percent of PIA for the couple (assuming she's entitled to spouse benefits under the dual entitlement rule). When the worker dies, the widow's benefit steps up to 100 percent of the PIA. The household income drops from 150 percent of PIA to 100 percent of the PIA. Still, for most women, 100 percent of the husband's PIA is more than 100 percent of her own PIA, so she gets the widow's benefit rather than her own worker's benefit. Most men, on the other hand, will not collect widow's benefits, because their own work record provides a PIA that exceeds 100 percent of their wife's PIA. The widow's benefit under Social Security is a godsend to women — no pension provides a 150 percent benefit to a married couple, and a 100 percent benefit to the survivor, without a reduction in the primary benefit.

A Gender Bias in Favor of Women

As we've learned, not all gender biases work against women. Social Security, loaded with unintentional biases, features some *intentional* biases that favor the lower paid — women and minorities chief among them. First, Social Security benefits are proportionately larger for the lower-paid worker than for the higher-paid worker. The worker earning $10,000 per year can expect his or her Social Security benefit to replace over 50 percent of the wages; a $20,000 worker, only 42 percent. A worker earning over $50,000 may see less than 25 percent of his or her wages replaced by Social Security.

> **This feature means that you should apply for your own worker benefits even if you are married to someone who earned more than twice what you did. If your husband earned $50,000 per year, while you earned $23,000, you might think that your spousal benefit of 50 percent of his PIA will outshine 100 percent of your own PIA. But it won't, because your lower pay earned higher benefits. Always check out all of your entitlements.**

Of course, before you become too enthusiastic, know that although the average retired man's 1994 Social Security benefit is $735, the average retired woman receives only about $562. And, too, all workers pay the same 7.65 percent payroll tax up to $60,600 of income, and nothing above that (these are 1994 figures). The payroll tax is therefore regressive, and a bias against the lower paid — the very women and minorities favored by the benefit structure.

Confronting the Earnings Test

Social Security was born in the deep depression of the early 1930s. Part of its function was to keep money flowing into the economy; the other part was to open up jobs by enabling older people to retire. To discourage older people from staying on the job, a limit on earnings was imposed. If you earned over a certain amount — and drew Social Security benefits as well — your Social Security would disappear. Over the years, Congress has reduced this unpopular penalty, but it still is a factor for beneficiaries through age sixty-nine (workers older than that, Congress evidently feels, have enough problems without Social Security adding to them — the earnings limit disappears on your seventieth birthday). Up until age sixty-five, your Social Security worker's benefit is reduced $1 for every $2 you earn over $8,040 annually; from sixty-five to sixty-nine, it is reduced $1 for every $3 you earn over $11,160 (1994 figures). Of course, if you choose not to draw benefits while you're working, the earnings test does not apply — your long work record will add a bonus to your eventual benefits, as we'll see below. Congress, every session, entertains at least one bill to further reduce or eliminate the earnings test. Be sure to check with Social Security for the current situation by calling the toll-free number given earlier.

For women, the earnings test presents a special dilemma. Over the last decade, labor statistics demonstrate that men are taking early retirement in droves; at the same time, mid-life women are entering the labor force in record numbers. Men in their fifties are leaving their jobs as fast as women in their fifties are applying. This means that a much higher proportion of Social Security–eligible women than men are working at entry-level, low-paid positions, and are in the worst position to lose their benefits. Take Nola and Brian, for example, both age sixty-five. Nola earned $15,000, and her Social Security PIA was $3,600 per year. Brian earned $85,000, and his PIA was $8,000. When the earnings test was applied, Nola lost

$1,280 per year from her Social Security. Brian lost all of his. But Brian, with $85,000 left to live on, was far better able to sustain the loss than Nola, with only $17,320.

> **Note that the earnings limit applies only to compensation. You can have millions in investment or pension income and be unaffected. The earnings limit, besides favoring men, favors the rich.**

The silver lining for women? More of us will reach the privileged age of seventy when the earnings limit disappears altogether.

A Bonus for Late Retirement

If you delay your application beyond your full retirement age, Social Security will give you a bonus — an increased check for the rest of your life. The amount depends on when you were born, with the maximum being 8 percent per year of delay for those born in 1943 and later (the minimum is 1 percent per year of delay for those born in 1916 or earlier). If you, born in 1935, delayed your application until age sixty-eight, your PIA would be 118 percent (6 percent × 3 years + 100 percent) for the rest of your life.

> **If you do delay your application past sixty-five, be sure you apply for Medicare, anyway. Delaying your Medicare application will gain you nothing and could be costly. More about that in Chapter 7.**

But there is a catch for women. Suppose you figured you'd delay retirement a few years to boost your benefit. You're pleased when you retire at sixty-eight with $708 monthly benefits instead of the $600 you would otherwise have been entitled to. Your husband's benefits are $800, so your 50 percent spousal benefits would be only $400 per month — you're ahead by taking your own entitlement of $708. But one month after you begin drawing, your husband dies. Now you are eligible for widow's benefits of 100 percent of his PIA, or $800. Obviously, you'll take the widow's benefits over your own benefit, so the years you delayed to boost your benefit were for naught. Had you drawn at sixty-five, you would have had thirty-seven months of $600, or $22,200, instead of one month of $708. Since women are overwhelmingly the surviving spouses, this is a gender bias aimed right at a widow's heart.

For married women, then, delaying retirement to increase the benefit is risky. You have to keep your husband's life expectancy, and your potential widow's benefit, always in mind. Before you decide to delay your application, sit down with Social Security and have them run the numbers for you, especially taking into account widow's benefits.

The Very Best Time for You to Apply

We have discussed how 100 percent of your PIA is payable at sixty-five (currently), and how you can reduce or boost this amount by taking it early or late, or reduce it by working. Social Security is complex, and sometimes you can maneuver your application date to take advantage of its complexity. Workers subject to the earnings test who are nearing their sixty-fifth birthday may benefit by applying for Social Security months before their birthday. In fact, every applicant has an optimum month to apply, and Social Security will help you find it. For this reason, have Social Security do some preretirement planning with you at age sixty. If you decide to apply at age sixty-five, be sure you visit Social Security a year ahead to learn if you would benefit by applying a few months earlier (with no lifetime reduction in benefits — a possibility for some subject to the earnings test).

Spousal Benefits

If your own work record does not produce a benefit equal to one-half of your husband's, you will probably be eligible for a spouse benefit, beginning as early as age sixty-two (reduced, or the full benefit if you wait until sixty-five). The exception would be the government pension offset discussed below. Men and women are equally eligible, but in fact few men are entitled to worker's benefits worth less than half their wife's, so the spousal benefit is a wife's benefit most of the time — one more example of Social Security's immense importance to American women. The couple benefit, then, is 150 percent of PIA, assuming both apply at full retirement age. The checks can be issued to each spouse separately or only to one.

After Your Husband Dies: Widow(er)'s Benefits

When the worker dies, the spousal benefit becomes a widow's benefit, and jumps from 50 to 100 percent of the PIA (reduced, of course, if the early retirement option was taken). But since the household Social Security declines from 150 percent PIA to 100 percent PIA, you should look at this as a 33 percent reduction rather than an increase when planning for your future. Widows can apply for (reduced) benefits as early as age sixty, or full benefits at sixty-five. A disabled widow can receive benefits as early as age fifty.

> **A decade or so ago, many older folks complained that they would love to marry their companion, but couldn't because they would lose their widow's benefits. A kind-hearted Congress took heed and ruled that widow(er)s and divorced widow(er)s over age sixty (fifty if disabled) could remarry and retain their entitlement to their former spouse's benefit.**

Divorced Spouse's Benefits

You can begin receiving reduced divorced *spouse's* benefits as early as age sixty-two, or your full amount at age sixty-five if:

- you were married at least ten years
- he is receiving Social Security, or is sixty-two and eligible
- you have never remarried

You can receive divorced *widow's* benefits if:

- your former husband has died
- you were married at least ten years
- you are at least sixty years old
- you did not remarry before age sixty

While your former husband is alive, you will be eligible for a benefit equal to 50 percent of his, paid separately to you. This will not affect his benefit, or his new wife's. A disabled divorced spouse can apply as early as age fifty. Similar rules apply to the wife: for you to qualify, your own work record must yield less than 50 percent of the benefit he is entitled to.

If your former husband is living, your remarriage at any age will end your benefits — however, after he has died, you may again be entitled to his benefits if your new marriage ends by death, divorce, or annulment.

Your benefit will not be lowered if your former husband's check is reduced due to the earnings test.

You will receive the largest of your various entitlements: divorced spouse, spouse, widow, or worker.

Government Pension Offset

You may lose your eligibility for a spousal or widow's pension if you receive a government pension. Teachers, government clerks, public-transit bus drivers — double-check with Social Security if you will get a government pension (state, federal, or local) and also hope to receive a spousal, widow's, or divorced spouse's benefit. Your Social Security dependent's benefit will probably be offset by your government pension — very possibly resulting in no Social Security benefit payable to you at all. Two-thirds of your government pension is deducted from your Social Security spouse's, widow's, or divorced spouse or widow's benefit — even if that results in zero Social Security. The offset does not apply to any benefit paid to you from your own work record, but watch for the windfall penalty rule, below.

The Windfall Penalty Rule

Although the government pension offset doesn't affect your own worker's benefits, the windfall penalty rule might. If you earned a government pension and earned Social Security in another job, your Social Security could be reduced by as much as 55 percent (but never more than 50 percent of the government pension). If your husband's benefit is reduced because of this rule, so will yours be as his wife, former wife, or widow. It is a complicated formula, and you should ask Social Security if the rule will apply to you.

Social Security and Taxes

Social Security benefits are completely tax-free for individuals whose total income (earnings, pensions, investments, one-half of Social Security income and "tax-exempt" investment income) falls below $25,000 for an individual and $32,000 for a couple (in 1994 — check with the IRS for changes). At most, one-half your Social Security income could be taxable. The taxable thresholds well exceed the average annual income of older women (and minorities), so this tax break is great for women.

For purposes of this tax, your *tax-exempt* income is counted in the total. Some people near the line switch from tax-exempt investments to *tax-deferred* ones, such as certain U.S. bonds or annuities. Since there is no current income from the annuity, there is nothing for the IRS to count. But remember that annuities can

pose serious gender-biased disadvantages for the woman investor, as well as the risks posed by the insurance company that sells them.

Social Security, then, is a major factor in any woman's retirement. The vast majority of American older women receive it, while the reverse is true for pensions. In the next section we'll talk about pensions for you as a worker, as well as pension benefits for you as a widow or divorced wife.

How to Make a Good System Even Better

Social Security was structured to fit the typical middle-class family of the 1930s: a working father, homemaker mother, dependent kids; a one-income family, in which divorce was unthinkable. Only widows were protected — not divorced men or women, nor widowed men unless they could prove financial dependency on their deceased wife. Times change, family structures have certainly changed, but Social Security — although it has added bells and whistles for divorced people and widowed men — remains fundamentally the same.

Women workers continue to trail men in their Social Security entitlements for reasons largely traceable to unfavorable gender bias:

- Many women are still paid less than men for the same work.
- ''Women's'' jobs pay less than ''men's'' (librarians versus plumbers).
- Many women move in and out of the labor market to assume family responsibilities.

Since Social Security benefits are computed on lifetime earnings, it is easy to see how the disparity arises. But it doesn't have to be this way. If we truly wish to recognize family values, then the years a parent stays at home raising children should be rewarded on retirement. Other countries credit the caregiving homemaker — male or female. The United Kingdom, for example, gives up to twenty years' social security credit for someone caring for a child up to age seven or a disabled adult. Under our system, the homemaker accumulates "zero years" during the time she (or he) is out of the paid labor force. These zero earnings years are included in the calculation of the final benefit — with devastating effect. Of course, this applies only to those who will draw their own benefits — spouse's and widow's benefits are not affected by zero years.

A fairer system would be something like community property. A married couple, when parting due to divorce, would add up their joint credits and split them down the middle. The contributions of each of them to the marriage — whether in the home or on the job — would be given equal dignity and worth on the demise of the marriage. This concept is called *"earnings sharing"* and has been debated by Congress for at least a decade — but so far to no avail, despite the backing of organizations such as the Older Women's League. Social Security is a federal, statutory system — meaning Congress is the proper forum to address reform.

If you're interested in this fascinating social system, and would like to know more — or help in its reform — here are a couple of organizations you should contact:

> **The Older Women's League (OWL), 666 11th Street NW, Suite 700, Washington, D.C. 20001, telephone (202) 783-6686; and the National Committee to Preserve Social Security and Medicare, 2000 K Street NW, Suite 800, Washington, D.C. 20006, telephone (202) 822-9459.**

PENSIONS

Pensions, as we've known them, appear to be candidates for the Endangered Species Act. The traditional pension, paid into by the employer over long years of employment, then paid out on a monthly basis to the retired employee until death, is fading in favor of a variety of voluntary retirement savings plans, such as the individual retirement account (IRA), deferred compensation plan (401(k) and 403(b), and simplified employee pension (SEP-IRA). The employer may or may not contribute to these plans, and their eventual value is anything but guaranteed. For younger workers, especially, traditional pensions are increasingly hard to find outside of government employment.

This trend will affect women differently from men. The traditional pension hasn't been kind to women, so its loss will not affect women's retirement income as much as men's; we've had only half as much pension income anyway. And things aren't getting any better. In 1976, single women received 74 percent of the pension income of single men; married women received 61 percent of the pension of married men. By the end of the 1980s, single women fell to 56 percent, and married women to 43 percent.

Women workers, with their greater job mobility, will benefit from the portability offered by the voluntary plans. As they move from job to job, they can roll over their funds, no matter how often they move or how long they work. But the voluntary plans mostly or entirely depend on employee contributions, something women, along with other lower-paid groups, will find difficult or impossible to fund. Also, the tax aspects of these plans are tilted heavily in favor of the higher paid. Single moms, responsible for tuition, child care, and other heavy costs, will find it all too easy to look on their retirement funds as emergency funds — and there goes the retirement. Traditional pensions, at least, are locked away until drawn.

In this section we'll assume a traditional pension is in your present or future — either on your own record or as a widow or former wife — and we'll take a womanly view of each pension particular, to form the best strategy for you. First, we'll look at the pension you earned at work, then survivor's and divorced wife's benefits on your husband's work record.

Sorting Out Some Jargon

Traditional pensions are known as "defined *benefit*" plans, because the employee is told from the beginning how much the pension will be, based on length of employment, age, and pay level.

Ask your plan administrator (PA) or personnel office for a copy of your plan's Summary Plan Description (SPD). You are supposed to get one annually. It will explain how your pension will be calculated.

Employer-sponsored voluntary savings plans are called "defined *contribution*" plans, because the employee and perhaps the employer make a certain contribution periodically — but how much the payout will be depends on how well the investment does over the years. There are a variety of defined contribution plans, including

- 401(k)
- 403(b)
- Keogh
- ESOP
- SEP-IRA

The 401(k) and 403(b) plans (named for the sections of the internal revenue code that defines them) are employer-sponsored investment programs. Through a payroll deduction, some of your pay is diverted to the plan. The employer may or may not contribute as well. Because you contribute pretax dollars, and the investment income is not taxed until you withdraw it after age fifty-nine and a half, these devices grow much more rapidly than the same amount of money put into ordinary savings. A Keogh is a similar program available to the self-employed. You can contribute more to these programs than you can to your IRA, and your contribution is tax-deductible *and* tax-deferred, a double tax break that may not be true for your IRA. On the other hand, you are freer to invest where you want with your IRA. Your employer approves the investment vehicles for your 401(k) or 403(b).

> **If you don't like your employer's choices (and the company may very well have yielded to a high-pressure salesperson in its choice of funds), have a little chat. It is actually quite easy to broaden the selection. If you have a favorite family of funds, they will have forms you can give your employer to get them on board. Call the fund's retirement advisory.**

One kind of retirement program popular in the corporate world is the employee stock ownership plan (ESOP). In an ESOP, the corporation transfers its own stock into employee retirement accounts. Some companies have been sued by former employees after managers "looted" the sinking ship — thus rendering the stock (and the ESOPs) worthless. Obviously, an ESOP, even more than a 401(k)/403(b), is a heavily restricted investment vehicle. You have no choice of investment and no diversity.

If your company contributes to an ESOP for you, obviously you'll take it. But because of its lack of diversity, it is too risky to bank your entire retirement on. ESOP owners should be particularly eager to build other investments and diversify them religiously.

An SEP-IRA is an IRA to which your employer contributes. It is also available to the self-employed. You can select just about any investment you'd like, and your employer makes its contributions directly to the fund. Your SEP is in addition to your regular IRA. SEP-IRAs are very easy for your employer to set up. Large investment houses (like a bank or a mutual fund family) will happily send a kit with everything you need, including IRS forms. The investment house will administer the SEP, and all your employer has to do is authorize the contribution. If your employer is pension-shy because of "all the hassle," a SEP-IRA may be just the thing.

SEPs: What Small Businesses Need to Know can be
ordered for $1 from the Government Printing Office,
Washington, D.C. 20402-9325. Ask for stock number
045-000-002-560.

If you have self-employment income, you can set up a SEP-
IRA for yourself. It will be tax-deductible and tax-deferred,
regardless of whether you or your husband have a pension that
otherwise disqualifies your regular IRA from deduction. You
can also contribute more to your SEP than to your regular IRA
— up to 13 percent of your adjusted gross income.

You can set up as many programs as you're eligible for,
although there is a top limit of combined tax-deductible
contributions.

**Do your level best to fund your tax-deferred programs
to their limit, especially if your employer matches
your contribution. Even if your company puts in only
$1 for every $10 of yours, that raises your 6 percent
return to 16 percent — unbeatable today. You want to
keep some emergency money on hand, of course, but
don't be too intimidated by the 10 percent penalty for
early withdrawal of retirement savings. After a few
years — perhaps as few as five — you'll make more
in your tax-protected account even if you do take the
penalty along the way.**

Retirement planners have long favored defined benefit
plans, because they project stability, are employer paid, and
are generally protected from premature withdrawal by the employee. Nevertheless, voluntary retirement savings programs
are beloved by younger workers, probably because they can
see their money grow more visibly than with the traditional
plan. Traditional plans declined 20 percent in the 1980s, while
voluntary plans doubled. By the end of that decade, only 44
percent of the work force (predominantly middle-aged males)
was covered by a pension. Younger workers' enthusiasm for

voluntary plans and the weakness of the labor movement, with its long insistence on sound defined benefit plans, combined to accelerate the decline of the traditional pension.

Public Versus Private

Generally, the best pensions are in the public sector — a break for women, since taxpayers employ armies of women, such as clerks, typists, teachers, and postal workers. Government pensions are the traditional defined benefit kind, except that the employee makes substantial contributions to the plan. Voluntary savings plans are also available to government employees. The 403(b) (formerly known as tax-sheltered annuity, or TSA) was originally developed for teachers and nonprofit employees.

Just like any other voluntary plan, a 403(b) is only as safe as the underlying investment. If you invest your funds in aggressive stock funds, be prepared to enjoy the roller-coaster ride. If you have an annuity, be certain you are tracking the health of the insurer — your employer will not be, nor will the agent who sold it to you. Usually you can switch your money out of a fund that you've lost confidence in. Check with your benefits clerk for a list of approved vendors.

Federal pensions are the Cadillacs — averaging over $13,000 per year. State and local pensions average about 75 percent of that, and private pensions are only about half. Up until the mid-1980s, federal employees did not earn Social Security, nor did many state and local employees. Now it is a rare public servant who does not also earn Social Security — teachers are chief among those who don't.

If you are offered the opportunity to pay into Social Security, you need to sort things out. First, if neither

you nor your spouse qualifies for Social Security
when you're sixty-five, your Medicare bill will be substantial — over $250 per month (Parts A and B) in
1994, and growing annually. Some government work-
places are allowing individuals to elect to pay the
Medicare tax (1.45 percent of your pay). You might
want to opt out of the Medicare payroll tax if you're
married to someone covered by Social Security. You
will not have to pay the Medicare premium if you qualify for spousal benefits — even if the public pension
offset disqualifies you from cash benefits. You should
also determine if the windfall penalty rule discussed
earlier in this chapter will reduce your newly earned
Social Security benefits.

How Safe Is Your Pension?

Most traditional defined benefit plans are insured by the
federal government. If the plan fails, the government will pay
the pension to the retiree. But one important group of employees — mostly women — is excluded from protection. Staffs
of professional offices with fewer than twenty-five employees
are not protected by government insurance — and just who
might these staffers be? Legal secretaries, office nurses, receptionists, clerks — an army of female workers targeted by their
kindly Congress to bear the burden of their employer's mis-
handling or misdeeds. Workers whose pensions *are* guaranteed
by the federal Pension Benefit Guaranty Corporation (PBGC)
are protected only up to a limit — under $3,000 per month
(adjusted annually for inflation).

The voluntary savings programs are not covered by the
PBGC or any other government insurance. Your 401(k), IRA,
and the like are subject to two risks:

- the soundness of the investment
- the honesty or competency of the trustee

ESOPs are particularly vulnerable. If the company fails, its stock (and, of course, your ESOP) will be worthless. ESOPs are not protected by the government and are especially vulnerable to investment risk, since by definition they are anything but diversified.

If you've had your ESOP at least ten years, and you are at least fifty-five years old, you can switch 25 percent of your money into other investments; and over the next five years, another 25 percent. Do this, even if your company is large and solvent. Single companies are much too risky a way to invest all your retirement savings.

Because traditional pensions are so heavily skewed toward the male work pattern, it seems especially unfortunate that so many of those women who do manage to secure one are excluded from the government guarantee. It seems the PBGC is a bastion of male protection — especially as more and more women put all their eggs in their (unprotected) 401(k) baskets.

Finally, the PBGC is not in good shape. Most of the ninety-five thousand pensions insured by it are sound, but enough big ones are tottering that alarm bells are ringing. Most experts agree that covered retirees need not worry — a PBGC default would be politically impossible. More likely, a bailout borne by the taxpayers will be the result. Women taxpayers will bail out a program that mainly benefits men.

Think through your retirement programs. Are they guaranteed by the PBGC? If not, consider a more conservative approach to your investments than might otherwise be appropriate. A nice, fat, guaranteed pension in your future frees you to accept a little more risk (and the possibility of greater reward) in your portfolio.

There is another way you can lose out on the PBGC's guarantee. Federal law allows your company to terminate your pension plan and use the funds for its own purposes provided it purchases an annuity that will pay the pension commitments. Cash-hungry companies legally "looted" their pension funds in the 1980s of $21 billion, replacing the funds with annuity contracts. Problem? The annuity contracts are not guaranteed by the PBGC. Another problem? Retirees almost always end up with smaller retirement checks than they would have had under the old plan. You have your thoughtful Congress to thank for this — would it surprise you to know that members of Congress draw pensions worth tens of thousands per year, and adjusted annually for inflation?

Should You Take Your Money and Run?

If you are a government employee, you've made substantial payroll contributions to your plan over the years. If you leave your job, you will be given the opportunity to take your contributions with you. The windfall looks mighty nice, and you may figure you can do a better job investing it for your retirement than can the plan. But be very careful. Franny, a schoolteacher, left teaching after fifteen years. She was offered the choice of leaving her $40,000 of contributions in the system (earning interest) until retirement or of taking them with her. She chose the latter and invested the funds wisely at 7 percent until she was sixty-five, ten years later — at which time the fund had doubled to $80,000. But had she left her funds in the system, her school district and the state would have each matched her funds. She would have better than *tripled* her money by leaving it in the system.

> **Any contributions you make to a pension, whether public or private, are yours whether or not you worked long enough to earn the right to draw a pension. When you retire, you'll be wise to check with all former jobs. You may have a small vested pension you aren't aware of. There is no law against drawing several small pensions — you might have enough to treat a friend to lunch every month!**

When you decide it is time to draw your pension, you may be offered the choice of lifetime payments (annuity), usually monthly, or a lump-sum withdrawal. Actuarily, the lump sum and the annuity add up to the same amount, but here is another opportunity to play your gender-awareness hand. Pension annuities, unlike those you purchase on the private market, are not allowed to discriminate according to gender. This means that in general, the annuity choice will be better for women than for men — because chances are better that a woman will outlive the unisex life-expectancy tables forced on the payer by law. For most women, then, the annuity over a lifetime will pay more than the lump sum (often the better choice for men).

When Your Husband Dies

All pensions offer a survivor's benefit of some kind — they have to by law. The retiree doesn't have to *elect* the survivor's benefit, but both spouses must consent in writing if the benefit is to be waived.

Unlike Social Security, which increases a married couple's benefit, pensions *decrease* the monthly payment if a survivor's benefit is elected. A pension runs on annuity principles, and since the payout period is longer when two lives are insured instead of one, the monthly benefits are reduced to compensate for the longer period. Some programs have a variety of options — the survivor's benefit can be 100 percent of the pre-death annuity, 75 percent, 50 percent — there can be many varieties.

You and your husband have an opportunity to develop a good strategy here. The election usually becomes irrevocable on retirement, so think through your options carefully. Since you are the likely survivor, you must be *very* sure of your future income before you accept a reduced survivor's benefit in exchange for higher present income. Of course, if you are in very ill health, or are significantly older than your husband, or are independently wealthy, then waiving the survivor's benefit might make sense. Otherwise, it is best to bite the bullet — accept lower current income in return for the highest future income you can manage. Your ordinary living expenses will *not* decline significantly when you're alone. And don't forget those long years of inflation ahead.

> **Beware this pitch, popular among financial planners who sell insurance: You and your husband will be urged to waive the survivor's benefit. Then, with the resulting extra current income, you pay premiums on a (surprise!) life insurance policy, which will substitute for the survivor's benefit when your husband dies. The salesperson will run some good-looking numbers and point out that if you die first, your husband will not have to live a lifetime with a reduced pension. First, it is unlikely you will die first — widows outnumber widowers six to one. Second, your pension, including the survivor's benefit, is probably guaranteed by the PBGC. The insurance benefit is not. The company could go under, or you could become unable to pay the premiums. If you have a government pension, it probably will include inflation adjustments. The insurance annuity almost certainly won't. In most cases, you'll be wise to show the salesperson the door.**

This is not to say that a good term policy on your husband's life is not an excellent idea. Shop around. You might find a $1 million policy on your sixty-year-old husband that costs less than $4,000 per year — or $500,000 for $1,700. Less than $1,000 might buy you $250,000. Term life insurance is an important part of any wife's future planning.

Federal pension law, which requires the written consent of both parties before the survivor's benefit is waived, does not cover federal, state, or local government pensions. Many permit the worker to waive the benefit in secret. Only at the funeral does the widow learn that the pension she expected was buried with her husband. This loophole covers a lot of ground, unfortunately. The biggest pensions in the country are government plans — the teachers of New York, for example, or the public employees of California.

> **If you are expecting a survivor's benefit from a government pension, ask to see a copy of your husband's election form — just to make sure you know exactly how to plan your future. Don't trust his memory — memories fade, retirement instructions can be confusing, and, unfortunately, some men just gamble that they will die last and a higher current income is more than they can turn down.**

Your Pension Rights After Divorce

Unlike Social Security, no pension offers an automatic benefit to a former spouse. But the divorce laws of most states consider the pension to be part of the marital property, and divisible on divorce. You will need a court order at the time of your divorce. The pension administrator will usually be ordered to pay two checks, so if you're in this position, you won't have to chase your ex every month for your share.

> **The Displaced Homemakers Network serves widows and divorced homemakers by educating them on their rights and advocating policy reforms. Contact them at 1625 K Street NW, Suite 300, Washington, D.C. 20006.**

How much will be your share? Depends on the state, the court, and your circumstances. If the pension was earned over the course of a long marriage, a greater share will be awarded the wife in most courts. Both defined benefit (traditional) and defined contribution (401(k), etc.) plans as well as IRAs are subject to division at divorce.

Some courts will order the pension divided immediately, even if your husband has not retired. The pension will be given a dollar value, and that amount will be offset (or traded off) with other marital property. Other courts prefer to split the payments as they're actually paid.

If your husband decides to delay his retirement, you can begin to draw your court-ordered share when he would otherwise be eligible to draw his. You don't have to wait until he retires.

If you live in a community property state, you have a better chance of getting more of the pension than if you live in a common-law state (see the discussion of marital property laws in Chapter 5).

The best treatment of pensions and divorce is published by the Pension Rights Center: *Your Pension Rights at Divorce.* **Call the center at (202) 296-3776 for the current price, or write them at 918 16th Street NW, Suite 704, Washington, D.C. 20006. This is a comprehensive, readable, and authoritative book, since the center is always at the forefront of reform measures and has paid particular attention to hidden biases against women.**

Your Right to Sue

If all goes badly, you have the right to appeal to the plan administrator — whether you be the worker, wife, widow, or former wife. And if the appeal goes badly, too, you can sue the plan in court.

The Pension Rights Center reports that because of certain court decisions, some lawyers are avoiding pension claims. In any case, you don't want a general lawyer for this type of specialty litigation.

The National Pension Assistance Project has a roster of several hundred attorneys in most states who are trained to represent pension claims. This resource, known as the National Lawyer's Network, can be reached at 918 16th Street NW, Washington, D.C.

20006. The U.S. Department of Labor enforces pension law: DOL, Office of Pension and Welfare Benefit Programs, 200 Constitution Avenue NW, Washington, D.C. 20210.

A System Crying for Reform

All nongovernmental pensions are governed by one comprehensive federal statute: the Employees' Retirement Income Security Act (ERISA), which was enacted in the mid-1970s as a reform measure. Abuse was rampant in the pension world — outright fraud as well as shady practices that amounted to the same thing: years of work under a pension system that in the end paid out nothing. ERISA, and its subsequent amendments, has gone a long way to mitigate these abuses, but for women it is fundamentally flawed.

ERISA was enacted with the male work pattern in mind. It, and therefore the pensions it regulates, rewards the well-paid, long-term, full-time employee of a large company — and that worker is most likely to be a middle-class white man. Women and minorities, with lower pay and more mobile work patterns, lose heavily — if they even get into the game to begin with — because ERISA's greatest failing was in not mandating pensions in the first place.

Twice as many men as women receive pension income, and those women who do receive it get half as much. The obstacles put in front of every worker are higher for women. For example, women predominate in the businesses that don't offer pensions in the first place. Then women tend to change jobs more frequently, failing to vest in the pension (usually a period of five years). Pensions, unlike Social Security, are not portable. A mobile woman worker can't work a few months here, or half-time there, and take her pension credits "with" her. Part-timers are excluded from ERISA protection, and women constitute two-thirds of the part-time labor market. Women's mobility, as they move in and out of the paid labor market in order to care for their families, is punished by ERISA.

Like Social Security, ERISA is a creature of Congress. Reform begins and ends there. If you're interested in looking into it further, the aforementioned Pension Rights Center in Washington, D.C., is the place to start. In addition to broad pension reform, they have paid special attention to the biases in the system against women.

SUPPLEMENTAL SECURITY INCOME

Supplemental Security Income, or SSI, is the federal welfare program for the aged, disabled, and blind. I won't go into it in depth here, because books on investing are generally irrelevant to SSI recipients, so stringent are the eligibility requirements. Nevertheless, you should know where the safety net lies, as part of your own financial strategies.

Like Social Security, SSI is adjusted annually for inflation, but in 1994 SSI federal maximums are $446 per month for an individual, $669 for a couple. Some states supplement these federal allowances. Eligibility is based on income and assets, which can differ among the states. Call the central Social Security phone number listed below for SSI information.

The asset limit in many states is $2,000 for an individual and $3,000 for a couple — but *not all assets count*. Your home, for example, is exempt, as are many other necessities such as cars, household goods, and personal effects (depending on value). You need not be a citizen to receive SSI, but you do need to be in the country legally.

If you are eligible for SSI, you will probably also be eligible for ancillary services such as Medicaid, food stamps, and local programs, including housing subsidies.

The central Social Security toll-free number, (800) 772-1213, serves SSI as well. Call to learn if your state supplements the basic SSI grant, and by how much, what the eligibility requirements are, and how to apply.

DO YOU UNDERSTAND YOUR RETIREMENT INCOME?

1. Have you filled out the Social Security (SS) PEBS?
2. Which is the short leg of your retirement income stool? The steadiest one?
3. Have you filed the SS toll-free "800" number?
4. Will you be (are you) dually entitled?
5. Have you calculated the cost and benefits of drawing early SS?
6. If you are over sixty, what is your optimum SS application date?
7. Do you know your full SS retirement date?
8. Were you married ten years before a divorce?
9. If widowed or a divorced widow, did you remarry after age sixty?
10. Do you know what your widow's benefit will be?
11. Do you know what the SS earnings test costs you?
12. Do you know the effect of your public pension on your SS?
13. Is there a traditional pension in your future?
14. Do you have a benefit estimate from the plan administrator?
15. Are you funding tax-deferred accounts to the maximum?
16. Do you know your husband's SS number? Does he know yours?
17. How much will your pension survivor's benefit be?
18. Will you be able to keep it after remarriage?
19. Is your pension insured by the PBGC?
20. Was your pension traded for an uninsured annuity contract?
21. If you are divorced, how much will be your share of the pension?

4

Wealth Is More Than Money
Housing and Jobs

Our wealth, indeed, is much more than our money. A nice, old-fashioned word for that is *means*. We have the "means" to travel, for example, if the combination of all our resources (cash and otherwise) *and* the cost of our trip are happily in harmony.

We've spent some time on investments and entitlement income. If all is well, those three legs of your retirement income stool are long and sturdy. But if you're still a little wobbly, now is the time to climb off the stool and look at alternatives. In this chapter we'll focus on housing and jobs, since these may be your resources of last resort.

HOUSING

Your house is more than your castle. Very likely it is also

- a substantial part of your net worth
- an important component of your estate plan
- a significant item in your budget
- your emergency reserve

and, maybe, your house is

- too large for your needs
- difficult to maintain
- not near enough to your children
- not well lighted, with too many stairs
- vulnerable to fire and crime

In other words, after so many years, your house could be both a blessing and a curse.

While you're still married, your house will probably be more of the former. Two people sharing an older, large home can work around many of the difficulties that one person cannot. If one has trouble with stairs, the other is the runner. If one falls, the other is there. One might do light maintenance while the other changes the bed. And of course, the couple provides its own companionship.

It is widowhood that brings on the curse. Loneliness, safety issues, reduced income, mounting maintenance — these nagging concerns begin to intrude on the plus side of the ledger: familiarity, memories, old neighbors — and inertia.

As a woman, you should look on your home very objectively. You will likely spend long years alone, and that is when the minuses may begin to overcome the pluses. More than your husband, you should get in the habit of thinking of it not only as your *home* (with all that implies) but also as a financial resource.

You'll need to be familiar with the following terms:

- *Equity*: Your "stake" in your house. If it would sell for $100,000, and your mortgage is $60,000, your equity is $40,000.
- *Basis*: What you paid for your house, plus improvements. If you paid $24,000, and added a room for $6,000 and a deck for $2,000, your basis is $32,000. When you sell your house for $100,000, you'll be subject to tax on the capital gain (selling price less basis) unless you come under

an exclusion, discussed below. Basis and death taxes are tackled in Chapter 6.

Of course, you already think of your home's dollar value (even if only vaguely). You cannot help but be aware of what similar homes sold for in your community — against what you paid years ago. Get used to thinking of your home (and your second home) as part of your net worth. When balancing your portfolio, your residential real estate belongs in the growth (not the income) sector of your investment program.

First you need to know what it is worth, even if you plan never to sell it. You can't balance the rest of your investments without knowing your full net worth, and how much of it is in real estate. However, it is doubtful you've had your house professionally appraised recently unless you're planning to sell it.

That is your first task. Get a professional appraisal, even if it costs you a couple of hundred bucks. You can find appraisers in the yellow pages. You don't need to do anything with the information. But for insurance, estate planning, and even for balancing your investment portfolio, you need to know what you own.

If you have plenty of other resources, you can afford to be sentimental about your house. However, if you are or will be living on the line — or under it — it makes no sense not to know exactly what your options are. You don't have to exercise your options, after all — but knowledge *is* power.

Here are some ways to keep your house a little longer if that's what you want — and other opportunities if you don't.

Getting Free and Clear

You've been paying off your mortgage forever, it seems — and maybe you've reached the nirvana of the paid-up house. If not, you can save tens of thousands or more in interest by paying it off faster. Simply double your principal payment, and you'll get there more than twice as fast.

But you don't have to double your principal payment to get fine rewards. If you pay back your thirty-year 8.5 percent mortgage in twenty years, you'll save $68,500 in interest on your $100,000 debt. Your mortgage statement probably has a checkoff option where you can indicate how you want extra payments allocated. If your total payment is $500, with $100 principal and $400 interest, pay $600 and check the box that allocates the extra $100 to principal. You will gain equity twice as fast and save thousands in interest.

Watch out for "mortgage reduction" services that charge you a fee to reduce your mortgage. They will simply tell you how to pay more principal. You can do that for free.

Fending Off Foreclosure

A faster mortgage payoff is all well and good if you've got the extra funds to do it. But what if sudden illness or other catastrophe empties your reserves and you find you can't pay the bank, the taxes, or the insurance?

The first place to look for "fat" is your home insurance. First, shop around for the lowest-priced policy. Call several agents listed in your yellow pages, and ask them for quotes using the same data (that is, same property value, same liability, same extras if any). You will be surprised how much the prices vary. Then go over your policy very carefully to see if you are overinsured. If your net worth (counting the equity in your home) is $200,000, you probably don't need $1,000,000 in liability protection. Your insurer offers several grades of home insurance — usually five — often denominated HO-3, HO-5, and so on. If you live on the Pacific coast, you probably don't need snow-load coverage. Theft coverage may not be important if your property has sentimental value only. See if HO-1 (or your insurer's most basic homeowner's policy) will suffice for a while until you get back on your feet. In any case, unlike your banker, should you default on your mortgage, your may feel differently. Just be aware that the RAM will significantly reduce your estate.

Some RAMs, like other annuities, use gender-biased actuarial tables. This would mean that a man and woman of the same age, with the same home equity, would get very different monthly checks. The man's could be as much as 20 percent higher than the woman's. Government-backed RAMs use unisex tables and so are a much better deal for women. As a woman, shop the banks until you find one that uses a unisex actuarial table. Your brother is better off with the gender bias.

Making Your Home More User-Friendly

Your house can become your enemy sooner than you think. If your dearest hope is to remain independent in your own home for all your days, think through every detail of your home as if you couldn't

- manage stairs
- see well in halls or at night
- rise off the toilet
- climb out of the tub
- hear the phone or doorbell
- twist doorknobs
- bend over to plug in the vacuum cleaner
- always remember to turn off the stove

Assume that in one degree or another all of these limits will be yours in time. You don't want to end your days in a nursing home only because you and your home become incompatible. You probably won't have to do much to make your home a much friendlier place to grow old in. If you're remodeling, improve the lighting in dark areas. Have the electric outl moved up to chest high so you won't have to bend over. bars can be installed near the toilet and the tub, quite ine sively, during a bath remodel. Interior and exterior do be framed so that they can be widened to take a wh

insurer won't foreclose on your home if you drop the insurance — although your lender may well insist you carry at least fire protection. Be sure your policy is for *guaranteed* replacement. Simple replacement is not enough and often costs nearly as much as guaranteed replacement.

Your second task, if cash is short, is to have a talk with your mortgage holder *before* you miss or reduce a payment. Explain the situation. Banks hate foreclosures, and your bank will probably work with you to come up with something you can live with. *There is no shame in this* — restructuring loans is an everyday business practice that your bank is well-equipped to accommodate.

Third, contact your utility companies. Phone, water, electric, and gas companies frequently offer "lifeline" or basic rates to low-income or senior households.

Finally, consider property taxes. When you miss or underpay the tax, sooner or later the county will place a tax lien on your property — and can sell your property at public auction if the delinquency goes on too long. Of course, you can "cure" the delinquency at any time by paying the tax due plus penalties and interest. Ask your tax department how long between

- delinquency and placement of a lien
- lien placement and foreclosure

If it will be five years between the recording of the tax lien and foreclosure, for example, you'll have some time to make plans and cure your default.

Many states and localities protect senior citizens against tax foreclosures by going no further than recording the tax lien. In other words, when you (or your estate) sells your house, the taxes due will be collected — but while you're living in the house, there will be no forced sale. Ask your tax department about this.

The important thing to remember is not to panic. Fore-closure, the worst-case scenario, takes lots of time. You'll be given plenty of chances to get back on track by all parties concerned.

And if it looks like your cash-flow problem will be more than temporary, consider applying for a reverse annuity mortgage, discussed next.

House Rich and Cash Poor:
Reverse Annuity Mortgages

In recent decades women, especially, have found themselves in a difficult position. After years of paying off their mortgages, they find that they own their beautiful home free and clear but don't have the money to live in it. House rich and cash poor became a familiar term among mature women everywhere. As real estate values burgeoned, many women came to realize that on paper they were quite well off, despite their penurious circumstances with respect to income. For many, the decision was to sell the house and invest the proceeds for income. Others were loathe to sell the house they had spent a lifetime in, raising their kids and making a home.

Bankers took a look at all that locked-up equity and saw an opportunity. Enter the reverse annuity mortgage (RAM). The bank would loan the homeowner a certain amount, to be paid in monthly installments for a period of years (often ten). At the end of that time, the loan would be due in full, or the bank would foreclose. When you paid your mortgage, every month you paid the bank and every month you owned a little bit more of your home. The reverse mortgage is just the reverse. Every month the bank pays you, and every month you own a little *less* of your home. Instead of building equity over the years, you lose it — meaning that in the end your home could be foreclosed. A woman of seventy-five could outlive the term of the loan, and at eighty-five find herself homeless.

There had to be a better way, and now there is. T government backs some RAMs, but only those that d in foreclosure after a period of years. A very few ba guarantee payments for life; more will for so long as in the house. Here is where the annuity aspect enters bank figures your RAM by determining your equity in the and your life expectancy. A monthly sum is calculated, ideally would result in your equity running out on the day you die. If you die earlier, the bank wins; if later, you After your death, your executor or trustee will sell your h to repay the bank. Some RAMs work like a line of credit. stead of a monthly check, you withdraw what you need wl you need it — up to the credit limit.

> **Equity worth $100,000 might bring you $450 p month as long as you live in the home; $250,000 coul improve your monthly bottom line by more than $1,000!**

Think through the effects of a RAM on your mobility. Rod and Jessie were strapped for cash after he retired from his high-paying executive position. They unlocked the equity in their large home by taking out a RAM that would pay for as long as either of them lived in the home. Rod died two years later. Jessie wanted to move across the country to be near their daughter, but she couldn't afford to lose the $1,000 RAM income. Although selling the house would give her some funds to invest, the guaranteed $1,000 per month for as long as she lived in the house was more than she could afford to walk away from. Jessie and Rod would have been much better off getting a RAM that paid for life, regardless of where the annuitant lived.

Be sure you understand the little extras — points, fees, appraisal fee, closing costs — as well as any extra charge added to cover the lifetime annuity feature. Shop around! And don't forget, even with a lifetime RAM, your loan will end with fore-closure. Your estate will turn your house over to the bank, or sell it to pay off the loan. I happen to believe your duty to ourself exceeds your duty to provide for your heirs, but you

very easily if the time comes. Stairs can be ramped. Microwave ovens turn themselves off automatically, so forgetting to turn them off is not a problem. If you have a two-story house, consider making the half-bath downstairs into a full bath — in case you can't climb the stairs in your later years. Make sure that one phone in each room is low enough to be reached by someone who has fallen. Over the years, keep accessibility in mind as you improve and maintain. The payback will be enormous in terms of peace of mind and actual dollars saved by avoiding that trip to the nursing home in your last years.

The "smart" homes of the future, if properly designed with the maturing population in mind, will be a lifesaver for those who want to live independently despite some physical limits. Already, houses exist in which from your bed you can control all lights; start the coffee; engage the security system; set the thermostat; and talk to someone at the door. It shouldn't be long before your computer can talk to your son's across the country every night — assuring him that you have turned off all the lights and the stove, the doors are locked, and the security system is on. Maybe he won't hustle you off to a nursing home ahead of your time just for *his* peace of mind.

In France, older adults use the Teletel system, which allows them to bank, shop, arrange for housekeeping, and even review restaurant menus right from their homes. Something similar is inevitably in our future, too.

> **The Centers for Independent Living across the country are eager to help anyone with disabilities, including those that are age-related. Call them. They can tell you about all sorts of adaptive devices for any kind of impairment, such as visual, hearing, or mobility.**

Cashing Out Your Home

Women, ending their lives older and "aloner" than men, face a special problem when the house they've loved for a lifetime becomes an albatross: too many stairs, too many rooms, too many taxes, too far from the grandkids. Many widows, mindful of the tax advantages of bequeathing the home (see Chapter 5), feel stuck. They'd like to downsize, but the prospect of an immense capital gains tax is daunting. If this is your situation, you can employ some strategies to lessen the blow.

Keep in mind that saving taxes should not be the highest order of business. You have a life to lead, too. If you will owe the IRS tens of thousands of dollars on your $200,000 profit — perhaps that's a reasonable price to pay to watch your granddaughter grow up, or enjoy the convenience and companionship of more suitable quarters.

If you've decided to make the move, your first consideration will be the $125,000 exclusion from capital gains available to anyone over fifty-five *one time only*. To qualify, you must

- be fifty-five or older on the day of sale (either spouse, if married)
- have lived in your house three out of the last five years
- have never taken the exclusion before (either spouse)

If you take this exemption while married, both you and your husband are disqualified from taking it again for the *rest of your lives*. This spousal policy is biased against women, because a woman is much more likely to experience a drastic change of lifestyle (widowhood) leading to a need to downsize her residence. This spousal joint exemption becomes particularly aggravating when widows and widowers seek to remarry. If either has taken the exemption in the prior marriage, both are excluded from exercising it in their new marriage. Joyce and Tom, both widowed, married and bought a home. Five years later, they decided to sell. Their $25,000 profit was fully exposed to tax because Joyce and Lee, her deceased husband, had taken the exemption — although Tom never had.

There is a way to get an exemption for each spouse, but it is drastic. People whose divorce is *final* before

the home is sold will each get an exemption. The husband, say, can use his when the house is sold after the divorce, the wife will use hers whenever she needs it in the future. The $125,000 break for someone in the 28 percent tax bracket will save about $35,000 in taxes — much more than an uncontested "friendly" divorce would cost. Of course, if you remarry each other in the future, you could be accused of illegal tax evasion, so your divorce should be viewed as final. As with all tax matters, the law changes frequently. Check with your tax adviser before you change your life because of taxes — a dumb idea, anyway.

June and Bill, both widowed, fell in love. June and her late husband had taken the exclusion when they became renters in a retirement village. Bill had never taken the exclusion, and his house had appreciated by $250,000 in the thirty years he owned it. If June and Bill marry, then sell the house, June will "taint" Bill, and he will lose tens of thousands of tax dollars. Bill can sell his house before they marry, or they can decide to live together without marriage.

Assume, though, that you have sold your home, have used your exemption, and are still looking at plenty of profit. You have two years from the date of sale to buy a new house — *and fix it up* before the tax on your profit is calculated. Of course, if you spend as much or more on the new house, your tax is deferred. But the older woman, living alone, is likely to buy something smaller.

Your strategy is to think through all the improvements and repairs you'd like to make to your new home "sometime in the future." Every one you make within your two-year grace period carries a big subsidy from Uncle Sam. Defer furniture purchases until after the two-year period, in favor of replacing the roof.

You can escape tax on your home's appreciation entirely if you keep it until you die. Your heirs will owe no tax on any appreciation up to the date of your

> **death. See the discussion in Chapter 6 for an explanation of tax basis and the "stepped-up" basis rule.**

Many women, when moving to smaller quarters, choose to buy a condo or co-op rather than rent an apartment, to avoid the capital gains tax. If the $125,000 exclusion is available to you, you could buy a place worth $125,000 less than the one you're selling and owe no tax. Obtain tax advice before you do this, though, because figuring the basis for your old home can be more complicated than just remembering how much you paid for it.

If a retirement residence is in your future, be aware that sometimes you can buy into these rather than renting. This is even true of some "life care" communities. Many women choose to buy as a way to roll over their home appreciation so as to qualify for the stepped-up basis after death.

As always, see your tax adviser before applying general information such as this to your own special circumstances.

> **The IRS has toll-free numbers for your convenience. But be aware that their record for accuracy over the phone is spotty. If you act according to their wrong advice, *you* are liable for the tax and penalty, anyway. For big matters, you can ask for a written opinion. It will take a couple of months, but the IRS will stand behind it. For tax questions, call (800) TAX-1040. For forms and publications, call (800) TAX-FORM.**

Joining Together

Collective housing has been a boon to many mid-life and older women. Some are informal roommate arrangements, with everyone sharing rent. Others are more formal, usually involving shared ownership. For single adults, shared housing is often the answer to the loneliness, expense, and insecurity of the large family home.

Several friends (or relatives) might buy a single-family residence and live there as *tenants-in-common*. We examine
tenancies-in-common and joint-tenancies in Chapter 6, but you
should understand what happens to your share when you die
before you buy into either arrangement. If you own your house
as tenants-in-common with three friends, you could end up
sharing with a stranger when one of you dies and her share
is sold by her heirs. Of course, you could choose *joint tenancy*
with rights of survivorship, so that when an owner dies, her
share goes to the remaining owners. The problem here, of
course, is that your heirs are shut out. Talk to a property lawyer
before you sign the deed — you and your friends don't want
surprises.

Taking In a Boarder

Of course, there is one way to turn your home into income
that's been a mainstay for widows for generations: share your
home. In college towns, students rent rooms along with kitchen privileges; in other places, recent immigrants fill the role.
Often chore services can be negotiated in lieu of full rent —
a particular help to someone needing extra personal services.
Zoning laws that prohibit these arrangements are ignored in
most communities, because the need for affordable housing
for the young, and income and security for the elders, is
recognized.

Adult Communities

Adult communities feature individual living units (rented
or owned) in a planned setting. Usually there are security, rec-
reation, planned activities, and rules. In some, meals are provided; in others, not. Many provide for tiers of care within the
community — individual living, semiassisted living, nursing
care. There are always age restrictions. You need to know the
following:

- Can you be moved to a higher-care tier over your objection?
- Can your thirty-eight-year-old daughter move in with you?
- Can her ten-year-old visit you overnight? How long?
- Can your twenty-year-old grandson inherit and live in the unit?
- If under life care, can you get your money back after a trial period?
- Are there limits on how high your periodic fees can rise?
- How financially sound is the corporation?
- What is your position if it goes bankrupt?
- Where is the residential nursing facility located?

As stated earlier, whether you buy into or rent one of these facilities may have important income (capital gains) tax consequences when you sell your home. Always check.

Becoming a Renter

If you're over fifty, you belong to the ''homeowningest'' segment of the American population. But as you move along in years, you may find yourself renting a place for the first time in decades, or even your life. Aside from the tax consequences of moving from owner to renter, you'll need to be aware of your new rights and responsibilities.

Most likely, the landlord will ask you to sign a *lease*. Often this is a standardized form that may or may not comply with local law. If your community has rent control, the standard lease form may not reflect that. The eviction procedure in the lease may not comport with local practice. Just remember that if you get in a squabble, check out the lease provisions with a landlord-tenant lawyer before you concede your case to the landlord. (Landlord-tenant lawyers, like all specialists, advertise their specialty in the yellow pages under the general heading of ''attorneys.'')

Usually, you will be asked to provide the first and last month's rent in advance, as well as a security deposit. As this can well be a few thousand dollars, most communities have regulations that govern the maximum amount allowable, as well as the conditions under which the security deposit is returnable to you, and whether you or the landlord gets the interest from its investment in the interim.

Generally, the landlord owes you a "habitable" unit. This is a legal term of art that may differ between communities. Usually, habitability means adequate lighting, heat, and ventilation; operating utilities; no water leaks or pests; and safe stairs, elevators, and other structures, as well as reasonable security. Anything affecting public health, such as leaking sewers, is always a condition of habitability.

Although laws differ, the usual remedy for violations of habitability is withholding of rent. However, to avoid eviction you usually must comply with certain procedures, such as placing your rent in an escrow account. Don't ever withhold rent without knowing your rights first. Many communities have tenant's-rights organizations that can answer any questions for you. Look in the yellow pages under "tenants" or "real estate management." NOLO Press, the reliable do-it-yourself lawbook publisher, has excellent landlord-tenant books written for non-lawyers, which you can order by mail or through your local bookstore. You can reach NOLO at 950 Parker Street, Berkeley, California 94710; telephone (800) 992-NOLO. Your library or bookstore has others.

In addition to withholding rent, you can sue your landlord in court for money damages. For example, if you suffered a permanent back injury from falling down a broken stairway, simply withholding your rent until the condition is fixed is hardly enough. You'll need money for medical bills, assistive devices, future attendant care, and pain and suffering. Or if you are assaulted in the dark parking lot — and your landlord had notice of the dangerous conditions but chose not to install lighting — you probably have a good lawsuit. See a personal-injury lawyer.

If you are being hassled over your pets, some places have laws that permit seniors to have pets even if the landlord doesn't allow them otherwise. You might also look into rules regarding seeing-eye and hearing-ear dogs. If your pet qualifies, you may be able to keep it despite the apartment rules. The Centers for Independent Living, or perhaps your local senior center, would probably know about these exceptions.

WORKING AFTER RETIREMENT

If you are a homeowner, your equity can bail you out of a tight situation — think of it as your next-to-last resource. Your last resource? Perhaps it's you! Turn your own skills and energy into money if all else fails.

If you're a woman past age fifty entering the paid labor market for the first time, or returning after some years, consider yourself part of a trend. Labor statisticians tell us that although the trend is leveling off, men over fifty are taking early retirement as soon as they can manage, while women of the same age are entering the job market in droves.

Your career needs after fifty are probably different from your husband's. While he is wrapping up a career spanning thirty years, you may have only ten to fifteen years under your belt, probably for several employers and with time-out taken for family care. He wants to rest; you want to pick up where you left off before the kids came. You want to build your Social Security, possibly a pension; he is fully qualified on his.

And some of us find ourselves alone for the first time in years, through widowhood or divorce. A job for some of us is a plain necessity.

First some bad news. Young women earn close to the same wages as men of the same age and education ($.92 to the male $1.00 for eighteen- to twenty-four-year olds). Thereafter, the ratio steadily declines, until women of fifty-five to sixty-four earn only $.54 to the $1.00 of similarly educated men. Part of this is explainable by the fact that far more mid-life women are beginning workers than men. And part is because "women's" jobs pay less than "men's." And part of it is flat-out age and sex discrimination.

The good news is that mature women are now in vogue among employers. Airlines are advertising for flight attendants in their late forties, motel chains are seeking out mid-life and older women for their front desk operations — and everyone knows the fast-food joint wants you. On the lower end of the pay scale, the reason is a shortage of teenagers.

Unfortunately, there is another reason, too: discrimination against moms. Employers won't admit this out loud (because it is illegal), but older women don't have young kids — who get sick, want dinner on the table, and add to the health policy bill.

One way or another, if working is part of your survival strategy, you need to know your rights and make the right moves. In this section we'll talk about preserving your rights as an applicant, an employee, or a near-retiree (your Social Security and pension rights after retirement were discussed in Chapter 3). We'll also discuss self-employment, increasingly popular among mature women.

Civil Rights for People over Forty

The federal Age Discrimination in Employment Act (ADEA) prohibits age discrimination in hiring, promotions, fringe benefits, firing, demotions, layoffs, training, and retirement by employers of twenty or more. Many states have age discrimination statutes as well. No longer, except for those in some safety-related jobs, such as pilots and police officers, can you be forced to retire at any age. The end of mandatory retirement is especially good for women, since the trend is for older women to join the labor market and for older men to leave it.

Employers cannot, for example, say that they have nothing against older people — but that customers expect a youthful image. Employers can't hide behind their customer's prejudices. Nor can they say that certain physical abilities (commoner to younger folks) are a job requirement if the job can be perfectly well performed without them. An employer can't require 20/20 uncorrected vision if the job can be performed with 20/40 best corrected eye.

Lisa, age fifty-one, passed all the written and skills tests for the emergency home response paramedical team. She was denied the job, however, because she was heavier than the "light frame" weight standard used by the department for female applicants. Male applicants could qualify based on the "heavy frame" standard. Lisa won the job when she (and her employment law attorney) proved that the weight tables were discriminatory against females and people over forty, and had no relevance to the actual job, since many of the active paramedicals were much heftier than the weight table's guidelines.

ADEA biases against women? There are two of them. First, age forty is too high a threshold — women are blatantly discriminated against in their thirties for many "image" jobs such as TV talent, cocktail waitresses, receptionists, and so forth. But the ADEA doesn't protect them. And second, the ADEA covers only employers with more than twenty employees. The majority of small-business workers are women, unprotected by the high minimum.

> **Run — don't walk — to the nearest office of the federal Equal Employment Opportunity Commission (EEOC) or your state's fair employment practices office if you feel your age has been used against you. The statutes of limitations can be quite short — 180 days. If you're afraid your employer will retaliate against you, know that retaliation is a separate offense against the ADEA. You can win a retaliation suit even if you lose your main claim. As soon as it appears likely that the EEOC will close your case (the most likely outcome, regardless of the merits), see an employment law attorney. Look in the yellow pages, or write the National Employment Lawyers Association, 535 Pacific Avenue,**

San Francisco, California 94133, for its directory of employment lawyers nationwide.

Be alert to subtle signs of age discrimination:

- Your responsibilities are diminished.
- Your worksite is downgraded.
- You miss out on important training.
- Your history of good evaluations turns sour.
- There are hints that older workers are costly.
- There are hints that you are near retirement.

If your phone conversation with personnel was upbeat, but your personal interview is a bomb — consider age discrimination a possibility.

Lynn, a mid-level executive of sixty with thirty-five years on the job, learned that certain employees were being selected for a special training program in advanced computer use. She was not chosen, nor was anyone older than fifty. The company pointed out that the training was expensive, and it wouldn't pay the business to train people nearing retirement. Lynn knew the trainees would be first in line for career advancement and contacted the EEOC. The agency explained to her supervisor that the ADEA prohibited discrimination in training on account of age, and the company removed the age restriction.

As an applicant, watch out for that old piece of baggage "overqualified." We women have long understood that "overqualified" was a code word for "too old." We recognized this long before men did, because historically we were the ones applying for entry-level positions at age thirty-five after our kids were all in school, while men hung on to their careers until retirement.

But things are changing. More mature men are hitting the pavement than ever before — and the hated word now stares them in the face with its cruel, clever challenge. Rebut the charge? How? By pleading that you're not overqualified at all —

in fact, your qualifications are so deficient you'd have problems getting to work on time? Desperate applicants revise their resumes, downgrading them to leave out professional degrees or technical experience. But of course it doesn't help, because what is out of line is not the experience, it is the dreaded appearance of passing years.

So it was a fine day in early 1991 when the U.S. Court of Appeals (2nd Circuit) agreed that "overqualified" could be a code word masking illegal age discrimination. The fifty-nine-year-old appellant's job had disappeared in a reorganization, and his dozens of applications for other positions with his large employer were routinely dismissed with the excuse of "overqualified." Of course, the court didn't mean that anytime "overqualified" is used as a reason for rejection, the hapless applicant will win a lawsuit. It simply recognized that "overqualified," as a reason for rejection, needs some explaining if the employer is to successfully defend itself against an age discrimination suit.

When this prestigious federal appeals court handed down its opinion, it wrote, "Denying employment to an older job applicant because he or she has too much experience, training, or education is simply to employ a euphemism to mask the real reason for refusal, namely, in the eyes of the employer, the applicant is too old."

Plainly stated, and amen.

Your Job Rights as a Woman

Ever since the Civil Rights Act of 1964, sex discrimination in employment has been illegal except for very narrow exceptions where gender is an inescapable requirement (a model for women's fashions, for example). Like the ADEA, Title VII (as the employment section is known) is biased against women and minorities because of its exclusion of small businesses. For federal law to protect you, your employer must have at least fifteen employees. However, many state laws extend protection to smaller businesses, so be sure you check before counting yourself out.

Laura applied for a warehouse job but was rejected when she couldn't load 135 pallets per day, the entry-level standard. When she proved that the average loader on the job was held to a standard of 122 per day, a quota she consistently met, she successfully argued that the artificially higher standard discriminated against women who on the average are less well muscled than men. It was not a "bona fide occupational requirement" because veteran loaders weren't held to the higher standard.

When Lou, a sheriff's deputy, applied for promotion, she learned that applicants with two year's jail-guard experience were given preference. Because male deputies had the opportunity to fill twenty jail-guard slots, and female deputies only two, the experience criteria discriminated against female deputies, and after a call from an employment law attorney, the procedure was revised.

As with age discrimination, you begin by complaining to the EEOC or your state's fair employment office. If that effort fails (likely), see an employment lawyer forthwith.

A New Law Full of Possibilities

Although the ADEA is usually thought of as the principal job law for older Americans, the recent Americans with Disabilities Act of 1990 (ADA) should prove enormously helpful in keeping older Americans on the job. The ADA simply requires that employers with fifteen or more employees after July 26, 1994, (twenty-five until then), make "reasonable accommodations" in the workplace to assist employees (or job applicants) with disabilities. No longer can an employer practice age discrimination under the subterfuge that an applicant's difficulty seeing in low light, for example, is the reason for dismissal. Now the employer will have to improve the lighting — or make other reasonable efforts to make the workplace barrier-free.

Although Congress had in mind the more than thirteen million working-age Americans with disabilities when it enacted the ADA, experts predict that older workers will be the primary beneficiaries because disability rates rise with age. The definition of disability is broad and includes chronic medical conditions such as diabetes and AIDS. Although the law is too new to determine all its ramifications, it is not beyond reason to assume that some types of appearance discrimination might be redressable under the ADA. An overweight individual rejected for employment on the premise that he or she will cause the group health insurance to rise in cost might successfully claim unlawful discrimination against a medical condition. So, too, the individual with an unsightly skin condition or other factor that affects appearance only and is not traditionally thought of as a disability.

The EEOC enforces the ADA. Damages of up to $300,000 are authorized, in addition to back pay, reinstatement, and attorney's fees.

Is It Worth It to Work?

Any worker eligible for Social Security must calculate the real worth of staying on the job. This is especially true for women because they are much more likely to take marginal jobs in their later years than men. One of the principal reasons is to supplement their Social Security, which for millions of older women is their only income. See the Social Security discussion in Chapter 3 for more on the earnings test; here we'll calculate it along with other work costs to see the real value of a paycheck.

At sixty-five, Eloise got a job in a mall paying $400 per week to supplement her Social Security. Her annual salary of $20,800 exceeded the 1994 earnings limit of $11,160 for beneficiaries aged sixty-five to sixty-nine, so she lost $3,213 of her annual Social Security benefits. Of course, as a worker, she had to pay Social Security and Medicare payroll taxes of 7.65 percent, or $1,591. Her federal income tax (15 percent) increased $3,120 because of her earnings. Her $20,800 is now $12,876, or $247 per week instead of the $400 she was counting on.

And that's before state taxes, commuting costs, and clothing costs are considered. The Social Security payroll tax applies to the first $60,600 of annual income (in 1994), so all of Eloise's income is taxed.

The Eloises of this world are probably not in a position to give up their jobs, but they must discipline themselves to be ruthlessly realistic in apprising the true costs of their jobs, or their budget strategies will be painfully out of whack.

Armies of older workers deliberately keep part-time hours to stay under the earnings limit. This is throwing out the baby with the bathwater. Despite the limit, you still keep more than you lose.

When job hunting, here are some *rough* translators:

- **Half-time job = 1,000 hours per year**
- **Full-time (40-hour week) = 2,000 hours per year**
- **$5/hour = $10,000 per year full-time (you double the hourly wage and add three zeros)**

Protecting Your Fringe Benefits

The Older Workers' Benefit Protection Act generally requires employers to provide older workers with benefits of equal value or equal cost to those provided younger workers. However, the employer is permitted to offset some benefits against each other. Lorna, for example, was entitled to three months' severance pay when she retired, as well as continuing health benefits. Her employer was within its rights when it deducted the cost of the health insurance from her severance pay.

Even if you'll continue in the group health plan, be sure you apply for Medicare three months before your sixty-fifth birthday, or no more than three months after. If you miss that "window," you could end up paying higher Medicare premiums for the rest of your life. See Chapter 7.

What About the Golden Handshake?

Since forced retirement is now illegal in most jobs, employers have come up with a more agreeable way to ease (expensive) senior workers out. If you've been offered a sweetener to take early retirement, you'll want to *carefully* consider your options.

Golden handshake packages vary — but most are variations of

- a lump sum, payable immediately
- a pension supplement for life
- a Social Security supplement for life
- a benefit such as health coverage (may be limited in time)

Since these benefits will probably *not* be protected by the PBGC, you need to worry about your company's future health. You want to be sure the company will be there to pay the benefits out of its assets.

What to do? Women are less likely than men anyway to be offered the golden handshake, since far fewer women hold the highly paid positions the company wants to eliminate. Still, if the early retirement offer comes your way, there are some considerations. A sound employer weighs in favor of taking the offer. If your company is troubled, however, it could go under, taking you and your job with it.

Your employer may ask you to waive your rights to an age discrimination claim, but such waivers will not be effective against a federal ADEA claim unless they comply with the Older Workers' Benefits Protection Act. To be legal, such a waiver must

- **be written in plain English**
- **mention you are waiving your ADEA rights**
- **not waive future claims**
- **advise you to see an attorney before you sign**

- **give you twenty-one days to consider signing**
- **give you seven days after signing to revoke it**
- **pay you something in return for the waiver**

The EEOC enforces this act.

Here are some questions to ask yourself if you've been offered a sweetened-up early retirement:

- Will your income replace 100 percent of your final earnings?
- Will your employer be financially healthy for your lifetime?
- Has your employer guaranteed all benefits? How?
- If the supplement is an annuity, is the insurer sound?
- Will the survivor's benefit be supplemented? Is it insured?
- Will cost-of-living adjustments be paid?
- What about other benefits, such as health and life insurance?
- Can you get another job if need be? With your employer?

Everyone's Dream:
Being Your Own Boss

When a man ends a forty-year career working for others, the idea of starting a little business after retirement may seem sweet indeed. He sees it as liberating, fulfilling, and a way to fill up his time. Since he can't be forced into retirement anymore, going out on his own is his choice.

For a mature woman, the process is different. She is usually pushed into self-employment because nobody will hire her — so in effect she hires herself. She goes into real estate, becomes a consultant, an interior designer, a caterer, a tax preparer, a freelance writer, or a piano teacher — all fine, if you can survive. The Small Business Administration reports that 20 percent of small businesses today are being started by men and women over fifty.

Here are some issues to consider if you decide to work part-time or become self-employed:

Part-timers (defined by federal law as those who work fewer than one thousand hours per year or twenty hours per week) need not be included in the company's fringe-benefit programs — no pension, health insurance, or sick leave. Of course, mandatory payroll taxes still apply. Part-timers build Social Security and Medicare, and are covered by worker's compensation, unemployment, and disability benefits.

Consultants not only don't get the fringes, they also don't get payroll benefits such as Social Security and Medicare that even part-time staff gets. These they have to pay themselves — including double the Social Security tax they paid as employees — a whopping 15 percent! Some companies try to characterize some jobs as consultancies when in reality they are employees. It is cheaper, because the company doesn't have to pay expensive payroll taxes. It is also an illegal tax-avoidance scheme, in many cases, in the eyes of the IRS. If your consultancy seems more like a job to you, be aware that you are dangerously unprotected (worker's compensation and disability insurance, for example, in case of injury), as well as outside the scope of fair labor practices acts — and possibly afoul of tax and labor laws, too.

In your negotiations with the company, put a price on these benefits and include them in your contract price. Your Social Security costs double as a consultant; you have to (or should) buy your own disability policy, retirement program, health insurance — and you'll lose pay during vacations or while sick. Your tax situation is more complex — you will owe estimated taxes, and be subject to all sorts of schedules and forms that salaried workers aren't. The cost of your tax work will soar. Dollar for dollar, the salaried worker paid $1,000 per month is probably at least 30 percent "richer" than the $1,000 consultant.

Owning the Store

Part-timers and consultants answer to others. If you want to be your own boss, join the million entrepreneurs who go it alone every year. Most fail, but you don't have to be among them. You already have a head start. You have maturity and the experience that goes with it.

You're way ahead of the twenty-two-year-old. Life has taught you caution, perhaps a healthy dose of skepticism. You've spent a lifetime confronting a budget, procuring goods, evaluating suppliers, negotiating disputes, scheduling tasks, meeting deadlines — and satisfying your customers, including your husband and kids. You've learned tact and patience. Long ago you tempered your optimism. You don't like surprises.

If you're going to hang out your sign or shingle, work out your plan in detail first. Pay particular attention to financing. Even if you don't think you'll need a loan, apply for one at a local bank. The questions the banker asks will help you think through your plan.

The Small Business Administration (SBA) has an advisory program of retired business managers who will be delighted to help you prepare. Its Service Corps of Retired Executives (SCORE) emphasizes (free) assistance for the "not-yet" businessperson, so don't hesitate.

The Small Business Administration has lots of information for you on all aspects of running a business and particularly welcomes inquiries from women and minorities. For their publication list, write SBP Publications List, P.O. Box 1000, Fort Worth, Texas 76119. You can reach SCORE (and the SBA) at this toll-free number: (800) 827-5722; or write SCORE at 1825 Connecticut Avenue NW, Washington, D.C. 20009.

As a woman, you have more healthy years to develop your business than a man of the same age. This puts you at a tremendous advantage. You are eight years younger at sixty than he is — so take advantage of this priceless gift of time, and turn it into money. This is the invisible fifth leg of the woman's retirement stool — earned income.

Make the most of it.

PLUMBING YOUR HIDDEN RESOURCES

1. Have you had your house appraised in the last three years?
2. Your house is what percentage of your net worth?
3. What do property taxes, insurance, and interest cost you?
4. How much has your house appreciated since you bought it?
5. What would be your capital gains tax if you sold now?
6. List all the reasons you should keep your house all your life.
7. List all the reasons you should not.
8. Are you house rich but cash poor?
9. How much equity do you have in your home?
10. Could the equity in your home be a source of income?
11. Will your house become your enemy as you acquire disabilities?
12. Are you becoming marginal at work as time goes on?
13. Are you alert to the subtle signs of age and sex discrimination?
14. Have you calculated the real costs of your job?
15. Have you thought through the golden handshake?
16. Are you an employee masquerading as a consultant?
17. Are you being held to part-time hours to avoid fringe benefits?
18. If self-employed, have you talked to the SBA? A banker?
19. Can you afford to lose the money you'll put into a business?

5
Willing It Your Way
Estate Planning, Wills, and Probate

Estate planning is suffused with a masculine aura: wood-paneled offices embrace lawyers, accountants, judges, bankers, insurance agents, and clients — all male, at least in the main, even today.

And it's a shame, because creative estate planning should really be a female domain. Since — unlike our husbands — we probably won't have to provide for a surviving spouse, we women, in the end, can weave a more interesting tapestry. Free of dependents, we can manipulate our estates to equalize the situation between our children, give comfort to an old and dear friend, or make a substantial and meaningful gift to our favorite charity. Final plans that would be irresponsible for a married man are entirely righteous for a widow.

We have at our disposal many tools. In weaving our tapestries, we can select a trust as the solid background, a joint tenancy as one accent, a pay-on-death account as another, and a pour-over will as the integrating theme. We'll learn about each of these as we go along, so that our plans can serve our purposes with a precision that comes close to art.

Making your tapestry the beauty it should be is the purpose of this chapter and the next. Read them together, because estate planning is best understood as a whole. Together we will learn about the nuts and bolts of estate planning, the goal being to familiarize you with the elements. Once you are conversant with the concepts and understand the vehicles, you'll be ready to take an active part in directing the professionals in your life — instead of, as is too common now, letting them direct you.

The problem for women starts with the professional estate planner. Most ignore this important reality: estate planning for women should be different from that for men. This is true because of these all-important factors:

- More than four out of five wives outlive their husbands.
- Widows outnumber widowers six to one.
- Eighty-five percent of women die single.
- Eighty-five percent of men die married.
- A typical woman of sixty-five has 33 percent more life left than a sixty-five-year-old man.

In brief? Your husband's final plans will probably be focused on providing for you. And yours won't be concerned with him at all.

Professional advice that doesn't take into account these differences in our lives serves women poorly. The extra years, the gender biases in marital property laws, and the economic disadvantages of the unmarried state contribute to the doleful reality that three out of four older Americans living in poverty are women.

In this chapter and the next we'll walk through the basics of estate planning, keeping in mind the special strategies women need to compensate for the subtle gender biases wrought by biology, law, and tradition. In this chapter we will talk about how to use an estates/probate attorney, wills, probate, and what happens if you do nothing at all. Trusts, other probate-avoiding devices such as joint tenancies, and death taxes are the subjects of the next.

The idea here is not to duplicate the general estate planning guides already widely available, but to recast each estate issue into a woman's perspective. What cautions should *women* bring to a living trust that a man need not? Why might a husband's will be more important to a woman than her will is to him? Why do seemingly gender-neutral inheritance and probate laws impact men and women very differently? How about death taxes? Can you avoid them? And we won't leave out attorneys — how to find one, how to deal with them — especially with respect to common assumptions held by too many probate attorneys about the capabilities of women. Some components of many estate plans, such as powers of attorney and medical directives (right-to-die instruments), are discussed in Chapter 7.

Children of Eve

The unavoidables in life are death and taxes, so it is said. Of course, we make things so complicated trying to avoid them anyway that, given the choice, we would no doubt skip the final experience of our lives just to avoid the hassle.

And really, what should be more simple? In the privacy of our homes we contemplate the drawing of our last breath, and in peace and dignity we write a loving little note designating our few treasures to our friends and favorite charity. Then we conclude our lives in the peaceful certainty of harmonious equanimity.

The problem with this picture, of course, is human nature — *we* are the reason for the probate process. Thousands of years of human experience have taught us that wherever there is property, we are embarrassingly likely to fight over it. We do it at divorce, and — although we suspect it is unseemly — we do it after a death, too.

That is the unattractive little secret that every probate lawyer knows — even good, loving friends and family members fight over property. Nobody expects the fight, of course. Each has a perfect understanding of the proper way the estate should be distributed — and assumes everyone else is equally endowed with such clear vision. Alas, the beloved decedent had a different idea, and so the heirs begin their uncomfortable little quadrille. Sometimes a settlement is reached among them to alter the distribution. But all too often, the argument ends up in court.

Most of the time, though, the estate is distributed as originally written, with hard but unspoken feelings breaking up friendships and spoiling family relations for years. "Sue should have left me more — after all, it was I who cared for her in her last illness." "No, Sue knew what she was doing — I loaned her money to buy her business years ago." "Both wrong. I am Sue's only child — I should have it all."

So much for harmonious equanimity.

One way or the other — with a will or a trust, or even if you do nothing at all — your assets cannot be simply left up for grabs. Society has an interest in avoiding the spectacle of family fights, as well as seeing that creditors and taxes get paid. Whether the estate goes through probate, or is distributed according to a "will substitute" such as a trust or joint tenancies, the law prescribes an orderly process, even if you have made no plans whatsoever.

Estate Planning Is
Different for Women

For women, estate planning has a special significance. This is one more area where biology dictates different planning for men and women. More than four out of five of us will be the survivors of our marriage. If you are a wife, it is overwhelmingly likely that you will be the one who ends up living with the plans very likely made by your husband and a lawyer without you.

The wife needs to plan for two deaths: his and hers. The husband generally expects only to plan for his own. More than your husband, you need to understand life insurance, probate, administering a trust, distributing a will, death taxes, and executors. Unfortunately, all too often the family lawyer confers with the husband, plans the estate with him, and outlines the will or trust with him, and the wife is brought in only for her signature. Consequently, women often are not certain about the status of many important matters, including how title appears on deeds and other assets, the implications of will or trust provisions, and what formalities will have to be dealt with after her husband dies.

Men make the plans, women execute them. Well, what else is new — except that this paternalistic practice sets a woman up poorly for the rest of her life, which she'll most likely live as a single woman. Active and understanding participation in estate planning *before* the death of either spouse is a must for both partners. Typical estate planning by traditional probate attorneys has caused a lot of problems for women, who, newly widowed, find their assets tied up in trusts or eaten up in fees — or even learn they've been disinherited in favor of a mistress, charity, or children (especially of a former marriage).

If, like many men, your husband is reluctant to contemplate his own demise, you must step in and take the initiative. Good estate planning really should be all about *your* life after he's gone — fifteen years of widowhood if you're average. The estate plan should have your mark all over it. After all, you are most likely to live it.

If you are unmarried (single, widowed, or divorced), you are in a much better estate-planning position than a wife. You have only one death to plan for. You still need to know the basics about wills and trusts, and how to manipulate them to carry out the last detail of your wishes. If you have children, you have an opportunity to protect the spendthrift, equalize things between siblings who may not have received equal funds from you during your lifetime, guarantee regular income to a beloved friend, or make a great gift to your favorite charity. If your plans include a longtime companion or partner, you absolutely must prepare a careful plan, and understand the underlying formalities and what happens after a death. You also need to know what happens in your state when someone dies without a will or trust. But all in all, as a single woman, you are really a much freer soul than the wife when it comes to final planning.

We can't take the mystery out of death, but let's take the mystery out of the laws that surround it. We can begin by taking a look at the folks who could do so much to demystify the process but, alas, so often don't: attorneys.

Finding the Right Attorney

Too many women find themselves stuck with a lawyer that just doesn't fit. All too often the husband selects a lawyer, while the wife merely comes along for the ride. This may be appropriate for business counsel, if the husband runs the business. But for estate planning, you should do the selecting, because you are much more likely to be the one who will have to live with the choice when it counts. The pleasantries in the lawyer's office while the wills are drafted are often the high point of the relationship. It's easy for the lawyer to be accommodating then. But when the going gets tough — when you need to talk several times a week about estate details — you want your lawyer on the other end of the phone, not "out to lunch" or "in a meeting."

You should probably select your estate attorney from one of the following:

- elder law attorney
- probate attorney
- general practitioner
- your family lawyer

Your first task in selecting a lawyer is to decide whether you want to go with your old *family retainer* who practices general law. If yours will be a routine estate, and you like him or her, there should be no problem in going with that lawyer. Ordinary wills, trusts, and probate are the bread and butter of general law practices, so they should present no challenges your lawyer can't handle.

If your family lawyer won't do, you might consider locating an *elder law practitioner* in your area. This is a new specialty that goes far beyond ordinary probate and estate planning. An elder law specialist will take into account the possibility of catastrophic long-term care costs and will show you some remarkably clever ways to accomplish an estate plan that will protect family assets in the event of such a catastrophe. A good elder law attorney is the way to go if one is available to you. This is especially true for women since elder law really developed around the plight of women whose marital assets went down the drain because of the costly custodial care required by their husbands. An elder law attorney is oriented toward the needs of the wife.

Probate attorneys are the traditional choice for estate planning, and still not a bad one if your community does not have an elder law specialist whom you like. Traditional probate practice, unfortunately, often patronized the wife or widow. Marital assets were tied up in trusts "to protect her" or "help her manage." She was told not to bother her pretty head about details of estate management — the law office would provide everything she needed.

Sometimes the advice given her was self-serving to the lawyer. Some probate lawyers held onto estates far longer than necessary, partly because the estate grew while idle, and the attorney fees were figured on the final value of the estate. Some probate lawyers brush off questions from the widow about establishing a probate-avoidance trust — because the attorney is eager for the probate fee after her death. Remember, because the attorney's fee will probably be a percentage of the estate, he or she stands to earn more per hour by spending the least amount of time on the estate possible. And don't think for a minute that calculation isn't a factor in the service you receive and the availability of the lawyer. No question, plenty of probate attorneys are excellent. Just keep your eyes open, be politely persistent with your questions, remember you can fire a lawyer, and understand that if you feel uncomfortable with some response or practice, you are probably not out of line. Demand information you can understand. You're paying for it.

A lawyer with a general civil practice who handles probate routinely can manage your ordinary estate. If the estate is complex, go with a specialist. What is a complex estate? One that

- might be subject to death taxes
- may be contested
- contains out-of-state property
- will involve the sale of real estate
- includes gifts over $2,000 to minors
- includes a testamentary trust

Once you've decided which specialty is appropriate, how do you narrow the field to just the right lawyer? The traditional advice is to ask friends. This will get you a lawyer your friends like — but doesn't guarantee good lawyering, or sensitivity to you as an intelligent woman. A female may work out better for you, but you can't count on it. Your local bar association probably runs a referral service, but usually it is on a rotating basis and caters to lawyers just starting out. Your local senior center or senior law clinic might be helpful.

Here is something you might try if you really have no place else to start. Look in the yellow pages under "attorneys." Pick five whose offices are convenient to you, and who claim to be elder law or probate specialists. Call each one, following this script:

You are the daughter and sole heir of an eighty-eight-year-old widow who has around $100,000 in assets and is in good health with a sound mind. You've heard of living trusts and wonder

- whether the lawyer recommends one, and
- how much, approximately, would it cost?

After calling all five, judge the attorneys on the following:

- Did the attorney return your call promptly?

- Did he or she speak to you personally?
- Was he or she frank and forthcoming, or evasive?
- Did you feel you were given a hard sell?

The right attorney may not be the cheapest but should not be wildly out of line with the others. He or she should have welcomed your inquiry and candidly offered an opinion free of charge. The opinion should include a rough estimate of costs saved by going with a trust over a will — this hypothetical situation is borderline. There should be no pressure to get you into the office before a "horseback" opinion is given, but he or she would be justified in explaining that you should not rely on the advice, because all the factors aren't yet known. You might want to eliminate the one who did no more than refer you to the secretary to make an appointment or wouldn't speak personally to you in the first place. An accessible lawyer who is willing to talk candidly to you for no charge is a promising start. And be sure to do this anonymously or pseudonymously, in case you find an attorney you like and don't wish to admit to your little test.

Now let's take a look at wills and probate, starting with an all-important fundamental: what assets do you own, anyway? You may be surprised.

Community Property Versus the Common Law

If you have been a homemaker most of your married life, chances are good that you don't own what you think you do. The things you and your husband refer to as "ours," including your home, investments, furniture, and "your" car, are legally his in most states. If his earnings acquired them, he has the right to sell them, borrow on them, give them away, waste them, and *will* them, in forty-one of our fifty states. In the remaining nine, wives and husbands each own half the assets acquired during the marriage (except gifts and inheritances), regardless of who earned the money that bought them or whose name is on them.

These profound differences in property rights derive from a historical split among our states. The forty-one common-law property states use the English common law with respect to marital property, meaning the asset belongs to the spouse whose earnings acquired it. A wife in a common-law state can acquire property only by inheritance, gift, or her own earnings. The same law applies to her husband, but that he has had the lion's share of the earnings, and therefore owns the lion's share of the marital property, is much more likely. In the nine community property states, in addition to gift, inheritance, and earnings, each spouse *also* acquires assets through the efforts of the other. In other words, it doesn't matter whose earnings bought "your" car in a community property state — you and your husband own it fifty-fifty. Community property comes to us through Spain, and the original eight community property states were Arizona, California, Idaho, Louisiana, Nevada, New Mexico, Texas, and Washington. Wisconsin joined the fold in the 1980s.

Where you live your married life, therefore, can mean everything to you as a widow. If you are a community property wife, you own half of the marital property outright, so your husband cannot disinherit you from your half, nor will you lose it if he dies without a will. If you are a wife in a common-law state, you have much less protection — and this can translate into real dollars.

Throughout this chapter and the next, we will refer to the differing rights of common-law and community property wives and widows. If you have lived in both types of states during your marriage, and have property acquired under both systems, you will need expert advice if you end up with fewer marital assets than you believe you're entitled to.

Just keep in mind that as a wife in a common-law state, you probably own much less property than your husband does and will have to plan quite differently from he. You can protect yourself by ensuring your husband has made a will in your favor and is keeping it up-to-date. A good will can protect you in ways your state law will not.

The National Organization for Women (NOW) is working to bring community property principles to the common-law states. You can reach NOW at 1000 16th Street NW, Suite 700, Washington, D.C., 20036; telephone (202) 331-0066. Ask about the Task Force for the Rights of Women in Marriage.

When Someone Dies

Let's suppose the unthinkable happens, and your healthy, active husband drops dead tomorrow. Will you know what to do? The people who will suddenly become a part of your life know what to do, even if you don't. At the very beginning, medical professionals will be involved, even if only to declare death. The doctor, or hospital, will prepare the death certificate and ask you what to do with the body. The funeral home will transport the body, or the hospital will arrange transportation if the body is to go to a medical school. The funeral home will often order multiple copies of the certified death certificate. You will need at least one for every account you will be changing into your name. Get plenty of *certified* copies — virtually no one will accept copies you run off on a copier. You, or someone you ask, will call your family lawyer, if you have one, and he or she will produce a copy of the will and get in touch with the executor. If you have the original will, locate it.

There is no great rush at this point. You and those close to you have time to focus on the wake, service, or whatever, before you need to be involved further.

After things have calmed down, work with the attorney and executor to "marshal the assets." Turn over copies of bank and brokerage statements, deeds, insurance policies; inquire of his pension administrator about survivor's benefits and death benefits. Notify Social Security. Track down all debts, and learn if credit insurance was involved. If so, the debt may be paid in full. If your husband died in an accident, especially on a public carrier like a bus or plane, be sure to ask your credit card carriers if they insure such a loss; many do. In some places, a safe-deposit box may be frozen until the estate is officially inventoried, but your lawyer should be able to get you in to locate the will, if necessary.

Here is an emerging high-tech problem: personal computers. Often only one spouse likes computers — and probably has all sorts of fancy financial programs loaded onto the hard disk, and the family's financial records as well. If he or she suddenly dies or becomes incompetent, how can the computer-phobe retrieve the files? All too often, the survivor has no idea how to turn the machine on, much less access its files. Indeed, he or she may well have no idea the records are on the computer in the first place. If you are caught in such a situation, be sure to have a data recovery service get the records out. Look in the yellow pages for such a service — if none is listed, call a computer dealer for a referral. In the meantime, be prepared. The computer whiz should conscientiously print out the data once a month or so, and file it where the other knows where to find it, along with a list of financial software in use. If the deceased used a computer at the office, get data recovery to search it, too. Many workers keep personal files on the office computer under secret passwords.

In general, your probate or trust lawyer will guide you, but you are entitled to full explanations at all stages. The important thing to remember is that you're paying the medical and legal professionals to see you through this, and you should expect to be gentle to yourself during this time. Let the pressure be on them, not you. The lawyer will take care of all court filings and legal notices and will guide you and the executor through the whole process. If a tax expert is needed, the attorney will see that one is hired and paid out of the estate. Your job will be to provide the attorney and the executor with the documents they need. Expect at least a year to settle even a relatively simple probate estate. An allowance from the estate will be arranged for you to live on in the meantime.

When you feel up to it, change the names on your credit cards, bank accounts, and car registrations, and revise your own will or trust.

The AARP has a popular program for widows and widowers operating across the country. The groups meet locally, offering mutual support and companionship. The Widowed Persons Service can be reached in care of the AARP at 601 E Street NW, Washington, D.C. 20049; telephone (202) 434-2277.

When There Is No Will

The technical word for a will is *testament*, thus the person who makes a will is a *testator* (in older terminology, a female willmaker was a *testatrix*), and when someone dies without making a will, lawyers refer to it as *intestacy*.

All states have rules governing *intestate succession*, the process by which an estate is distributed to the heirs if there has been no will or will substitute. The intestate estate goes through probate (more about this later), its debts and taxes are paid, the administrator and the attorney are paid their fees, and the probate court orders what's left distributed to the heirs.

It is here that you are most likely to have an argument with the state. The heirs under your state's laws may not be the same people you have in mind. Although it differs somewhat from state to state, typically your assets would go first to your spouse (perhaps with a portion to your children); but if no spouse, then to your children; if none, then to your parents; then your siblings; then on to your remaining blood relatives by degree. Usually the entire estate goes to the first class of relatives entitled before one penny goes to the next ones in line. In other words, your parents (or siblings) will get nothing if children exist, who will (in many states) get nothing if a spouse is living. Of course, nothing whatsoever will go to nonrelatives, including in-laws and charities. If you have no relatives, no matter how remote, the property will go to your state's treasury (*escheat*).

Consider Kathy's problem. Her developmentally disabled daughter, Alice, lived at home with her. Her other daughter, Kim, was a news anchorwoman at a small radio station across the country. Kim was a single mother of three sons, and every day was a struggle. Kathy planned to leave her entire $300,000 estate to Kim, so that Alice would continue to qualify for SSI disability (welfare), which would cover her expenses in a local group home. Kathy died without a will — meaning Kim and Alice (through a guardian) shared equally in the estate. After debts, fees, and taxes, each daughter received $130,000 — not enough to secure Kim's future, but too much for Alice. The sum disqualified her from SSI, meaning it went to pay the group home until it was spent down, after which SSI was reinstated. In effect, $130,000 that could have gone to Kim went instead to the taxpayers in lieu of SSI payments to Alice. Some will say this is appropriate — but yes or no, it was not Kathy's plan. A good will would have put her thoughtful wishes into effect.

Perhaps you believe that you don't have enough property to worry about, so a will or trust would be a waste of money. But if you have personal mementos of sentimental value that you wish to leave to a friend or a particular child, it would be best to give it to that person while you are still alive (but read the section in the next chapter on death taxes before you give away art or antiques that have appreciated substantially in value). You may feel a note left among your modest belongings will be enough to guide your friends after your death, but you must realize that by law they cannot informally give away your assets. You *can* handwrite a simple will that will do the job; see the section on holographic wills below.

> **You may think you own nothing. Actually, you have no idea what will be in your estate after you die. If the hospital you die in is negligent, your executor would sue for malpractice. If the drunk driver who kills you**

is rich, your executor might settle for hundreds of thousands of dollars. Your will would ensure that the damages go to your named heirs.

Certain assets, such as life insurance, pension death benefits, joint-tenancy accounts, passbook "trust" accounts, some retirement savings such as IRAs and 401(k)s, and, of course, inter-vivos (also called *living*) trusts, will go to the beneficiary you named, whether or not you have written a will. It is possible to pass thousands, and even millions, of dollars of assets through these "will substitutes" without ever writing a will. However, it takes sophisticated and careful planning. We'll cover these in more detail in the next chapter.

> **Consider intestacy to be as much an estate planning choice on your part as writing a will or trust. In other words, it is irresponsible to put off writing a will or trust just from indecision or inertia. You don't have to write a will. But read some books on estate planning before you choose not to. NOLO Press has books on estate planning written for consumers (see Resources at the end of the book).**

That's enough about you. What about your husband, if you're married, or a close friend or relative if you are not? Has he or she made a will? Should you be in it? If the answer is yes, ideally you should have a copy of it. If that is not possible — or too awkward — consider your position should the expected bequest fail to materialize.

Vicky gave up her job and her apartment to provide twenty-four-hour care to her mother in her mother's home. Her mom had enough money to support them both and always promised she'd leave the house to Vicky. But before she had a chance to write her will, she became incompetent following a stroke. When she died without a will, the court had no choice but to pool all the assets, including the house, sell them, and divide them equally among Vicky and her five brothers — none of whom had done more than call on Mother's Day. After debts and probate fees were paid, Vicky, age sixty, ended up with $23,000 of the $200,000 estate. She had no job, no prospects, and was two years away from claiming a reduced Social Security check, minimal because of her years out of the paid labor market caring for her mom. Her brothers were sure this was the way mom wanted it — after all, she could have written a will leaving the house to Vicky, couldn't she have?

Sylvia and Nancy were inseparable for twenty years before Nancy's death. As partners, they combined their resources and paid jointly for everything. They lived in Nancy's house, but jointly paid for all improvements, including adding a bedroom and remodeling the baths and kitchen. They didn't believe in state-sanctioned formalities, so in the presence of good friends, they pledged their intentions to leave everything to each other. They even typed out instructions reflecting their intent. But when Nancy died suddenly, Sylvia lost the house to Nancy's long-estranged husband, her only legal heir because there had never been a divorce. The typed instructions and the pledge before friends had no meaning in law. Nancy had died intestate. Sylvia was able, at great expense and heartache, to recover from Nancy's estate part of the costs of the home improvements, and to prove that some of the money in their common accounts was hers — but thousands of dollars were not recoverable. A simple will or trust would have carried out their expectations to the letter.

> **A wife has a special incentive to urge her husband to write a will (or trust). In many states, she will not inherit all the marital assets if he dies intestate. They will be shared with her children, leaving her much poorer in widowhood than in marriage. In many states, her share of the marital assets would be only *one-third*, meaning she may well receive more of the marital assets through divorce than widowhood.**

Donna and Butch worked hard through their forty years of marriage. From time to time they wrote wills, but tore up their last ones when they had a falling-out with their only son.

Donna had always been a housewife, so Butch's earnings had paid for their $200,000 house, and $100,000 in investments. Butch died before they had a chance to write new wills, so under the intestate succession laws of their common-law state, two-thirds, or $200,000, went to their son, and $100,000 went to Donna. She had to sell the house in order to settle with her son and was left with only the $100,000 — and no home to live in for the rest of her life.

In a community property state, only one-half of the marital assets would be subject to the intestate laws. The other half, belonging to the living spouse, is left intact. Therefore, Donna would have kept her half and received at least one-half of Butch's half, for a total of $225,000. Many community property states, and some common-law states, would pass all the marital assets to the surviving spouse.

> **Your first job is to learn the intestate laws in your state. Any probate lawyer can tell you, or call your local agency on aging or senior law center. Even if you know your husband has a will, it is not a bad idea to have this information — pass it along to your friends.**

And remember, intestacy is easy to avoid. Read on.

WILLS

A will is a time-honored device for passing property after death. The right to determine for yourself who will get your property after you're gone is a great right. In earlier centuries, laws decided such important things. The right of the first-born son to inherit the land and title was his birthright — not yours to give by will. Married women, being nonpersons in the eyes of the law (quite literally), could not inherit, nor could they will their possessions to others — since they owned none. Married Women's Acts, passed in all the states in the mid-nineteenth century, gave American married women the right to own and will their assets.

Of course, you can't will what you don't own, and that poses a real problem for wives in common-law states. If all your marital assets were acquired through your husband's earnings, you probably cannot legally will anything — you don't really own anything to begin with. Community property spouses can will only their half of the marital property; the other spouse always retains his or her half. The retained half does not go through probate since it wasn't (couldn't be) willed in the first place.

In this section we'll take a look at some of the ways you can use wills to carry out every detail of your plan. These include

- formal wills
- holographic or handwritten wills
- pour-over wills
- codicils

Formal Wills

You remember the scenes from the old movies. The dear one has departed, the grieving heirs assemble in the lawyer's office, the will is read in stentorian tones. Longtime probate practitioners can pull from their files old wills written on black-bordered paper, perhaps beginning with the prudent salutation "In the Name of God, Amen."

Things are a little different nowadays. The modern will is most likely produced on the office computer — a simple fill-in-the-blanks procedure in many cases. Black borders and prayerful openings are long gone. The will is seldom "read" in a formal gathering. Rather, it is mailed to the named beneficiaries, as well as to those who would inherit if the will were to be thrown out.

But one thing has not changed in the least. Formal — that is, typed and witnessed — wills remain suffused with formalities that must be observed *to the letter* if the will is to be valid. This is why many lawyers who long ago discarded the after-death reading insist on assembling the witnesses and the testator (willmaker) in their office for the signing. Depending on the state, certain words must be said in front of the witnesses; certain acknowledgments made in return. This exacting little ritual may seem silly but is not done to run up the lawyer's bill.

Doris, or rather her intended heirs, got caught by formalities. She had her will notarized rather than witnessed in the precise way set down by her state's law. The notarized will failed for lack of valid witnesses, and her estate passed to relatives she hadn't seen in years rather than her best friend as planned.

> **Take care in selecting your witnesses. Be sure they are not named in your will, are likely to survive you, and will be locatable when you die. They need not read your will, only witness your signature. Your executor will need to contact them so that they can sign the declarations to "prove" (*probate*) your will.**

Aside from the formalities, a will is a relatively straightforward instrument. It opens with a simple declaration of your intent to will, then names your beneficiaries, the executor, and your bequests, and concludes with a catchall clause that names someone to receive everything else you own. Lawyers call this the "residuary clause," and in many wills it is the major bequest.

It is often good planning to keep your "specific bequests" to a minimum, so you don't have to keep changing your will every time you change your property. You might, for example, leave your heirloom silver to your sister (a *specific* bequest), then the residue of your estate to your two children, half and half (the *residuary* bequest). Anything you acquire in the future will pass under the residuary clause, making it unnecessary for you to keep changing your will every time your possessions change. If you sell your silver, your sister will be out of luck. She will not be "owed" anything by your estate because of the absent bequest. If your sister should die before you do, most states would pass the silver to her heirs, but in some it would go to the residuary beneficiaries — your kids.

If you are married, don't forget your community property or common-law rights. If all your property is community property, you can will only your half. If you've lived all your marriage in a common-law state and own no separate property of your own, you may have very little to leave by will.

JoAnn and Richard lived in a common-law property state. They each drew up wills disposing of their marital assets to each other; but in the event they failed to survive each other, JoAnn willed her assets to her alma mater. Richard willed his to his nephew. They were killed simultaneously in an auto accident. All the assets went to Richard's nephew, none to JoAnn's college — because none of the marital assets legally belonged to JoAnn at her death. She didn't really own her "half," so she couldn't will it.

In states that have passed the Uniform Simultaneous Death Act, each decedent is treated as having survived the other. The practical effect of this, in JoAnn and Richard's case, would be that the college and the nephew each inherit half of the marital estate. Had Richard and JoAnn lived in a community property state, half the assets would have gone to the nephew, the other half to the college. JoAnn's hard work over the years in maintaining their resources would have been recognized in her right to will her half of the marital estate to further a cause she believed in.

> **In both community property and common-law states, separate property can be acquired by gift or inheritance. In other words, your husband can give you some of the marital assets, making them yours to will, and you have the right to will your inheritance from your mother, provided you have kept it separate from the marital assets.**

Do-It-Yourself Wills: Holographs

Wills can be very simple or quite elaborate. You can write one yourself, perfectly legally, with the help of any number of do-it-yourself books. A *holographic* will is one you write yourself in your own handwriting. Obviously, this cuts costs. It also provides privacy — even a lawyer need not know your secret heir and lover — although the public *will* know when the will is filed with the probate court after you die, which is an argument for the greater privacy of a trust. It also ensures flexibility. Change your mind about your heirs? Rip it up and do it again.

The entire holographic will *must be in your handwriting*. To be safe, don't even type your address or use letterhead. It must be dated and signed. Check your state's law about witnesses and holographic wills — witnesses are not required in many states, and might even invalidate the holograph in some.

Be very careful if you write your own will. Testamentary law is archaic and suffused with formalities. You must follow the rules for your state *exactly*, or your will will fail and your assets will be distributed as if you never wrote the will. Be sure any guide you use is up-to-date, *and for your state*. You might call your state bar association — some have form wills. Also consult the senior citizen's law centers — perhaps they would read over your will to make sure it suffices. Attorneys should also be willing to look over your will for a reasonable fee. Just be careful you don't end up paying more for a consultation than you would for the attorney to write the will.

Changing Your Will: Codicils

Whether or not you write a simple holographic will on one page at home, or pay an attorney to draft an elaborate, multipage one, formally witnessed — there comes a time when you may want to change it. All wills are modifiable. You can either revoke the will and start over with a new one, or you can modify it by *codicil*. A codicil is just another name for an amendment.

A formal, typed will drawn by your attorney can be modified by you with a handwritten, holographic codicil, provided *always* that all technicalities governing holographic wills (which are generally the same for holographic codicils) are observed *to the letter*.

Of course, you can always have your attorney draw up a formal codicil, which will require witnesses, as does a formal will. Or you or your attorney can simply draw up an entirely new will or holograph, revoking all earlier wills.

Whatever you do, you mustn't mark up the existing will. Do *not* line out, scratch out, cut out, insert words, or otherwise change the face of your will without legal advice. It is terribly easy to invalidate the provision you are trying to change, or even the entire will. Codicils, whether formally drawn and witnessed, or simple holographs, must be written on separate paper from the will they are amending.

After a new grandchild was born, Gabrielle decided to change her will to include the baby. She simply added the child's name to those already listed in her typed, witnessed will. She initialed and dated her change. When her will was probated, the new grandchild was not permitted to share in the estate, because proper formalities had not been observed. Had Gabrielle handwritten a codicil, signed it, dated it, and left it with her will, her wishes would have been carried out in most states.

A Will to Go with a Trust: Pour-Over Wills

You may have heard that wills are obsolete — that the good estate plan now uses trusts instead of wills. Is this true? Yes and no. The problem with wills is that they lead directly to probate — and as we shall see later, probate is lengthy and expensive. Drawn carefully, the right trust can give the same result as a will, yet without probate. You avoid probate fees (the executor and the attorney) with a trust, but unless you draw it up yourself, you will pay an attorney to do it for you. We'll examine the costs of trusts in the next chapter, but for now, you should realize that the cost of a will versus the cost of a trust is not as simple as comparing the costs of distributing the assets.

Even if you do use a trust to shelter all your known assets from probate, your adviser may recommend a *pour-over will* to complete your estate plan. A pour-over simply bequeaths all your assets, whatever they may be, to the trustee of your trust. This way any asset you forgot to include in your trust will go through the trust to your trust beneficiaries (the millions from the uncashed lottery ticket found among your effects after your death, for example). Like any other will, a pour-over can be formal or holographic and must conform to all technicalities. See the discussion on pour-overs in Chapter 6.

Picking Your Executor

Your executor (in times past, women were called *executrixes*) will work with an attorney to see that your assets are all accounted for, taxes and debts paid, probate and court fees paid, and the estate distributed to your beneficiaries. Although an executor is not required to hire an attorney, most do, because probate can be a frustrating technical mine field for the uninitiated. The executor and the attorney are then paid out of the estate.

Many people choose one of the principal heirs to be the executor, with the idea that the fee increases his or her share of the estate. Others expect a family executor to waive the fee, or you can set a fee in the will that is lower than the state maximum.

Although the attorney who wrote your will may not volunteer the information, the executor is not required to hire him or her to be the attorney for probate.

Your executor can be anyone you wish, provided he or she is not a minor. You can even name an out-of-state executor, but most advisers discourage this, because it is handier if the executor is near the property. He or she may have to do some legwork, such as clean out your residence, close accounts, sell some assets. You want someone capable of this activity. You can name coexecutors, but again, the inconvenience and delay of getting multiple signatures on every document argues against that. Your named executor can decline the nomination — you cannot force someone to execute your will.

You can name a professional fiduciary, such as a bank or an attorney, to act as your executor, but a family member or friend can do just as well with the estate attorney's guidance and will get the fee as well.

Unless you waive it in your will, your executor will probably have to post a bond, and the fee for that will be paid from your estate. This protects your heirs in the event your executor makes off with the funds.

> **It is common for family members named as executor to waive the fee. As a probate attorney, I always felt the executor's efforts were worth compensation. It is not an enormous job, but it is exacting and can be tedious. I think executors should not be intimidated into waiving their fee by other beneficiaries. If the estate is quite large, and the fees would amount to several hundred dollars per hour, perhaps a scaled-down fee would be appropriate. The executor will earn it.**

The Unspoken Word: Disinheritance

Although not recognized as such, disinheritance is a women's issue.

Remember that 85 percent of men die married? This means that the overwhelming majority of American men will write their last will as married men and have the opportunity to disinherit their wives. The reverse is true for women. Since 85 percent of women die single, most women leave no spouse to disinherit.

What does this mean? It means that when one spouse disinherits the other, it necessarily will usually be the husband who does the disinheriting. In addition, since two-thirds of American women live in common-law states and therefore own few assets compared to their husbands, when they are disinherited it is usually for a substantial loss.

Disinheritance, of course, is often a mutual plan — in the event of a second marriage, for example — where each has ample assets and wishes to leave them to his or her own children. But the old-fashioned variety, where the widow learns of the disinheritance only after the death, can be devastating.

In a community property state, of course, the disinherited wife cannot be disinherited from her one-half share of the community property. She *can* be disinherited from her husband's separate property, if any, and his one-half share of the community assets.

But in a common-law state, the rights of a disinherited wife vary widely. Generally speaking, the disinherited widow in a common-law state can force the executor to pay a proportion of the estate to her, regardless of the disinheritance. At most, this *forced share* would be one-third of the estate. In some states the forced share affects only personal property; in others, only the real estate. In some it is lower than one-third.

Even a wife who has not been fully disinherited but was left less than the statutory forced share should be able to bring her share up to the forced-share amount. She needs a probate attorney.

Fifteen percent of husbands leave their wives less than their forced share. Since most wills are attorney written, it must be assumed that this percentage would be larger were the drafter not constrained by his or her knowledge of the forced-share laws.

If your claim or grievance against the estate is denied, you will need another attorney to represent your interests. The executor and his or her attorney are ethically bound to represent the interests of the estate. A forced-share claim, for example, would not be in the interests of the estate, so you should look to outside representation, no matter how much you like the estate's attorney, and how sympathetic he or she personally is to your claim.

Not only are women more likely to be disinherited by their husbands than the reverse, women are also more likely to be in a position to disinherit other relatives than are men. Since most men die married, their wills usually contemplate their wives as their major heir. Most women, dying single, have adult children to consider. Anytime such a woman doesn't leave her entire estate to her children in equal shares, she is technically disinheriting someone.

Martha willed her prize teacup collection to her best friend, $500 to the local hospice, and left the rest of her estate in equal shares to her three children. Technically, they were disinherited from her teacup collection and the $500. A disinheritance occurs every time someone gets less under a will than he or she would have received under intestacy. Had Martha died intestate, the teacup collection, the $500, and everything else would have gone to the kids in equal shares. This is why there are will contests.

There is no forced share for children or other relatives. They can be fully or partially disinherited, but it is important that you name all your children in the will even if you leave them nothing (or, in some states, leave a token bequest such as $1). Forgotten children can claim a share of the estate, so naming them in your will proves you didn't forget them. Some people simply name their children and their birth dates, then set out their bequests without including the children as beneficiaries.

Rosie and her brother's relationship had been troubled for years. She didn't want to make this private matter public in her will, but she didn't want him to share in her estate, either. She solved the problem gracefully by leaving a bequest in his name to her favorite charity.

Solving Special Problems

You can use your will (or trust) to solve particular problems. Jayne, for example, had a housekeeper, Elva, who had been with her for years. Jayne knew Elva would have only a modest Social Security check to live on after she retired. Jayne wanted to secure Elva's future with a monthly check rather than a lump-sum bequest, because Jayne didn't want Elva to run out of funds in her old age. So Jayne, in her will, instructed her executor to purchase an annuity for Elva with $50,000 from the estate. When Jayne died, Elva had a life expectancy of twenty-one years, so the executor paid a $50,000 premium to a life insurance company who computed the annuity and paid it monthly to Elva for her life. If Jayne had wanted to leave a definite amount per month to Elva, let's say $500, she could have instructed the executor to pay out of the estate whatever the cost such a lifetime annuity would incur.

> **In general, it is better to avoid too many specific bequests. If you will Jerry $50,000, Susan $35,000, and Pete $40,000, and then die with an estate worth only $10,000, someone is going to be disappointed. It is much better to divide your estate by proportions — for example, 20 percent to one heir, 80 percent to another. This way you don't have to keep changing your will as your own fortunes wax and wane.**

Gretchen had assets worth $800,000 when she wrote her will leaving $200,000 to her favorite charity and the balance of her estate to her daughter. Later, Gretchen had a stroke, requiring her to stay in a nursing home for five years before she died. When probated, her estate was worth only $150,000 because of the catastrophic costs of her care. Because her will gave $200,000 to the charity and the rest to her daughter, the charity received the entire estate, her daughter nothing. If Gretchen's will had stated "one-quarter of the estate to charity, the remainder to my daughter," her desire to have her daughter receive most of her estate would have been carried out.

Wills and trusts can be custom-crafted to take care of special problems. We already saw how a stream of income for life can be included through the purchase of an annuity. An annuity is also appropriate to protect a spendthrift or a minor child. If you are wary of making a lump-sum bequest to someone who might use it unwisely, an annuity will take care of the problem. You can arrange for it to pay for a certain number of years, say ten, then have the remainder revert to the beneficiary in a lump sum. Or you can have it pay out for life.

Remember, because of gender-biased actuarial tables, annuities can be costly for women. If you are an executor charged with the duty to purchase an annuity, shop around and compare the premiums and payouts of gender-based and unisex annuities before you decide on one for your female or male beneficiary.

Debts can be forgiven in your will or trust. Or provisions can be included that square your children economically. Betty, for example, had paid her oldest son's college tuition of $30,000. Her oldest daughter had borrowed $20,000 for a down payment on a home. Her youngest daughter had borrowed or been given nothing. Wanting to equalize her lifetime gifts, Betty provided in her will that her college son receive $10,000, her first daughter $20,000 plus forgiveness of her debt, and her third child, $40,000. She explained this to them ahead of time, so there would be no hurt feelings.

If your husband owns his own business, especially if he has partners, be sure "after death" arrangements have been carefully drawn. Will you take his place? Do his associates know that? Do you expect to sell it? Do they know that, too? It is estimated that over half of the small businesses in the country have made no arrangements for the death of an owner — an open invitation to expensive litigation down the line. Of course, if the business is entirely his (or your) property, the will or trust will dispose of it. But businesses are more than sticks and stones. Flesh-and-blood people may have expectations that don't jive with yours. You and your husband should both be in on the succession planning. A good estate plan should include the business succession plan, including tax and debt structuring.

Pets are an important consideration for many women. In our single old age, many of us turn to pets for companionship. Legally, your pet is your property. You can will your pet to another, or instruct your executor to find a good home, or have the animal put to sleep. But you cannot force anyone to accept your bequest, so be sure you've talked it over first with your intended beneficiary. Some people like to leave a small legacy to the pet's new owner, just to help out with the inevitable expenses and to show appreciation for taking on a task that at times will be at least inconvenient.

Wills, then, are delightfully flexible, frustratingly technical, and relatively easy to draft and amend.

Wills are also an opportunity to hurt and punish folks who did you wrong, without any possible risk of retaliation. *Don't do it*. Every probate lawyer has that certain client who keeps the attorney's payments on the Porsche going because she changes her will every month, as this nephew or that grandchild falls in or out of favor. Manipulating people through your bequests is a tired and pathetic game, and your dignity, in the end, is the final loser. Instead, use your will as a loving instrument to create peace where there was disharmony. An unexpected bequest, even if small, to someone long estranged could be your most important and lasting legacy.

The major problem with wills? Willed property, except that willed to a spouse in some states, goes through probate.

PROBATE

Probate is simply the process by which the administrator locates and accounts for the assets; pays taxes, debts, and administration fees; and distributes what is left to the heirs — all under court supervision. The probate process is much the same whether *or not* the individual leaves a will. Without a will, the administrator will distribute the estate to the heirs set by state law. You can avoid probate, which is lengthy and expensive, by planning ahead. There are a number of probate-avoidance devices, and we will look at them in the next chapter.

Generally, all wills are probated, although in some states very small, simple estates are permitted a streamlined procedure. Many states also allow estates that pass in their entirety to a spouse to proceed without most of the formalities. For the rest, probate is usually a lengthy procedure, often taking more than a year for the average, uncomplicated estate.

Demystifying the Probate Process

Many states have similar probate procedures, because they have enacted the Uniform Probate Code, a model procedure developed by an unofficial body of legal scholars. If your state is one, probate will be something like this:

- Within thirty days of learning of the death, the executor files the will with the probate court and a petition to open probate. If there is no will, a similar procedure is followed, except that someone (a relative, a friend, or the decedent's lawyer) will petition the court to become the administrator of the estate.
- A hearing is set to approve the will and empower the executor (or administrator).
- Notices of the hearing are sent to all beneficiaries under the will and to all the disinherited (that is, those who *would* have inherited had the individual died without a

will; they are notified so that they have a chance to con-
test the will and force the estate into intestacy, thus inherit-
ing the estate themselves). For an intestate estate, notices
go out to all the relatives entitled to inherit by law.

- If no one contests the will at the hearing, the judge will
admit it to probate on the strength of written declarations
of the witnesses. If it is an unwitnessed, handwritten will,
the declaration of someone familiar with the handwriting
will be used. At this time, "letters testamentary" are issued
to the executor, authorizing him or her to administer the
estate (or "letters of administration" to the intestate administrator). The executor/administrator now can open accounts, pay debts, and otherwise act for the estate.
- Notice of death is published in newspapers, giving the
executor/administrator's address, and notifying creditors
that they have four months in which to make their claims
against the estate.
- The executor/administrator marshalls the assets, and pre-
pares an inventory of the estate, may sell some or all of
the estate property (at a court proceeding in many cases),
and readies the estate for distribution.
- Another court hearing is set to approve the final distribution. Again, notices are sent to the beneficiaries and other
interested parties. If no questions are raised, the court
approves the accounting and the distribution.
- The executor/administrator pays claims, taxes, and fees,
and distributes what remains to the beneficiaries.
- The executor/administrator is discharged by the court.

The waiting periods set by law for notices, claims, hearings, and so on are responsible for much of the time lost in
probate. It's not all dillydallying at the law office. The petitions
are generally routine forms, prepared by the lawyer's clerical
staff. The court hearings are usually also routine, and if they
are uncontested, in many cases the attorney and executor/
administrator need not even appear. An uncontested probate
is a rubber-stamp procedure in most overcrowded courts.

If someone asks you to be his or her executor, you should be aware that the attorney you select will take care of the procedural formalities and tell you what to do. You will have to sign a lot of papers, and perhaps do the actual clearing out of the home, readying it for sale, or hiring appropriate professionals or services to handle this. You will also open and close bank accounts, so you should be comfortable with the idea of some legwork. You can also administer a simple estate yourself without an attorney's help — there are reliable guidebooks for this (the aforementioned NOLO Press offers one). But since the estate pays for the attorney, you may want to make your life easier by appointing an attorney to take care of the complexities. Probate can be unnervingly technical, and much time can be lost doing things over if the court finds fault.

Probate's lengthy process is one very good reason to avoid it. The other is fees. As we discussed above, probate fees come out of the estate, which may work out better for you than paying for a trust up front. Lots of older women are house rich and cash poor. When the executor sells the house, there will be plenty on hand to pay fees. Still, unless the executor and attorney have agreed to lower fees, typical probate fees can be pretty hefty.

Here is one state's scheme. The executor and the attorney each receive

- 4 percent of the first $15,000;
- 3 percent of the next $85,000;
- 2 percent of the next $900,000;
- 1 percent of the next $9 million;
- ½ percent of the next $15 million; and
- for more than $25 million, a fee to be determined by the court.

In this state (California), encumbrances are ignored when calculating the estate's gross value (the mortgage isn't deducted).

Here is how fees are calculated for a $140,000 estate:

- 4 percent of $15,000 = $600
- 3 percent of $85,000 = $2,550
- 2 percent of $40,000 = $800
  Total = $3,950 × 2 (attorney and executor) = $7,900

For a trust of the same amount:

- $800 to draft the trust
- $500 each for attorney and trustee on an hourly rate of $100 to distribute the trust estate to the beneficiaries after death.
  Total = $1,800

In most states, the probate fees are set by statute *unless you negotiate otherwise.* It is a sad fact that too many lawyers — perhaps even most lawyers — will neglect to tell you that you can negotiate a lower fee (but not a higher one). This goes for the executor as well. You can set these terms in your will (for the executor) and by agreement with the attorney. Get it in writing from the attorney and give that writing to your executor. Usually, you can't dictate to your executor who he or she will use as the attorney for the estate, but you surely can make suggestions. Your executor can then decide whether or not to accept the position with the lower (or even nonexistent) fee.

So probate is lengthy, clumsy, and expensive. Even the settlement of small, simple estates can be protracted because of the notices, hearings, and so on.

Are there ever any reasons *not* to avoid probate? The fact that some trust fees are paid during life, and probate fees after death, will sway some. Others don't want to bother with the hassles of trust administration and record keeping during their lives (discussed in the Chapter 6). Some attorneys believe it wise to put the estates of certain professionals (mainly doctors and lawyers) through probate because the four-month claims period precludes malpractice actions against the estate later on. But that's about it.

There really is very little desirable about probate for most people, and unfortunately, wills and intestacy generally lead right to it.

People often wonder what happens if the estate has been probated, distributed, and closed, and then more assets are discovered — a forgotten bank account, or stock, for example. Get in touch with the lawyer who did the probate. There are procedures for handling "after-discovered assets," as they are known to the law.

The good news is that probate is easily avoided through a number of devices, and trusts are chief among them. We'll cover them, other will substitutes, and death taxes in the next chapter.

CHECKING UP ON YOUR WILL

1. Have you planned for your (average) fifteen years of widowhood?
2. Did you pick your lawyer? If not, are you fully satisfied?
3. Is there an elder law practitioner in your area?
4. Do you live in a common-law or community property state?
5. Have you thought through your state's marital property system?
6. Have you written a will?
7. Do you review it annually?
8. Does your husband have a will? Is it up-to-date?
9. Have you seen it?
10. Do you know where your "important papers" are kept?
11. Do you have the key to the safe-deposit box?

12. Do you know which lawyer wrote your husband's will?
13. Do you know your husband's Social Security number?
14. Do you know in detail what your husband owns?
15. Do you know what you own?
16. Do you know the details of what either of you owe?
17. Do you know where the life insurance policies are?
18. Do you know who your husband's insurance agent is?
19. Have you an idea of who you want for a probate attorney?
20. Do you have an emergency-fund account in your own name?
21. Have you estimated the probate fees on your gross estate?
22. If you die without a will, how will your estate be distributed?
23. If your husband dies without a will, what will be your share?
24. What will be your forced share if your spouse disinherits you?
25. Will your executor likely outlive you?
26. Will you be an executor? Do you know what that entails?
27. What will become of your estate if your heirs die before you?

6

Avoiding Probate
Trusts, Joint Tenancies, and Death Taxes

The nicest thing you can say about probate is that you can avoid it. You can do this in a number of ways — lawyers call these devices *will substitutes*, because like a will, they pass along property after a death. The most popular will substitutes are

- revocable, inter-vivos (living) trusts
- joint tenancies
- pay-on-death accounts (also known as Totten trusts)
- life insurance

Just like a will, each has advantages and disadvantages. And — no surprise — the implications and appropriate use of each one are different for most men and women. In this chapter we will learn the basics about these things — and death taxes, too — especially taking a woman's view.

TRUSTS

Trusts are very popular these days as probate-avoidance devices. You can use a trust to dispose of your property to your heirs, friends, and charities just as you can a will, but without going through probate and incurring its delays and fees.

Women and men should look at trusts quite differently, because of that salient truth: vastly more women die single than men. In many states, trusts are better left until after the first spouse dies. This is because in those states, property passed between spouses does not go through probate, so paying for trusts to avoid a procedure that won't happen anyway is a waste of money. Usually, that will mean a woman may want a trust once widowed, while most men may never need one. Married couples with estates exceeding $600,000 (1993) will want to look into trusts for death tax planning, as we will see below.

> **If you and your husband have willed everything, or substantially everything, to each other, and you live in a state that passes property between spouses without probate, you should closely question any estate planner who is recommending you write trusts. In 1993, there was no federal estate tax on estates under $600,000 (the IRS does deduct your mortgages, liens, or other encumbrances to arrive at this amount). Congress has debated lowering the exempt amount — be alert. For information on your state's law, call any probate lawyer listed in the yellow pages; he or she should answer this simple question over the phone for free.**

If a planner recommends a husband-wife trust, and there will be no probate on the first death because all property is passing to the surviving spouse, you have to know what the benefit will be to you, the likely survivor. If the traditional answer is given — that is, a trust will help you manage your resources — think this through. If you are sure you want someone else to manage your finances, and you well might be, or are using trusts to plan around estate taxes, or are making special use of a irrevocable trust for long-term-care planning, you probably won't want to buy a trust until after your husband's death.

What Is a Trust?

A trust, if you will, is a bit of lawyerly metaphysics. Trusts are an imaginary device first invented to serve monastics under a vow of poverty. The vow, strictly interpreted, meant the monk or nun could own nothing whatsoever, not even the habit he or she wore. A problem arose when the order needed property to live in. How could they own the monastery and still be true to their vows? Philosophical minds devised the trust. A trust simply divides the *ownership* of property from its *benefits*. With a trust, the monks could live in the monastery but not own it. The *trustee* held the title, and the monks had the use (the benefit). Of course, they could have avoided ownership by *leasing* the monastery, but a landlord would be under no obligation to continue the lease down through the generations of monks to come. A trustee is under a very heavy obligation to administer the trust property for the benefit of the beneficiary, whereas a landlord manages the property for the benefit of the landlord. The trustee's obligation to the beneficiary is called a *fiduciary duty*.

There are institutional trustees, such as banks, very willing to charge a fee to handle your trust. Attorneys, too, frequently act as trustees. You can appoint a relative or a friend. You can have a beneficiary also act as trustee — you can even act as trustee yourself. (More about that later.) All trustees are fiduciaries to the trust beneficiaries. The fiduciary duties owed by the trustee to the trust and its beneficiaries are the highest known to the law. For breach of fiduciary duties, a trustee can be forced to pay the trust back, and can even be removed from the trust. There are many fiduciary duties; for instance, a trustee has a duty to segregate the trust funds, to account to the beneficiaries, to invest prudently, and many others. Absolutely, except for trustee's fees, the trustee cannot use the trust property to benefit him- or herself — even if the trust gains as a result of the transaction. Bank trustees usually charge an annual fee based on a percentage of the trust assets (usually around 1 percent or less). An individual trustee's fee is usually set forth in the trust instrument, or it can simply be referred to as a "reasonable" fee. A reasonable fee will probably be an hourly fee, and it will be up to the beneficiaries to object if they feel the fee is unreasonable.

A trust begins when someone (we'll call that person a *trustor*) decides to split the interests in a piece of property he or she owns. The trustor selects a trustee and beneficiaries. The trustor decides the terms of the trust. How many trustees will there be? Who will succeed them if they die or resign? How will they be paid? Or will they? Who are the beneficiaries? Do they receive income from the trustee? How much? When? Do they ever receive the principal? What if they die? When does the trust terminate?

A trustor, a trust instrument, property, a trustee and a beneficiary. You might say the trustor provided the meat; the trust is the stew pot; the trust assets are the meat and potatoes; the trustee is the chef; and the happy diner is the beneficiary. That, to stretch a metaphor, is a trust.

A Device with Many Uses

Trusts are used for many things besides probate avoidance. Minor children, because they generally can't own property in their own names, often have their property held by trustees until they reach majority. Trusts can also be very useful in handling the affairs of the very old or incapacitated. Some trusts are used for tax planning, others for nursing-home expense planning, yet others to benefit charities. Trusts can be

- inter-vivos (living) or
- testamentary;
- revocable or
- irrevocable.

In this chapter we will concentrate on the revocable inter-vivos trust for probate avoidance, but first a brief explanation of testamentary and irrevocable trusts.

Testamentary Trusts

Remember the pour-over will? In the pour-over, the willed property is poured-over into an existing trust. But you can also write a trust into your will itself, to take effect only after your death. Because the trust is created in your will (testament), a trust that begins its life on your death is a *testamentary* trust.

Testamentary trusts are useful if you want to leave something to someone who can't handle a lump-sum bequest — a minor, for example, or a spendthrift. In your will you name a trustee to receive the bequest and administer it for the benefit of the beneficiary, under whatever terms you like. Income for ten years, perhaps, then the remainder free of trust. Elizabeth wanted to leave $50,000 to her twenty-one-year-old granddaughter, but she didn't feel the young woman was mature enough to handle the $50,000 just yet. In her will, she provided for the sum to go to a bank as trustee, which was instructed to accumulate the interest, distribute it to the beneficiary when she was twenty-five, thirty, and thirty-five. On her fortieth birthday she was to receive the entire bequest, free of trust. For this service, the bank charged an annual fee, which came out of the trust estate. But if you want to avoid probate, testamentary trusts *do not do the job*. As the creature of a will, the estate goes through probate before the trustee, like any other beneficiary under the will, receives the funds.

What If You Change Your Mind?

When the trustor decides on the terms of the trust, one of the first considerations is revocability. An *irrevocable* trust is just that. The trustor, forever, cannot change its terms. Because of this sobering feature, irrevocable trusts are used only in very limited circumstances. Irrevocable trusts are sometimes used in planning for long-term care, where an application for Medicaid is contemplated, and the individual's assets must be either secured in an irrevocable trust or spent down. If this is your situation, see an attorney specializing in elder law. Irrevocable trusts are also used in tax planning.

The Wonderful Inter-vivos Trust

For probate avoidance, you want an *inter-vivos* trust. Many people call these *living* trusts, because unlike testamentary trusts, they take effect while the trustor is still living. But to avoid confusion with *living wills*, I will refer to them by their legal name — inter-vivos. A living will is something quite different. With a living will, you tell your relatives and doctors how you want to die — with tubes and heroic measures, or without (more about that when we talk about death and the use of medical directives in Chapter 7). An inter-vivos trust is a fiscal device; it has nothing at all to do with end-of-life medical decisions.

Revocable inter-vivos trusts are what most estate planners use for probate avoidance. In the trust instrument you will list which property you want included in the trust. You and your trustee will work with your bank, brokerage, and other institutions to convert your holdings from your name to that of your trustee. If you have real estate, you will sign a deed over to your trustee and make sure it is properly recorded.

Now here is the trick — *you* can be the trustor *and* the trustee! You can even be one of the beneficiaries — in fact, in a probate-avoidance trust you usually are. You cannot be the only one playing all three roles, however. There has to be a division of interest at some point for it to be a valid trust.

Eleanor had $100,000 in a brokerage account, $50,000 in a CD, $3,000 in her personal checking account, and a $155,000 house. She estimated probate fees of $14,620 and decided in favor of a trust. With the help of a reliable do-it-yourself guide, she wrote a simple trust, in which she (as trustor) appointed herself as trustee of the Eleanor Trust. She described each trust asset so it could be identified. She listed the brokerage account, the CD, and her home. She did not list her personal checking account, because it was small and fluid — and since she frequently changed banks, she didn't want to amend the trust instrument every time. The trust instrument she drafted instructed the trustee (herself) to administer the trust for the benefit of herself and her two sons as beneficiaries. Since Eleanor was not the sole beneficiary, she was able to fill all three roles. The terms of the trust were simple. During her lifetime, she, as trustee, would pay to herself, as beneficiary, income from the brokerage and the CD, and she would have the use of the house. On her death, the successor trustee (named in her trust instrument) would distribute the trust assets to her sons equally. The trust would then terminate.

Trusts avoid probate, because technically the owner of the property does not die. The owner is the trust, which continues undisturbed under the successor trustee whenever a trustee dies.

Eleanor found that setting up the trust was more involved than writing a will. She had to change the title of her holdings from her name alone to herself as trustee of the Eleanor Trust. Her brokerage account, for example, now reads Eleanor, Trustee of the Eleanor Trust (instead of simply Eleanor, as before). She signed a deed to her house — from Eleanor, to Eleanor, Trustee of the Eleanor Trust — and recorded it along with the trust instrument, as required in her county. Her bank changed her CD to herself as trustee. She found that these financial professionals were well prepared to make the changes — no hassles there. Still, there was some legwork involved, and if Eleanor had been unable to get around, someone would have had to work with the financial institutions to get the paperwork to her.

Furthermore, now Eleanor must remember to amend the trust instrument to include newly acquired property, and to delete closed accounts. She has to abide by the terms of her trust — pay interest to herself, for example, and cut into the principal only under the terms permitted.

Eleanor did not have to worry about locking herself into something she would later regret. If she should find that interest income is not enough, she retained the power to invade the principal for health, education, and support. She could amend the revocable trust at any time, or even revoke it altogether. Each time, however, she must amend the trust in writing and have the change notarized.

So there are some strictures around inter-vivos trusts that don't exist with a will. For this reason, some people prefer to put large, stable assets like real property into trusts, and leave small, changeable holdings to pass under the will (and probate). The trust property, at death, will pass relatively quickly and cheaply; the will or intestate property (the probate estate) will take longer and cost more. The pour-over will discussed below will leave everything not already in the trust to the trustee, who will then distribute it to the beneficiaries according to the terms of the trust.

Inter-vivos trusts are marvelously flexible. Most of the things you can do with a will can be done with a trust. You can instruct the trustee to purchase an annuity for an old family retainer, you can forgive debts, you can equalize lifetime gifts between your kids. You can also protect a spendthrift by continuing a trust for that individual for a period of time, or even for life. Gail thought her forty-five-year-old daughter was prudent and careful but had doubts about her thirty-seven-year-old son, who had a history of disastrous business ventures. She knew he didn't have any retirement savings, and she worried about his future. She instructed her trustee to divide the estate in half after her death, distribute one half outright to her daughter free of trust, and continue administering the other half for her son, paying him incremental amounts from the principal on his fortieth, forty-fifth, fiftieth, and fifty-fifth birthdays, then distributing the remainder to him free of trust at age sixty. She could have had the trustee pay him income every quarter, or monthly for his life, with the remainder going to his children. Gail can almost do anything she wants with a trust.

Writing inter-vivos trusts has become highly competitive, with lawyers advertising package deals in the newspapers, which may include a trust, medical directive, pour-over will, and other instruments for under $500. Because these instruments are readily produced on the attorney's word processor (by the secretary or paralegal, most likely), the law office makes money on volume, not price. If your wishes fit into the computer program, this will probably work fine. Some "free" seminars are offered by insurance salespeople, who will even offer a free trust if you buy their product. Caveat emptor! Even kits costing less than $10 are advertised for do-it-yourselfers. If you use one of these, please buy a half hour of a lawyer's time to go over it, to make sure it conforms to your state's law and your expectations. Finally, if you have a computer, there are reliable will and trust programs you can buy for under $100.

Another advantage of trusts is privacy. Because the trust is privately distributed by the trustee, it escapes the public eye. Many celebrities and the very rich pass their property on via trusts for reasons of privacy as much as for reasons of cost. The public does not know the value of the estate, for example, as it can with the public records of probate. Nor does it know the beneficiaries.

The Economics of Trusts and Wills

You will generally pay a lawyer less for a will than for a trust — not because a will takes less time or expertise to draft, but because the lawyer hopes that later he or she will take the estate through probate, which is where the real fees are. In other words, the will is sold by many attorneys as a loss leader — a Thanksgiving turkey, so to speak. With a trust, the attorney has to get his or her fees out early, because there will be no probate fees later on.

This means that you can pay a lawyer $500 to $2,000 for a trust now, or much less for a will. After death, your *estate* will pay the probate fees (will) or administration fees (trust). It costs more to draft the trust, less to administer it after death. But with a trust, *you* incur the higher costs, because they happen while you are living. It is your *heirs* who reap the savings of a trust as probate is avoided. You need to decide if the $1,000 cost of a trust is harder for you to pay now than it will be for your heirs to pay probate fees out of the estate after you're gone. In addition, if you choose not to be your own trustee, you may well incur annual trustee's fees during your lifetime.

To decide if a trust is worthwhile, you need to know what probate fees are in your state. In the last chapter, we demonstrated how some states set probate fees. Setup fees are not the only trust expenses. If you use a professional trustee (bank or lawyer), you may pay around 1 percent of the trust assets annually as a fee. If probate fees will be 3 percent each for the attorney and executor, you don't have to be a genius to see that after six years the trust is more expensive than probate. You may have to file separate income tax returns for the trust, and that may cost you, too.

Christy, a divorced woman living on $1,200 a month, owned her mortgaged home and $15,000 in savings. Her home's fair market value was $125,000, but her equity in it was only $25,000. After paying her monthly house payments, she had to live very frugally. Her children were urging her to write a trust rather than a will, in order to avoid probate and its fees. She inquired at her local senior citizens' law center and learned that in her community a simple will would cost about $100, and a trust would cost about $800. With a will, the probate fees would be $7,900, but the cost of distributing a trust would be about $1,000. Obviously, the trust is much cheaper in the long run, but in the short term it was too costly for Christy, strapped as she was, to purchase. She talked it over with her children, who agreed that since the savings were for them, they would pay the difference between the cost of a will and a trust.

I think it is perfectly fair for you to negotiate this with your heirs. If a will, costing you $200, will cost them

$10,000 in probate fees after your death, then they should be more than willing to pay the difference between the will and a $1,000 trust. Unless you're well fixed, why should *you* spend more tight dollars now to save *them* bucks later?

This negotiation is more relevant to women than to men, because most men will leave a widow; in many states, property passing between spouses does not go through probate. It is much more likely to be a woman's will that will trigger high probate costs as her property is distributed not to a spouse but to children, friends, and charity.

Another reason some people still prefer wills over trusts is convenience. A will, properly drawn, will dispose of all the property you own, including things you don't even own yet. A trust disposes of trust property only, so if you neglect to include some assets, they won't be distributed under the trust. Some people, especially those younger than sixty, feel the hassles of adhering to trust formalities for decades is more than they want to deal with, so they prefer to use a will until they're older.

Using a Pour-Over with Your Trust

As mentioned in Chapter 5, many estate planners like to prepare both a trust and a pour-over will. The trust lists the ultimate beneficiaries, and the will lists the trust as its sole beneficiary. This means that any property not within the trust is "scooped up" by the will and "pours over" into the trust on death. Then it is distributed to the beneficiaries named in the trust. A simple pour-over will might read as follows:

I, Frances Leonard, declare this to be my will in the manner following: I designate Joan Rowe to be my executor, and I bequeath all of my property, of whatever kind or character, and wherever situated, to the trustee of the Frances Leonard Trust, under the declaration of trust dated March 1, 1993.

Do not use this language as a model. It is generic and may not work in your state. Like any other will, the pour-over must conform to formalities, for either holographs or witnessed formal wills.

Of course, the poured-over property goes through probate first since it passed under a will, so you wouldn't want major assets to pass under a pour-over if you're trying to avoid probate fees. One disadvantage of a pour-over is that it delays the closing of the trust. The trustee has to wait until the poured-over property is probated before he or she can finally distribute and close the trust. For this reason, some estate planners prefer not to use a pour-over, instead writing a will that simply names a beneficiary to receive "all the rest and residue" of the estate. This residuary beneficiary then receives all the property that for whatever reason wasn't included in the trust. This can be the same beneficiary as under the trust, of course.

There are other cautions in using both a will and a trust — obviously, giving the same property away in the will and trust to different people invites a lawsuit. Just keep this in mind: there is trust property, and there is property free of trust. One instrument concerns itself with one type of property, the other takes care of the other. Don't confuse them. Having different executors and trustees working to distribute your estate could also cause delay and confusion. Have the same person act as executor and trustee.

Sally owned her $150,000 house free and clear, and $50,000 in certificates of deposit. She placed her house in a trust, and every time she took out a new CD, she titled it to the trust as well. But her car, household items, art, and jewelry were not placed in the trust, because she changed them often enough that she didn't want to bother with the formalities. When Sally died, her home and CDs went straight to her heirs via the trust, with minimal cost and fuss. Her personal effects were probated, but their net value was less than $20,000, so probate fees were in the $1,000 range (this differs widely by state). In this way, Sally kept her large, relatively stable assets free of probate, and accepted relatively minor probate fees for her low-worth fluid assets in exchange for the convenience of not maintaining them as trust property.

> **Certain kinds of income tax–planning trusts popular a few years ago no longer hold water with the IRS. This is particularly true of those involving children. If you have one, be sure to check it out. You don't want nasty surprises.**

Some Caveats for Women

Trusts, for all their usefulness, have a downside, especially for women. Traditionally, the lawyer would sit down with the husband, and draw up a trust (or trusts) that would leave the husband's estate in trust to his wife. The attorney might act as trustee, or perhaps name the local bank, and the wife/beneficiary would be at their mercy for the years of her widowhood. Because, in common-law states anyway, it was likely that virtually all the marital assets belonged legally to the husband, all the assets were now out of her reach. When the terms of the trust limited her to the income from the assets (as is typical), widows commonly found a stranger-trustee standing between her and her life's dream of a cruise through the Greek islands. At her death, the trustee would distribute the funds to the children (or charities). She would have nothing to pass along to her own favorite charities or heirs, because technically she never inherited anything from her husband. The *trustee* did. In a community property state, she at least will still have her half of the marital assets free of trust.

> **If you have a trust standing between you and what you think of as your marital property, see a probate or elder law attorney. You may be able to force some of the assets out of the trust under your state's forced-share statute. The sooner you do this after your husband's death, the better your chances.**

Most trusts that leave only income to the widow also provide that for certain emergencies (usually health, education, maintenance, and support) the trustee has the power to invade the principal for the widow/beneficiary. However, it is demeaning and frustrating for the widow to have to plead her case before a banker or lawyer before money is freed up for her needs. And in too many cases, the trustee will see his or her duty as preserving principal for the *remainder* beneficiaries (usually the children or a charity). As the *income* beneficiary, the widow's interests necessarily conflict with those of the remainder beneficiaries — the more conservative the trust investments, for example, the more will be there for the remainders; but the income beneficiary will pay for it with low interest.

As a beneficiary of your husband's trust, you may not have the power to amend or revoke the trust, or change the trustee. If you're dissatisfied with the arrangement, you must find ways to defeat the trust, or at least some part of it. For that you need a lawyer.

> **Examine your husband's estate plan while he's still living. Scrutinize any trust, and be very sure you understand your powers and entitlements under it. You may prefer that his trust distribute the assets to you free of trust. Later, you can draft an inter-vivos trust for probate-avoidance purposes according to your own design. This is important for both spouses, but usually it is the wife who ends up surviving the marriage only to come under the thumb of a stranger-trustee.**

Some Limits of Trusts

Because of legal technicalities, some things you must do with a will because they won't work with a trust. Usually the only way you can disinherit your own or adopted child (even if adult) is through a will. If you leave a child out of your trust, but forget to also do so expressly by will, in many cases the child can successfully claim he or she was "forgotten" and receive a share as if there had been no will or trust at all.

Charitable Remainder Trusts

A charitable remainder trust is an agreement between a donor and a charity that allows the donor to contribute assets to the charity in trust. It works like this: Analiese, realizing her home was too large for her, but reluctant to pay the large capital gains tax that would result if she sold it and rented an apartment, arranged a *charitable remainder annuity trust* with her local nonprofit hospital. She formed a trust, with herself as the income beneficiary and the hospital as the remainder beneficiary. The trustee sold the home and invested the proceeds. A fixed income from the investments was paid to Analiese annually, and after her death the principal went to the hospital. Analiese paid thousands less in income tax at the time of her gift, instead of incurring substantial capital gains tax on a sale. Under the terms of the trust, her income payment was guaranteed to be a certain amount — if the trust income failed to cover it, the principal could be invaded to make up the shortfall. Larger charities will be happy to set one up for you at no cost. Just call the development office. For a smaller charity, you will probably need the assistance of a lawyer. Maybe the charity could share the cost.

> **Charitable remainder trusts are great devices, but women should keep in mind the effects of inflation on their income over the years, as well as their possible need for long-term care costing well over $100,000. These trusts are *irrevocable* — you will not be able to amend or revoke one. Don't remove your assets from your control unless you are *very* sure you won't need them for yourself. Saving taxes isn't worth it.**

OTHER WILL SUBSTITUTES

A will substitute is simply a way to pass property on your death directly to an individual or charity without going through probate or even the modest distribution hassles of a trust.

One time-honored use of will substitutes is to make a secret gift. Lovers, children born out of wedlock, a special companion — these are traditional recipients of remembrances that could not be made public (in the way of wills) or open to the other beneficiaries (in the way of trusts). Although all of these devices are included in the *taxable* estate, none is included in the probate or trust estate, and therefore, properly handled, can remain very private.

None of these devices is a stranger to you. None is esoteric or difficult to set up. In fact, one of their chief problems, as we shall see, is the very ease with which they can be obtained, as well as their misleading familiarity, which can sometimes lead to rude surprises. We're grown-ups now — we don't need surprises. Let's head them off.

A Woman's Perspective on Life Insurance

Life insurance is an old friend, of course — sometimes a friend who promises much and delivers little; sometimes even a friend with two faces. But we're well acquainted, just the same. We discussed the role of insurance as part of your portfolio in Chapter 1. Here we'll limit our discussion to its use as a will substitute.

Life insurance, of course, goes directly to your named beneficiary, rather than through probate to the beneficiaries named in your will.

You can name your estate, rather than an individual, as the beneficiary of your life insurance. This way, the proceeds will be divided among your heirs as your

will designates. *But see your tax adviser* **before you do that — there could be unfavorable estate tax consequences if the insurance benefit pushes your estate past $600,000 (still the federal exempt amount in late 1993, but always check for changes).**

Perhaps more than any other estate planning device, life insurance plays very different roles for women and men. If your husband is living, and he has life insurance, you are probably the named beneficiary. This is logical, since most likely he will die first, and you will have years left to fight inflation.

However, insurance on the life of a married woman past middle age has to be closely considered. Unless you have reason to believe your life will be shorter than your husband's, paying large premiums for his unlikely benefit may not be the best use of your money.

Generally speaking, if you're a mid-life or older woman, good reasons to insure your own life would include the following:

- providing for a dependent, incapacitated relative
- expanding a modest estate for the needs of grown children
- making a generous charitable gift on death

In the first case, be careful to understand the effects of your gift on the dependent's income if it is based on need. Social Security disability income would not be affected, but SSI disability probably would be. Your premiums would be better invested elsewhere if your benefit is going to render the individual ineligible for income support until your gift is spent down to the eligibility level.

The second idea is a good one if your grown children have a substantial need they will find difficult to provide for themselves, such as college tuition for their children, or a down payment on a house. You must, of course, decide for yourself if you can comfortably afford the premiums. You have no duty to provide an inheritance, and too many women deny themselves severely in the latter part of their lives trying to provide one to adult children who will use it for luxuries. Nevertheless, if your cash position is comfortable but your asset level is low, a term life insurance policy is one way to swell your estate.

Finally, if you yearn to give an important gift to the small museum at which you're a volunteer docent, but know that your small estate can support a gift of only $500 or so, consider joining an organization that makes group life insurance available to its members. You might be surprised how little the premiums would be on a $5,000 policy — a nice gift for a small nonprofit organization. Even a substantial death benefit can be surprisingly affordable. In 1993, for example, a sixty-five-year-old woman could buy a $100,000 death benefit for a one-time premium of less than $35,000 — or periodic premiums of much less. Of course, you don't have to join a group to get life insurance; the yellow pages are full of agents just waiting for your call. Group policies are cheaper, though. In any case, shop around. Premiums vary widely.

Anne found an interesting way to use life insurance to make a substantial charitable gift, while keeping the value of her estate intact for her two children. She and her tax planner realized that her stock portfolio had appreciated in value wildly over the fifteen years since her husband died, for a capital gain of $50,000. If she donated it to a charity, she would be able to deduct the current market value of the gift from her current income, thus saving thousands on her income tax bill, and avoiding a future capital gains tax as well. But Anne was reluctant to diminish her future estate by so much, since her children were not well off. Anne and her adviser figured out a way to make the gift and leave her estate intact as well. Anne made the gift and used the tax savings to pay the premium on a term life insurance policy with a death benefit equaling the value of her stock holdings — including estimated earnings and appreciation over her lifetime — and accomplished everything she wanted. She made an important charitable gift, thus taking a large charitable deduction on her current income taxes, and at the same time did not diminish her estate due to the eventual death benefit. Magic! All courtesy of Uncle Sam. As a bonus, her estate was reduced for estate tax purposes, because the portfolio no longer was in her estate on death, and the insurance death benefit, of course, went directly to her children. Estate planners call this the *capital replacement technique*. Of course, you'll need to see your tax adviser before trying something like this.

If you decide your estate plan includes life insurance, be very sure you buy *term* insurance, not whole or universal life. Remember, term insurance is pure insurance — it has no investment value, no cash value, no loan value. You pay only for what insurance does best — pay on death. The other varieties pay nice commissions (many times that of term insurance) so are pushed by agents, but they are not efficient ways to build savings. Other investment vehicles do this better. Do not be misled by charts and statistics. They are easily manipulated. Refer to Chapter 1 for more on term versus whole life insurance.

Your IRA and other retirement income accounts also give you an opportunity to name a beneficiary in the event of your death. Again, check with your tax adviser before naming your estate, rather than an individual, as beneficiary.

Annuities

Annuities, covered in Chapters 1 and 2 as investments, also work as will substitutes. We discussed the use of annuities as a bequest in your will (or trust), which will give the beneficiary a stream of income rather than a lump sum. But you can also purchase an annuity with no reference to your will or trust at all. Perhaps you'd like to make a private gift to a longtime companion and would prefer that it not show up in your will or trust. An annuity can do this. It can begin the payout immediately, or on your death, or on a stated event, such as the individual's sixty-fifth birthday.

**Don't forget the gender bias in many annuities. If your
intended beneficiary is a man, shop around for an annuity using gender-biased tables. If your intended beneficiary is a woman, look for a unisex policy.**

Pay-on-Death Accounts

Perhaps you'd like to set up a college savings account for
your grandchild. Maybe you'd prefer to leave control and ownership of the account in your hands, but payable on death to
the child's guardian. Many grandparents like to set things up
this way, because they want to leave the option open to use the
funds themselves for an emergency, or revoke the account entirely if the grandchild seems not to be college-bound. This type
of account, called a "Totten trust," or pay-on-death account,
will not be part of your probate estate, thus it will not enter
into the calculation for probate fees (death taxes, yes, if any).

Like other will substitutes, a pay-on-death account is also
a good way to leave a confidential gift. Perhaps you would like
to give money to a special friend or charity you'd just as soon
keep secret. Set up a pay-on-death account at your bank and
give the passbook to your friend. Usually you can add and
withdraw from the account during your lifetime, and you retain the right to close it.

In the past, pay-on-death accounts were simple passbook
savings accounts at your bank. Today, most investment companies, including the large families of mutual funds, will happily
set up your account this way. You can shelter large pieces of
your estate from probate through this kind of planning. Don't
forget, though, as illustrated below, that this and other will substitutes can wreak havoc on the scheme in your will.

With pay-on-death accounts, your beneficiary has no ownership interest in the account whatsoever until your death. Generally, you can do anything you want with it while you're alive.
The beneficiary need not even know of its existence, and because he or she has no ownership in it, no creditor of the

beneficiary can invade the account if the beneficiary falls on hard times. This is the critical difference between this device and joint ownership vehicles such as joint tenancies and tenancies-in-common.

Let's see why this matters.

The Good and Bad About Joint Tenancies

Cosigning on accounts and joint accounts is common to us women. We sign on to our parents' accounts to help out; we hold joint accounts with grandchildren, we cosign and own jointly with our husbands. But most of us have no idea what happens to the account after we die. We assume, of course, that our share quickly and easily becomes part of our estate, to be distributed to our heirs.

Co-ownership takes many forms and can have drastic consequences. The law in this area, and the terminology, date back to feudal England, so don't be misled by terms like *tenancies*. A *tenancy*, as used here, is an interest in property — it does not have to be real estate.

Joan added her daughter's name to her large bank account so that if something happened to Joan, her daughter would have immediate access to the funds. She trusted her daughter implicitly not to withdraw from the account, and she didn't. But one day, when distracted by the kids fighting in the backseat, the daughter ran a red light, killing a pedestrian. Wrongful death damages exceeded her insurance and modest assets, so the plaintiff went after Joan's bank account, on the theory that her daughter owned half of it as a tenant-in-common. Joan found herself involved in a lawsuit and paid plenty to her lawyer before she proved the funds were hers alone.

Cecilia and her two sisters inherited the family mountain cabin from their parents. They were careful to take title as joint tenants, because they understood that if one of them died, the two remaining would automatically assume ownership over the decedent's portion. Cecilia's business failed, however, and she went bankrupt. Her sisters were shocked to find themselves with a stranger co-owner when Cecilia's share was sold by the bankruptcy receiver to raise funds for the creditors.

Joint tenancies with rights of survivorship (JTWROS) and tenancies-in-common (TIC) are the principal methods of co-ownership of property in this country. For spouses, community property and, in most common-law states, tenancies-by-the-entirety are common in addition. Each has very different characterics, and the full ramifications fill volumes of lawbooks.

For this discussion on will substitutes, only joint tenancies really count. But you should know the difference between them on a death, so briefly, here it is:

- Joint tenants have the right of survivorship.
- Tenants in common do not.

Let's say Zak, Ivan, and Jacob each put $300 into a joint savings account as tenants-in-common. Ivan dies. Zak and Jacob each continues to own his $300 share, and Ivan's heirs get his $300.

If the account had been a joint tenancy, Zak and Jacob would each own 50 percent of the $900 account. Ivan's heirs would get no part of it.

Joint tenancies with rights of survivorship mean just that. If two or more people own property as joint tenants, the last one surviving will own the whole property, regardless of any provision in a will or trust to the contrary.

When you cosign on a bank account, the bank will usually consider it either a TIC or a JTWROS. If the account was a TIC, and you and your sister understood that 75 percent of the assets were yours and 25 percent hers — but there is no written record of your understanding — the bank will probably assume that half is available to her executor for distribution to her heirs. You could end up in a fight with your nieces and nephews over funds you and your sister understood perfectly.

So even though TICs are not will substitutes — because they pass under the will, not outside it — it is important that you understand the distinction between TICs and the true will substitute, joint tenancies, when making your own estate plans.

Not only do JTWROS, trust property, and the like avoid probate, but they cannot be willed even if you intend that they be. Your will, leaving everything to your best friend, means nothing if all your property is in joint tenancy with your son.

Joint tenancies are a serious estate planning tool. With them, you can pass property directly to the surviving tenant without probate and its fees. They are a snap to set up — just check off the box when you open your bank or investment account. But unlike a pay-on-death account, the joint tenant is presumed to have equal ownership with the other tenants and will have to sign papers when the account is opened. There can be problems if one tenant wants to sell out or is forced to by creditors. Unlike a pay-on-death, you will not have the right to unilaterally close out the account or use it for your own benefit, even if you contributed all the funds.

There are also *serious* income tax consequences to joint tenancies that you *must* understand before you use this form of ownership. We discuss them in the section below on death taxes.

The nasty surprise lurking behind joint ownerships is the mess they can make of a carefully thought out estate plan. We women, especially, with our readiness to ''share'' accounts as we get older, need to be very sure we know what we're doing when we set one up.

A bitter fight arose when Robin died. She and her sister and brother had lived together all their lives, never marrying. In their wills, each left his or her entire estate to the remaining siblings in equal shares. But, unfortunately, Robin's sister and brother did not share equally in her $200,000 estate as she had planned. Robin had $10,000 in stocks in her own name; she named her sister as joint tenant on a $100,000 CD; and she named her brother as beneficiary of a $10,000 pay-on-death account — and the remaining $80,000 was her equity in their home, held in joint tenancy. Although Robin didn't intend this, the only property affected by the will was the $10,000 in stocks. Each sibling got $5,000 from that bequest. Her sister, in addition, received the entire CD and half the surviving interest in the home, for a total value of $145,000. The brother got the $5,000 bequest, the $10,000 pay-on-death account, and his half of the joint-tenancy interest in the home, for a total of $55,000. He insisted bitterly that his sister should do the decent thing and give him enough out of her funds to even things up — after all, Robin's intent was for them to benefit equally, wasn't it? Robin's sister felt that Robin had known what she was doing, and refused to give up her share, so her brother moved out, forced the sale of their home, and they no longer speak. Another family sundered through inept estate planning. Every probate attorney has many such tales. A will leaving 100 percent of the estate to one heir will be ruined if the testator also owned property in forms that can't be willed, such as pay-on-death accounts and joint tenancies. This is sad, because it is so easily avoided.

Be very careful. Don't let this happen to you. Know the death consequences for every piece of property you own, or ask your probate attorney to explain it to you. You work hard to create harmony in your family, and you certainly don't want your death to create the spectacle of a family fight.

Planning Around Death Taxes

Many people assume that substituting a trust or joint tenancy for a will avoids death taxes as well as probate. Not so. Uncle Sam is not so dumb. Will substitutes, including pay-on-death accounts, trusts, and joint tenancy accounts, are calculated as part of the *taxable* estate, although not part of the *probate* estate. The probate estate, the trust estate, and the taxable estate are not the same thing, and a decedent's estate may consist of all three.

There are two kinds of death taxes — *estate* taxes and *inheritance* taxes. Estate taxes consider the size of the estate as a whole and tax it accordingly. The federal government has an estate tax, which currently (as of late 1993) excludes all estates smaller than $600,000. On those over $600,000, the tax is quite hefty — from 37 to 55 percent! If you think you have a taxable estate, see a CPA or tax lawyer. Don't rely on do-it-yourself guides, including this book, because planning can be quite complex and very individual.

Inheritance taxes tax the heir, not the estate. Each individual inheritance is taxed separately. Often, different types of heirs are taxed differently; for example, widow(er)s, orphans, and charities may receive a favorable rate, or even not be taxed at all. Some states have inheritance taxes, some have estate taxes, and some have no death tax. There is no federal inheritance tax. Depending on where you live, the size of your estate, and the nature of your heirs, you may well have two death taxes to plan around.

One popular way to reduce your taxable estate is through gifts during your lifetime. Of course, there are federal and state gift taxes depending on the size of the gift. The gift tax is on the donor, not the recipient, who receives the gift tax-free.

> **Under current federal law, gifts under $10,000 *per recipient, per year* are exempt from the gift tax. Since gifts are not taxable to the recipient, these gifts are among the rarest of the rare: a tax-free transfer of assets!**

Lillian and Richie's tax planner advised them to reduce their estate by $80,000. They decided on Christmas gifts of $20,000 each to their son and daughter-in-law. Because Lillian and Richie lived in a community property state, each had equal ownership of their marital assets, so each spouse was entitled to give $10,000 to each recipient. In this way, $40,000 was passed to their only heir and his wife free of tax on Christmas, and an equal gift was made on New Year's Day. Because the two gifts occurred in different tax years, the full $80,000 was legally moved out of the taxable estate in one week's time.

Certain trusts can also shelter you from some, if not all, death taxes. Jargon abounds, such as A-B trusts, Q-Tip trusts, credit shelter, and charitable remainder trusts. But women, because they are the likely survivors of the marriage, should scrutinize these tax-planning trusts before they agree to one. Some things are worse than paying taxes. Be sure you know the following:

- what you will own *free of trust* after your husband dies
- how much principal and interest you will regularly receive
- what the trustee can do for you in an emergency
- under what conditions you can invade the principal
- what the trust does for you versus the children
- that you personally know and like and trust the trustee

Balance your desire to reduce estate taxes against your need to protect yourself against catastrophic long-term-care costs later in life. For women, this is especially important, because of our longevity and because we can't plan on having husbands around to provide home care. Nursing homes can cost $30,000 to $50,000 per year, and around-the-clock home care can easily reach $100,000.

Nevertheless, for married couples with assets over $600,000, a consultation with an estate tax planner is a must, if only to work out the figures. Sally and Bruce had $1,400,000. When Sally died, all the property passed to Bruce free of federal estate taxes, because property passing between husband and wife is free of that tax no matter how large the estate. However, when Bruce died in 1992, only $600,000 passed free of tax. His children paid estate taxes on $800,000, amounting to more than $300,000!

Kathleen and Dick, with a trust arrangement that cost them $2,000 to set up, saved their children well over $200,000. Here's how: Kathleen and Dick set up a revocable, inter-vivos trust, called the Kathleen and Dick Marital Trust. During their joint lifetime, it paid them income — and they retained the right to invade the principal if necessary. When Dick died, the trust split into two: The first, designated the A trust, remained

revocable by Kathleen and paid her income for life, with inva-
sion of the principal permitted under the usual terms, then the
remainder to their children on her death. With the exception
of the amount designated to the second trust, the A trust received all the assets from the marital trust. The second trust,
the B trust, received $600,000 — interest to Kathleen for life,
invadable principal for the usual needs, remainder to their children on her death. The B trust was irrevocable. When Kathleen
died, the $600,000 in the B passed directly to her children tax-
free, as well as $600,000 from the A trust. In this way, Kathleen
and Dick passed $1,200,000 to their children tax-free. The chil-
dren paid tax on $200,000 of the $1,400,000 estate, or less
than $100,000. This tax magic is accomplished because techni-
cally, the B trust was never part of Kathleen's estate. Any probate
or elder law attorney can set up A-B trusts if you're interested.
In late 1993, a $1,200,000 estate would save a minimum of
$235,000 in estate taxes with an A-B (sometimes called a bypass,
credit, or marital deduction trust) arrangement.

If you're not married, the A-B hustle isn't available to you,
but you do have some options. One popular plan is to leave
your favorite charity the amount exceeding the exclusion. For
example, if your estate will be $700,000, you can leave
$600,000 to your daughter free of federal estate tax, and the
remaining $100,000 to your alumnae fund. Of course, your
exposure to your state's death tax may differ. Again, see a tax
planner, because gift, inheritance, and estate taxes are in con-
stant flux.

A Special Break on Capital Gains

In addition to estate and inheritance taxes, *income taxes*
play a special role at death. The slightest wrong move can cost
you tens of thousands or more. Take Brenda and Carleen, for
example, both widows. Each had lived in her home for thirty
years and owned it free and clear. Two years before death, each
moved into a retirement home for companionship and care.

At this point, each home was worth $250,000 more than the purchase price. Brenda sold her home when she moved; Carleen rented hers out. Because Brenda was not buying a new home, she owed income tax on the capital gain — less the "over-55" exemption. Carleen didn't buy a new home either, but when she died hers passed through her estate to her daughter, who sold it immediately. No income tax on the capital gain was due, because of a special favor granted by Congress only to heirs, called the *stepped-up* basis. For Carleen's and Brenda's heirs, the difference between carryover and stepped-up basis meant tens of thousands of dollars.

> **Brenda could have avoided the capital gains tax by *buying* into a retirement home rather than becoming a renter. Many seniors' residences are condos or co-ops, permitting the capital gains to be rolled over and deferred just as in the purchase of a new residence. Then, on death, the basis steps up to fair market value, thus eliminating the gain.**

Here is how this special tax advantage works: When an asset (such as stock or real estate) appreciates in value, the amount of the appreciation is taxed as a capital gain. The *basis* — that is, the value of the asset after you subtract the appreciation — is not taxed. You might think of bread as an appreciating asset, for example. You knead the dough, which then rises on its own — no additional input from you. The IRS might say the dough "appreciated" and tax everything except the original mound, which is the "basis." This "appreciation" in the bread is not the same as the increase in the stew you cooked. When you kept adding (depositing) carrots and potatoes, you got more stew, but only because of your additions. Your stew is more like a bank account, where only the interest is taxable. Bank accounts don't grow except through interest or your deposits. In other words, no capital gain.

Tax on capital gains works like this: Let's say you buy an original Ansel Adams print for $500 and sell it ten years later for $5,000. Your capital gain is $4,500, and you owe income tax on that amount. If you *give* the Adams to your best friend and she sells it for $5,000, she also owes tax on the $4,500 gain — the $500 basis is carried over from you to her. Tax people call this *carryover* basis. But if you *will* your friend the Adams (or leave it in a trust), the basis *steps up* to the print's fair market value on the day of your death. If your friend sells it before it appreciates further, she owes no tax. If she waits a bit and sells it when it is worth $5,500, she owes tax on the $500 appreciation from your date of death. A gift of the Adams one day before your death will cost your friend hundreds of income tax dollars — dollars saved if you leave it to her in your will or trust instead. Because the Adams is worth less than $10,000, your gift will pass free of *gift tax*, but your friend will still owe income tax on the capital gain. Remember, carryover and stepped-up basis applies only to appreciable assets such as art, antiques, jewelry, stocks, or real estate.

It is here in the never-never land of taxes that estate planning really gets complicated. Wills and trusts pass property with a stepped-up basis. What about the other will substitutes? As stated, life insurance benefits are not taxed at all, unless you name your estate (rather than an individual) as the recipient of the benefits. Then the insurance becomes part of the estate when its worth is calculated for the purpose of estate taxes.

Joint tenancies, on the other hand, have created major tax problems for the unwary. The IRS figures that the decedent's basis steps up, but the survivor's share does not. If you placed the Adams print in joint tenancy with your sister, for example, and she sold it after your death for $5,000, her half of the $4,500 gain would be taxable and your half would step up to fair market value on the date of your death. If, instead of a JTWROS, you bequeathed her the print, it would all step up and income tax would be due only on any appreciation over $5,000.

For husbands and wives in community property states, it is especially important to hold real estate and other appreciable assets as "community property" rather than as joint tenants. Community property assets step up in their entirety, while joint tenancies, even between husband and wife, step up only by half. This is a *major* tax advantage for community property spouses over spouses living under the common law.

> **Even in community property states, real estate deeds and brokerage accounts owned jointly by spouses are frequently titled in joint tenancy, due to the ignorance of brokers. If you live in a community property state, check the way your appreciable property, such as stocks and realty, is titled. If they are carried in joint tenancy, they can easily be changed to community property, possibly saving tens of thousands of tax dollars. The brokerage house can send you a form to change the title; for realty, a new deed must be recorded — an easy, and presumably low-cost, job for a lawyer, or perhaps even cheaper through a title company.**

Give your final plans a lot of thought. This is an opportunity to benefit those you love and assist them in carrying out their life dreams.

Review your will or trust on every birthday — or sooner if

- your spouse dies
- your spouse becomes incapacitated
- you divorce
- you remarry
- a beneficiary dies
- a beneficiary divorces or remarries
- a child is born or adopted
- your executor dies, moves, or becomes incapacitated
- you move out of state
- your assets or net worth changes significantly
- you get rid of assets you've specifically bequeathed

The power to bequeath is a great right. Women, more than men, have the opportunity to be creative, because most won't be leaving their worldly goods to spouses. It was less than 150 years ago that American women were given the right to own and will property. Cherish your right, and use it wisely.

IS YOUR ESTATE PLAN IN GOOD SHAPE?

1. Do you have a will?
2. If so, have you considered replacing it with a trust? Why?
3. Could your gross estate possibly exceed $600,000?
4. Does your state have a death tax? Will it apply to you?
5. Do you know how to amend your trust?
6. If you have a trust, do you also have a pour-over will?
7. What is the difference between a living will and a living trust?
8. If you don't have a trust, how much will your probate fees be?
9. If you do have a trust, how much are its future fees?
10. Do you have any tenancy-in-common accounts?
11. Do you have any joint tenancies?
12. Do you have any pay-on-death accounts?
13. If yes, do you understand how they'll pass on your death?
14. How much life insurance is on your husband's life?
15. How much life insurance is on your life? Why?
16. Do you understand the benefits of term life over whole life?
17. Do you understand the tax consequences of joint tenancies?
18. Will your estate benefit from the stepped-up basis tax rule?

7
Managing the Medical Money Monster

It was supposed to be so simple. Working people would be covered by group health insurance, poor people would be covered under Medicaid, and people over sixty-five would be covered under Medicare. But somehow it all went wrong, and now we have thirty-seven million uninsured, the poor can't find doctors, and Medicare pays well under half the medical costs of the people it is meant to serve.

And believe it or not, this big mess is mostly a women's problem. Women are the primary consumers of health care, and we dominate the uninsured because our jobs are much less likely to carry fringe benefits. Our extra years put us at greater risk for chronic conditions requiring long-term care. Medical treatment is consistently shown to be biased against women; and to medical research, women may as well not exist.

But things are changing. The president's health reform task force was headed by no less of a woman than his wife, Hillary Rodham Clinton. And women's groups are scrutinizing every word of every reform plan.

At this writing, all is still rhetoric. If any reforms were enacted, beware! Much of this chapter could be obsolete.

Money, of course, goes hand in hand with medical care, whether it be health insurance premiums, copayments, and deductibles; gaps in Medicare; financing long-term care; or the dreaded medical catastrophe. In 1991, the average person over sixty-five paid $3,305 out of pocket for medical care; invested at 5 percent, more than $80,000 dollars (taxable, state and federal, at 20 percent) would be needed to generate that amount. An $80,000 fund, dedicated solely to the costs remaining *after* Medicare and medigap pay their share — this is serious money. Fortunately, some strategies exist. We'll approach them with our gender in mind.

You can rein in the medical money monster with these:

- a sound medigap (if over 65) or health policy
- a sound, comprehensive long-term-care policy
- a good elder law attorney
- a living will or medical durable power of attorney

We'll begin with ordinary health insurance for people under sixty-five, then look into Medicare and medigap policies, and finally examine how to finance long-term care. Along the way we'll talk about avoiding the impoverishment of older wives, medical directives (living wills), and the right to die.

HEALTH INSURANCE

The modern American health care "system" began with a leap of faith. The idea was that businesses voluntarily would insure their workers in return for substantial tax advantages. Those outside the labor market, such as the poor and the retired, would be taken care of by Medicaid and Medicare. Free enterprise would ensure that businesses provided health insurance, because good employees would go elsewhere if they didn't. Likewise, free enterprise would guarantee that low-cost insurance would abound, as insurers competed for this lucrative market.

But no one counted on the effects of this giant infusion of funds into the medical establishment. Doctors, hospitals, and drug manufacturers responded to this largess by raising rates sky high. Their insured patients were now in a position to pay more, so the providers charged more — so much more, in fact, that by the mid-1980s, employers and insurers said "enough." Insurers raised their rates to match their costs; employers responded by cutting back on insurance. The American health crisis was born.

A Strong Gender Bias

Up to about age fifty (read menopause), insurers would rather insure a man than a woman. And wherever it is legal, they signal their preference with much higher premiums for women than for men of the same age. Insurers justify this by pointing to reproductive costs — birth control, prenatal, child-birth. These costs are loaded onto the female side of the ledger, as if these are unmentionable womanly realities that have nothing whatsoever to do with men. They dare not use race-biased tables (although equally predictive of health care consumption), but burdening women with the full cost of reproducing both genders of the species is thought to be both logical and proper.

At about age fifty, most health insurance premiums are about the same for women and men, after which men's premiums rise above women's — *but only for fifteen years*. At sixty-five, premiums become unisex due to the advent of Medicare. Because Medicare pays a little more than 40 percent of its beneficiaries' costs, insurers sell Medicare supplement policies (commonly referred to as "medigap" policies, because they purport to plug the gaps in Medicare). Medigap policies generally use unisex rates, another gender bias disfavoring women, since sex-based tables at that age would favor women. Health insurance pricing, therefore, disfavors women for all but about fifteen years. We'll talk more about medigap policies when we discuss Medicare later.

Don't confuse disability protection with health insurance. Disability pays you cash to live on when you become too disabled to work. Health insurance pays your doctor or hospital.

If you have insurance through your job, you cannot be charged more than your male colleague — that would be illegal sex discrimination. If your employer (with at least twenty employees) offers group health coverage, it must be equally available to workers over age sixty-five. Older spouses must be offered the same coverage as younger spouses. Past sixty-five, Medicare will back up your employment group — it will not be the primary payer.

If you lose your group coverage — watch out! You'll learn that if you're a woman over thirty-five, you are very likely uninsurable in whole or in part. Either no insurer will touch you, or the policy will exclude every medical condition you've ever had.

An otherwise reasonable policy that carries exclusions may not be such a bad deal. Many exclusions, under law or the insurance contract, terminate after a period of time — perhaps six months to two years. This means that if you had a cervical condition treated two years ago, after the policy has been in force one year, the exclusion may be lifted. In the meantime, your heart attack and breast cancer are covered.

If the agent offers you a policy, ask to see the rate charts for men of your age as well. If you're desperate, you might want to secure the first policy that will take you — but sign on for only a couple of months. During this time, shop around for a policy with premiums that favor women (if possible) or at least don't favor men.

You won't be shocked to hear that some agents are willing to deceive you. They'll sell you a policy with a nice low premium — but in a couple of months the premium soars out of sight. Always be sure to learn

how often and by how much the premiums can increase. You also want to know the company's cancellation policy, because in two years, when you're older and sicker, you don't want to be out on your ear.

Although you, as part of an employment group policy, may not be singled out for higher premiums because of your chronic condition, your employer might be singled out because of you. Small employers face stringent review by insurers. They may be refused insurance if, among their nine employees, one has a son with leukemia. Or their coverage might be canceled after five exemplary years, when one of their seven employees becomes diabetic.

Although your life savings may not be at stake when your health insurer goes under, countless people have been left holding the bag for thousands in unpaid medical bills when their insurers defaulted. All states have guarantee funds for up to $100,000 in medical costs — however, your carrier has to have been licensed in your state. You should also check at least two ratings: from A.M. Best, Moody's, Standard & Poor's, or Duff and Phelps. Ask your reference librarian, or call the companies at their numbers listed in Chapter 1. You can always try suing your insurance broker for negligently selling you a policy from a company on the ropes or one that is not licensed in your state.

When You Lose Your Coverage

As a small part of the massive Consolidated Omnibus Budget Reconciliation Act of 1986 (COBRA), Congress ensured that most people losing their eligibility for their employer-sponsored health plan would have a several-month grace period in which to find new insurance. Under COBRA, if you lose or quit your job for almost any reason except gross misconduct, you can continue in the group, paying up to 102 percent of your own share of the premiums, for up to eighteen months. You have eighteen-month COBRA rights if you lose eligibility because you were fired, reduced your hours, quit, went on strike, were locked out, or retired. If your family was covered with you, they will have the same eighteen-month entitlement you do.

"Gross misconduct" is undefined in COBRA, but most experts feel courts will require something very akin to criminal behavior before you lose your COBRA rights. Misconduct such as habitual lateness, or an unpleasant attitude, should not be enough. If you've been denied COBRA, you can sue. See an attorney familiar with employee benefits litigation.

Here is a nice gender bias in favor of women: If you're in the group as a dependent of the worker — wife, husband, child — and your dependency status ends (widowhood, divorce, a child marries or becomes too old), your COBRA rights extend thirty-six months. Because men are more likely to be the workers (eighteen months), and women are more likely to be "dependents" (thirty-six months), this quirk in the law definitely favors women. There's a reason for this. The Older Women's League (OWL), a national organization that focuses on the rights of mid-life and older women, lobbied hard for the dependent's bill, which was then merged with the weaker workers' bill, and both were subsumed under COBRA. (Here I will modestly assert that I drafted the original dependent's bill for state enactment on which the federal COBRA was eventually modeled.) Former dependents thus have stronger COBRA rights than the workers themselves — an anomaly for which you can thank the hard and clever lobbying of OWL's Washington staff. One million people per year now exercise their COBRA rights, a feather in the cap for OWL and its allies in the aging and women's movements.

COBRA, of course, does not solve the basic problem. It merely delays the crunch. The COBRA grace period was designed to give you a chance to obtain another job with good benefits, remarry someone with access to a group, or become eligible for Medicare.

In some cases, retirees and their widows who receive health benefits after retirement can qualify for *lifetime* COBRA rights if their company files for bankruptcy.

If nothing pans out within the eighteen- or thirty-six-month period, what to do? In many states, after COBRA expires, you have a right to convert, without medical qualification, to an individual (or conversion) policy. Conversion policies are often very costly, with minimal benefits — but not always. In any case, unless you've *already qualified* for a better arrangement, take the conversion policy until you know you can do better.

When you are first notified of your COBRA rights, call the plan administrator to learn if the conversion policy might suit you better. In some (rare) instances, the conversion policy offers a better value than the COBRA policy.

Our dependency on our private health carriers reaches into every corner of our lives. Just as we finalize plans to move closer to the kids, we realize that our health coverage is local only. Where the kids live, we'll be uninsured. Or when the new opportunity opens up in the office across town, we learn the group coverage is sadly inferior to our own. We can't afford to change jobs. We find ourselves stuck in the home and with the job we've outgrown — all because our health coverage is not portable or universal. We're held hostage by our insurers. Obviously, as the population segment most likely to be uninsurable — yet too young for Medicare — mid-life folks are hit the hardest.

Sometimes, if you plan far enough ahead, you can avoid this problem. COBRA requires that you be offered the identical medical privileges offered the regular employees. That means that during open enrollment, if a policy that covers a wider geographical area is offered, you are eligible to switch to it.

You can lose your COBRA rights if you are more than thirty days late with your monthly premium. Eligibility for

Medicare or a comparable health plan on another job will disqualify you, even if your eighteen or thirty-six months have not expired. But if the new coverage excludes conditions covered under your COBRA group, you can retain COBRA until it expires. Page left her job for a better one. The new job, however, offered coverage that excluded disorders related to high blood pressure for one year. Page was able to continue participating in her old plan under COBRA for eighteen months because of the exclusion at her new job.

You can also lose your COBRA rights by not paying attention. *You* have the duty to notify the plan administrator if you're divorcing or if a child is no longer eligible as a dependent. Usually this means he or she attains a certain age, or ceases to be a full-time student, or marries. If you fail to notify the plan administrator within sixty days of the disqualifying event, you will lose your COBRA rights.

COBRA can represent tens of thousands of dollars — or even much more — to you if you fall seriously ill. If your employer, divorce or probate lawyer, or plan administrator caused you to lose your rights, you have the right to sue in federal or state court. You want a lawyer familiar with employee-benefits laws.

COBRA excludes employers of fewer than twenty employees — a bias against women, since a preponderance of employees of small businesses are women.

> **If your employer had twenty employees on a typical business day during the preceding year, you have COBRA rights even if the staff is below that number at the time you lose your group coverage.**

Health Coverage for Retirees

Companies across the country are planning to renege on promises made to retirees. In a recent survey, 62 percent of companies polled by a major benefits expert stated that they intended to reduce retiree health coverage. If you're still working, chances are that retiree benefits will be severely cut back or phased out before you retire. This argues in favor of delaying retirement until Medicare eligibility at age sixty-five — something the average woman can do better than the average man, because she has more years left. If you are already retired, you are likely to see rising copayments or deductibles in the years ahead.

> **You have COBRA rights at retirement, and so do your dependents — eighteen months, like any other job termination. If you become Medicare eligible, your COBRA rights end.**

And If You Are Uninsurable?

If all else fails — COBRA runs out, there's no conversion right, and you find you're uninsurable — here are some strategies worth considering:

- Join an association that offers coverage to its members.
- Buy several cheap indemnity-type policies.
- Buy a high-deductible major-medical policy.

First, many large organizations, either voluntary like AARP, or professional such as bar associations or nurse's associations, offer group policies to their members. These are generally not as good as employer-sponsored groups — but any port in a storm.

Second, indemnity policies are available everywhere. These are the ones that pay you a certain sum (say $100 per day) for hospitalization. They pay in cash. Nothing should prevent you from buying several, so that if you can't get insurance anywhere else, you can at least get $500 or $600 per day to help with the bills. These policies are not very expensive because they are not very good. If you have basic coverage elsewhere, don't waste your money on an indemnity policy.

Finally, consider buying a high-deductible major-medical policy. Insurance agents listed in the yellow pages should offer them, as well as some large organizations as group policies. Even a $25,000 deductible — ludicrous at first glance — *does* limit the nightmare. You can plan your investments to fund the first $25,000, and no longer worry about losing your house. Major-medical policies are inexpensive, and sometimes available without medical qualification.

Quite a number of states sponsor "risk pools." These, for the otherwise uninsurable, offer basic coverage at a high price. If you can afford it, it's better than nothing. Call your state's insurance department to see if risk pools are offered.

MEDICARE AND MEDIGAP

Medicare, which began its life three decades ago in great hope of covering substantially all the medical costs of its beneficiaries, today covers less than 43 percent of the average older person's annual medical bills. Technical details concerning eligibility, applications, and extent of coverage are available by calling Social Security at (800) 772-1213. I won't recount them here. Our business is not to duplicate information readily available from Social Security, but to apply gender awareness to Medicare and its partners in the private sector, and come up with a few strategies that will save you real money and give you the edge.

Medicare and Medigap in a Nutshell

In general, *Medicare* is government health insurance for people over sixty-five and those who have received Social Security disability for twenty-four months. Medicare has two parts: Part A is hospital insurance, and Part B is for outpatient care. Part A is free to Social Security eligibles over age sixty-five; everyone pays a monthly premium ($41.10 per month in

1994) for Part B. Most of those ineligible to receive Part A for free can buy in. Since Medicare is paid for by payroll deduction, like Social Security, as well as the monthly premiums, eligibility is not based on need. *Medicaid*, described later in this chapter, is the program for the poor, regardless of age.

There are numerous exceptions to these generalities — especially involving government employees — so be sure to apply three months before your sixty-fifth birthday even if you doubt your eligibility.

Medicare carried a huge policy flaw when it was born nearly three decades ago. There was no cap on what a doctor or hospital (we'll call them both *providers*) could charge the patient. For outpatient care, Medicare would generally pick up 80 percent of *reasonable* charges — the patient was responsible for the rest. If Medicare determined that $60 was reasonable for an office visit, it would pay $48. The doctor was free to charge whatever he or she wanted — Medicare would pay $48, and the patient would pay the rest. If the office visit was billed at $100, Medicare paid $48, and the patient would be responsible for $52. This is called *balance billing*. It didn't take providers long to twist this system to their advantage. If their patients were able to pay $35 for an office visit before Medicare, then $35 was soon tacked on to Medicare's reimbursement rate. The patient pays the same as before — but the doctor is much richer because of the Medicare reimbursement. As a result of this fatal flaw, so much money flowed into providers' pockets during the 1970s and 1980s that the crisis we confront today was born.

Balance billing was never universal. Some doctors agreed to charge no more than the Medicare reasonable rate, in return for which Medicare paid them directly (this is called Medicare assignment). Doctors in poorer areas favored this method, because it ensured payment. Of course, the patient is still responsible for the 20 percent in excess of Medicare's reimbursement. Lately, a few states have effectively outlawed balance billing by making Medicare assignment a condition of a medical license. Others have limited mandatory assignment to low-income patients. Of course, some doctors in those states no longer accept Medicare patients — but this policy will never become widespread, because Medicare coverage is nearly universal among people over sixty-five, the biggest consumers of medical care.

Balance billing is more of a problem for women than for men, because women over sixty-five have only 60 percent of the income of men of the same age. Also, women are the majority of Medicare patients, so the $3 billion paid to doctors in 1991 over and above the fee recognized by Medicare as reasonable came mostly from the pockets of older women. Balance billing is a woman's issue.

> **Although there are exceptions, federal law as of January 1, 1993, provides that most medical services provided to a Medicare recipient cannot be billed at more than 15 percent above the Medicare fee schedule. If a reasonable fee is $100, your doctor can charge no more than $115. Medicare will pay $80, you will pay $35. Doctors are held to this fee limit even if the patient agrees not to involve Medicare at all. If you feel your doctor is overcharging, contact your Medicare insurance carrier. The phone number will be on your Explanation of Medicare Benefits form.**

There are numerous gaps in Medicare — deductibles, co-payments, uncovered services — which have spawned a healthy private insurance partner known informally as medigap ("Medicare supplement" policies is the formal term). Medigap policies are available in ten standard models (we'll talk more about that later).

> **The AARP's Medicare/Medicaid Assistance Program provides free assistance in dealing with Medicare (and medigap insurers, too). Write the AARP at 601 E Street NW, Washington, D.C. 20049. This service is available whether or not you are a member of the AARP.**

Medicare and Women

You owe it to yourself to become very familiar with everything Medicare covers, as well as how Medicare works. Two recently added benefits are the direct result of lobbying by women's organizations: mammography and Pap tests. Unfortunately, perhaps because they do not realize it is now available, well over half of women over sixty-five do not have regular mammograms, despite the fact that the risk of breast cancer increases with age. Medicare will pay only for a screening mammogram every two years, and then only partly — but it's a start. One in four cervical cancers occur in women over age sixty-five, but as in the case with mammograms, fewer than half the women of that age have regular Pap tests.

Medicare, like Social Security, is inherently biased *toward* women in a global way: both sexes qualify at age 65, but women as a class will have many more "Medicare years" than men.

Again, like most programs, Medicare also has biases that tilt *away* from women. For example, the deductibles and co-payments are the same for everyone, regardless of income. This makes them proportionately more expensive to lower-income beneficiaries — who, of course, are disproportionately women and minorities.

Whether Medicare is working for you or against you, you owe it to yourself to learn all its angles — because you will likely spend twenty years in Medicare's embrace.

Here is a problem for many women. Part A Medicare (hospital costs) is free to those eligible for Social Security, and available at a high premium ($221 per month, which when combined with the mandatory Part B premium of $41.10 exceeds $250 in 1994) for those who aren't. Part B Medicare is available to virtually anyone over sixty-five — a tie to Social Security is not necessary. Who is most likely to be excluded from Social Security? Teachers, that's who — two-thirds of whom are women — and relatively low-paid women, at that, who can ill afford the monthly Part A premium. Many school districts that still choose not to participate in Social Security (a mistake!)

now offer their employees the option of paying the Medicare payroll tax (1.45 percent).

Here is a strategy for you if you're offered that choice. Save your money (opt *out* of the payroll tax) if by age sixty-five you will qualify for spousal, widow's, or former spouse's Social Security on your husband's record. Even if your cash benefit will be wiped out by the government pension offset (see Chapter 3), you will be eligible for free Part A Medicare.

If you, like so many women, plan to work past sixty-five, apply for Medicare anyway, three months before your sixty-fifth birthday. Your earnings will not affect your Medicare eligibility. In any case, don't delay your application more than four months after your birthday, or you will have to wait until the annual enrollment period, January 1 through March 31.

Worse yet, if you miss your initial seven-month enrollment period, your monthly Part B premiums will be *increased* 10 percent for the rest of your life — and with your womanly longevity, that could be a very costly procrastination. Exception: If you delay your application because you are covered under a group plan at work, the increase will not be implemented. But don't assume you qualify for the exception: check with Social Security.

The Gaps in Medigap

Most of us women have to prepare for *two* catastrophic illnesses — first our husband's, then eventually our own. This means you should become the health insurance expert in your household. Because medical expenses can indeed be catastrophic, the time you spend learning everything you can about Medicare coverage, medigap and long-term care policies will probably translate into real dollars saved.

Begin by calling Social Security at (800) 772-1213 and ordering the free booklets describing Medicare and medigap policies. Your library and your senior center

**are other good resources. Many hospitals sponsor
health education centers, with books, tapes, and
seminars.**

Medigap policies, born to plug the gaps in Medicare, carry
numerous gaps of their own. Some provide only basic benefits;
others are fairly comprehensive. By federal law, all medigap
policies sold after August 1992 conform to at least one of ten
government authorized models (states are free to decrease this
number). All medigap policies are offered by private insurers,
and the company must offer at least the basic policy, and as
many of the other nine variations it chooses. If any policy suggests it is government sponsored, pass it by. It is not.

**If you are not yet on Medicare, *it is critical that you
understand this*: By federal law, you have six months
after your first Medicare application to enroll in a
medigap policy without fear of rejection for medical
reasons, and with no exclusions for preexisting conditions. If you miss this window of opportunity, you
will be subject to the whims and vagaries of each insurer's actuaries. Because of this six-month window,
it is all-important that you really make your first medigap decision a sound one.**

Your first task is to think through your own situation. How
much of your medical costs can you bear on your own? Don't
seek to insure every last penny of cost — it's just not worth
the premium. If you feel you can carry $2,000 per year in ordi-
nary outpatient expenses, buy a policy with such a deductible.
You'll save a heap of money, because high deductibles really
bring the premiums down. The ten authorized models range
from A coverage (the most basic) to J. All insurers must use
these letters, so you can easily compare one insurer's D policy
(and price) with another's. Before you buy one, get familiar
with all the coverages from A to J.

**One way to test the value of a policy is to ask about
its loss ratio. A policy that pays back sixty-five cents**

of each dollar paid in premiums has a loss ratio of sixty-five. For individual policies, the minimum loss ratio by law for medigap policies is sixty-five (but you should hold out for seventy-five to eighty if you can); for groups, the legal minimum is seventy-five.

Don't buy a medigap policy because you think it will pay for long-term care at home or in a nursing home. Despite some pretty misleading language, most will not. The nursing-home coverage is usually limited to the deductibles and copayments during the *Medicare payment period only*. The catch here is that Medicare pays very little nursing-home care — only about 2 percent nationally. Medicare will *not* pay for custodial care — and most nursing-home care is custodial. Custodial care is covered in special long-term care, or nursing-home care policies.

A big problem in recent years has been the oversale of medigap policies to the elderly. Although it is now illegal for an agent to sell a medigap policy to someone who already has one, many people still hold several policies sold before August 1992. If this is you, keep your best one and dump the rest. Complain to your insurance commissioner if an agent tries to sell you a second medigap policy.

Some shady agents may try to sell you replacement policies every few months. They get around the multiple policy prohibition by having you sign an intention to cancel your first policy. The agent makes a much larger commission on initial sales than on renewals.

Only if you lie on your application or don't pay your premiums can medigap policies be canceled or not renewed. Because a break in your coverage can make you vulnerable to waiting periods and preexisting-condition limits, it is especially important that you never default on your premium and that you replace existing policies with no break in time.

If you are switching policies, know that it is against the law for the new insurer to impose waiting periods or preexisting-condition limits.

When you buy your policy, make your check out to the company, not the agent. Expect the policy to arrive within thirty days — otherwise contact the company or your state's insurance department. Even after you've bought and paid for the medigap policy, you usually will have 30 days to reconsider and cancel with a full refund of your premium (in essence, you will have thirty days of free insurance).

Are you not quite poor enough to be eligible for Medicaid (see below), but paying for Medicare premiums, copayments, and deductibles is really a struggle? Women, especially, are in this position, since four out of five poor people over sixty-five are women. The Qualified Medicare Beneficiary program (QMB, or QUIMBY) helps people just above the poverty level pay their uncovered Medicare costs. This federal program is administered through the Medicaid office of your local social services department.

FINANCING LONG-TERM CARE

Long-term care is everyone's worst-case scenario. Whether it is in a nursing home or at home, long-term custodial care is costly in every way: lots of bucks, lots of tears. If someone you love needs custodial care, get all the support you can from books, groups, friends, and family. Here we'll let others dry your tears — we're going to concentrate on your bucks.

A Harvard study a few years ago demonstrated that half the retired couples in the country would be bankrupt just thirteen weeks after one spouse entered a nursing home. This is the nightmare that keeps Sominex in business. The sleepless hours should be double for women, since wives, at least, have to worry twice as much. Once for their husband's calamity, and once for their own.

Experts tell us that half of all women over age sixty-five will spend some part of their lives in a nursing home (compared to one-third of men). Women are the family caregivers, women are the nursing-home staff, women are the home attendants, and women are the majority of nursing-home residents. Long-term care is emphatically a woman's issue.

In this section we'll discuss some of the new wrinkles that can mean tens of thousands of dollars to you.

Pay careful attention to what follows — it is worth serious money to you, especially if you are married. Read this section twice if need be — but be sure you understand the twists, because many of them require advance planning, some well in advance of a medical catastrophe.

Choosing the Right Long-Term Care Policy

Medicare is a flop when it comes to institutional long-term care. Custodial care — the expensive, lengthy, tedious kind — is not *medical* in Medicare's eyes, whether in the home or in an institution. Medicare will pay for medical visits to the home or institution for administering of medication, therapy, and so forth, but nothing for custodial care. The $30,000 average annual nursing-home bill will be your responsibility.

The one hundred days of nursing-home care promised by Medicare is illusory in most cases, since not one day is permitted for custodial care. Since most nursing-home care is custodial, count on counting Medicare out.

Since few retired couples can fund a nursing home out of current income (and keep up the home for the at-home spouse), the dreaded spend-down begins soon after admission. This is the nightmare with a woman's face: The couple spends their savings until they are depleted. Destitute, the husband (four out of five times it is the husband who needs institutionalization first) qualifies for Medicaid, which pays for a minimum level of nursing-home care. Then the husband dies a year or so later. The wife, now impoverished, lives her final fifteen years in penury. This female nightmare is known as *spousal impoverishment*, and later in this section we will talk about clever ways to use the laws and regulations to your financial advantage.

Your first step, however, is to include a sound long-term care insurance policy in your insurance portfolio.

The true long-term care (LTC) policy will pay for custodial care, usually in a licensed nursing home (technically, a skilled nursing facility, or SNF). Some will also pay for home care, but because of insurer's fears that everyone wants to stay home with "maid service," most LTC policies have a bias toward institutionalization.

Medicare will pay for limited home visits for medical reasons, including nurses, therapists, and medical social workers, as well as medical equipment and supplies. Of course, it generally will not pay for routine chores of daily living, such as shopping, toileting, cooking, and housecleaning. Make sure you don't pay for a policy that duplicates Medicare coverage.

In finding the right LTC policy for you, gender awareness will be a valuable tool. Four out of five times, it is the husband who needs the custodial care, the wife who provides it at home. Eighty percent of chronic care is provided for at home — not in nursing homes — and 80 percent of those family caregivers are women.

Therefore, if you're married, you want to scrutinize every LTC policy with your needs in mind. Cast yourself in the likely role of caregiver for your husband. Will you be able to care for him at home? What services does the policy pay for at home? You want a policy that will supplement Medicare's meager respite service, because you *must* schedule adequate time for yourself away from your duties. Medicare will not pay for "chore service" such as household help, cooking, shopping, and patient personal hygiene. You want a policy that is strong on chore services.

Look out for policies that require a hospital stay before nursing-home coverage begins, and avoid those that exclude Alzheimer's disease or "mental or neurological" disorders.

LTC policies are still relatively new to the insurance world, so companies are still feeling their way. The policy is likely to be strictly limited in either of two ways. Either it will carry a lifetime dollar limit (perhaps $100,000), or a time limit (say, four years in a nursing home). A three- or four-year nursing-home limit in practical terms amounts to about the same as the $100,000 limit. In comparing policies with dollar limits against those with time limits, call four or five nursing homes in your area and ask for annual rates for a semiprivate room.

You may be concerned that the dollar or year limit isn't nearly enough. But here is a hard fact: most nursing-home patients die within four years, so in most cases you will be okay with a policy good for four years or the equivalent in dollars.

Look for a policy that pays a percentage of the room rate, rather than a fixed dollar amount per day. A policy that will pay 80 percent of a semiprivate room is worth more to you than one that pays $100 per day, even if that *is* 80 percent of the going rate. The insurer takes the burden of future inflation with the first kind, you bear the burden with the second. Your $100 per day is going to look paltry beside the $250 daily rate when you make your claim.

Medicare will pay for up to 210 days of hospice care. When the benefits run out, the hospice cannot evict the client.

When You Are the Caregiver

Four out of five elders who need assistance are cared for at home, and four out of five of the caregivers are female relatives. If you're married, that's likely to be you.

And, inevitably, money will be one of your many worries:

- Can you afford to care for your husband at home?
- How can you pay for adult day care?

- What about nursing-home care?
- Can you handle your household finances?

Your first task is to take a hard look at your LTC policy, medigap policy, and Medicare. Among the three of them, you might be able to patch together a useful set of services.

Medicare will pay for limited medical home visits, such as a visiting nurse, administering medication, providing certain therapies, and medical equipment such as oxygen tanks, hospital beds, and assistive devices such as walkers and shower stools. Of course, these must be ordered by your doctor. Medicare will pay for home hospice services as well, but only for a limited time, including respite services. This means you can hire someone to watch your husband while you take time off.

Your LTC and medigap policies may pay for adult day care, some chore service, some respite care, and maybe an attendant.

In addition, your community may have home services — home-delivered meals, for example — available for a sliding-scale fee. Some states have in-home supportive services, such as attendant care. Call your local senior center or hospital discharge planner for particulars.

After you've worked out what services you're entitled to, you'll need to take a hard look at your own finances. Be sure you have signing authority on everything. You don't know if your husband's slow decline could accelerate into a near coma overnight, thus rendering him legally incapable of adding your name to his accounts, deeds, powers of authority, and trusts. Then, to back up your cosignatures, be sure you get a general durable power of attorney authorizing you to sign in his stead on everything. You can have his Social Security or SSI checks changed to your name. Ask the agencies how to become a "representative payee."

Ordinary powers of attorney automatically expire when the principal becomes incompetent. Have your husband sign a *durable* power of attorney (don't confuse this with the durable power of attorney for health

care — here we're talking about the financial power of attorney). Durable powers continue to be valid after incompetency, which is crucial in a caregiving situation.

At all costs, you don't want to be forced into petitioning for guardianship (in some states, called conservatorship). Cosignatures, durable powers of attorney, and even a flexible inter-vivos trust will allow you all the authority you'll need to buy, sell, rent, withdraw, deposit — whether or not the asset or stream of income is his separate property. Guardianships are expensive, demeaning, and irritating to live with. However, all the alternative devices must be exercised while your husband is competent. After the stroke it may be too late. You could be forced into petitioning for guardianship overnight after your hale and healthy mate drops on the tennis court. Good planning means that both of you will have prepared for this by each signing the necessary papers well in advance of need.

If You Are Working

Not everyone is in a position to take care of a sick husband. If you aren't, first look into your company's benefit programs. Some offer family-care benefits that include adult care. Others allow you to use your sick leave to care for someone at home. Family-leave acts exist in some states, although not yet nationally, at this writing. If your state has such, your job will be protected for a period of time while you set things up at home. And don't forget Uncle Sam. The dependent-care credit on your income tax is not just for child care. If you work and pay someone to care for an adult at home, you are probably entitled to this credit.

Remember to check with the agencies that serve the disabled. They have a wealth of information you'll need on services, financial assistance, and resources. The disabilities common to aging are legitimately served by many agencies that serve the disabled.

Probably the most expensive part of home care will be the attendant. Your LTC policy, medigap policy, or Medicaid (if you are poor enough) may help to pay the attendant. Unless the services are medical, Medicare will not. But much more than cost is at stake. Anyone can offer him- or herself as an attendant — including convicted felons. Stories of theft and physical abuse are common. To protect yourself, call your local hospital's discharge planner to learn if there are geriatric-care managers in your area. GCMs do far more than arrange attendant care. They can pull together the entire spectrum of services you'll need, from home-delivered meals or groceries to check-writing services. GCMs are not guaranteed safe, either — they are not licensed as such in most areas. But an agency or service that uses licensees in established fields (RNs, social workers, licensed vocational or practical nurses) has its reputation to protect and so is a good place to begin. When you interview the attendant or GCM, you want to

- have a personal, not phone, interview
- have a friend with you during the interview
- avoid making a commitment during the interview
- give the interviewee a copy of written job expectations
- work out vacations, sick leave, holidays, ahead of time
- ask for *and check* references
- check your house insurance for employee injury coverage

Many communities provide in-home supportive services to the homebound. These may include home health, personal care, homemaker, chore services, meals, fitness programs, and respite services. Often these are offered on a sliding-scale fee schedule. Call your senior center.

Time for Yourself

The biggest problem you'll meet in caring for your husband at home is meeting your own needs for time off. Medicare will pay for limited *respite* services in the home.

You can also have several hours a day or week to yourself if your husband participates in an adult day-care program. Your doctor or senior center should know where to find one. Adult day *health-care* programs might qualify for insurance reimbursement — be sure to ask the agency that provides the service about that.

Call your senior center about support programs for caregivers. Even if you can participate only by phone, you will be helped immeasurably by the support and information these groups provide.

Avoiding Spousal Impoverishment

Although Medicare doesn't pay for custodial care, *Medicaid* does. *Medicaid* is the joint federal/state medical welfare program that pays over half the nursing-home costs in this country. Usually, you have to be very poor to qualify for Medicaid. However, in recent years, couples with one spouse in a nursing home get a small break. Too many women were left utterly impoverished after spending down to $3,000 to qualify their husbands for Medicaid and then living on the allowed $300 per month. Now, depending on the state, couples in this situation can insulate tens of thousands of dollars in assets and keep several hundred more to live on per month. These amounts change with inflation and vary among the states (subject to federal minimums and maximums). These days, with clever planning, a couple can insulate quite a lot of money from the spend-down. This is a situation where the right professional advice can save you thousands and thousands of dollars.

Your first line of defense against the dreaded spend-down is a good long-term care policy. Your second is a medical directive (discussed later in this chapter). Your third is a clever elder law attorney.

As stated earlier, elder law is a relatively new specialty developed with the problems of older women in mind: spousal impoverishment, Medicaid planning, survivor's benefits, wills, and trusts. Of course, elder law specialists can do the same things ordinary probate lawyers do — but they go way beyond that by ferreting out all the subtle but legitimate ways families can maximize their assets and income during periods, especially, of high long-term care costs. Elder law is too new to be certified as a specialty by state bars, which means that not everyone who calls him- or herself an elder law specialist cuts the mustard. Try to get someone with at least three years' experience in elder law (not ordinary probate or estate planning). Your local senior citizen center might have a list, and, of course, check the yellow pages.

The National Academy of Elder Law Attorneys, Inc., will provide you with local referrals: write to 655 North Alvernon Way, Suite 108, Tucson, Arizona 85711.

You don't have to be poor or marginal to be impoverished by a nursing home. Middle-class, and even upper-middle-class, couples can seldom pay the full cost of custodial care out of current income indefinitely. But desperate circumstances breed desperate strategies. Let's examine how two couples handled their health cost crisis.

In 1991, Helen and Alan were living on $30,000 per year (before taxes):

Income in Alan's name:

- $5,500 Social Security
- $14,000 pension

Income in Helen's name:

- $4,000 Social Security

Joint income:

- $6,500 from $125,000 invested at 5 percent

Alan suffered a sudden stroke, and Helen cared for him at home until her doctor told her she was close to collapse. The nursing home, a good one, cost $60,000 per year. Helen cut her expenses to $20,000 per year and used their savings to pick up the rest of the cost. Of course, as she exhausted the savings, the $6,500 interest vanished as well. After two years, her savings down to $10,000, and her (combined) annual income down to $23,500, Helen bowed to the inevitable and applied for Medicaid to pay for Alan's care. Medicaid, in determining Alan's eligibility, did not count the house, household furniture, Helen's car, or her personal effects. Helen was able to keep the $10,000 savings — all they had left. Because they lived in a state that allowed her the maximum living allowance, Helen was able to keep $1,662 per month for her own needs, and the rest was paid to the nursing home. Medicaid picked up the balance at Medicaid's reduced rate.

When Alan converted from a private-pay patient to a Medicaid patient, the nursing home was prohibited by law from evicting him, so long as the facility receives Medicaid or Medicare funds. Since nearly three-quarters of nursing-home beds in the nation are filled by Medicaid patients, few facilities take no federal funds.

A year later, Alan died. Helen lived the remaining eighteen years of her life on $12,500 per year: $5,500 widow's Social Security, and $7,000 survivor's benefit from Alan's pension.

Could Alan and Helen have given $100,000 to their children — sort of an early inheritance? Generally, no, not without running afoul of the "transfer of assets" rule, which would render Alan ineligible for Medicaid for thirty-six months after the transfer. Nevertheless, good professional advice can help you plan transfers of this type and still qualify for Medicaid when the time comes. This is why you should first seek advice at least *four years* before a nursing home admission.

In every particular, the incomes and assets of couple number two, Dean and Judy, were the same as Helen and Alan's. But Judy sought advice from an elder law attorney as soon as it was clear that Dean's illness would be long term. Following advice, Judy used $40,000 of the savings to pay off the mortgage on the house, $5,000 for a new roof and insulation, $8,000 remodeling the basement into a studio apartment, and $7,000 on a sensible and durable new car. Dean then applied for Medicaid soon after admission to the nursing home, and Judy was able to keep more than $65,000 in investments (this changes with inflation). Judy's expenses were lower than Helen's because she had no mortgage and lower utility bills because of the insulation. She was still allowed only $1,662 per month in income, but after Dean died, she was better off than Helen because she also had the income from the $65,000, the rental unit, and lower housing costs. The elder law attorney helped Dean and Judy convert their savings into exempt assets and made sure they applied for Medicaid before they had spent down too much (as had Helen).

There are many variations on these strategies. Because of opportunities to convert nonexempt assets into the exempt home, some advisers feel that older people are well advised to remain homeowners rather than renters in their later years. Certain irrevocable trusts can be used to protect assets from the spenddown — but the ordinary, revocable inter-vivos (living) trust will not do the job.

Be sure to ask your attorney about the possibility of a Medicaid lien against your estate. Sometimes the state repays itself for Medicaid funds expended out of the estate after the Medicaid beneficiary (and probably the spouse) has died. If you plan to leave something to your children, you'll want to know the particulars about this. Obtain competent advice *early*. Just as soon as someone becomes chronically ill, see an attorney. Even two years before institutionalization will be too late for some important tactics.

This area of the law is loaded with gender biases aimed right at women. For example, the at-home spouse can keep all the income that is in his or her name, even if it's several thousand per month. Guess which spouse is most likely to benefit from this rule?

Sometimes you can get a court order granting you more than the monthly income normally allowed. It is worth checking out. And, tragically, many couples divorce to preserve more of the assets. Kay and Roger had $200,000 in retirement savings, in addition to their house. When it became clear that Roger would live the rest of his life in a nursing home, they divorced. The court awarded Kay $100,000 plus the house. Roger spent his share on the nursing home and then applied for Medicaid. This way Kay kept $100,000 of her assets rather than only $66,000 (the allowed limit).

Let's not kid ourselves. The real reason Medicare doesn't pay for custodial long-term care (the genesis of spousal impoverishment) is that policymakers assume women are available to provide the care for free. And annoying as it is, they've been right. Medicare's default is a direct bias against older women, who provide at excruciating personal cost the care that other countries provide their citizens for free. The real villains in this sorry mess are the policymakers who refuse to fundamentally reform our health care system so that Americans can expect cradle-to-grave care like the citizens of virtually all other industrialized countries of the world.

We should recognize the refusal to pay for institutional care for what it is: a direct governmental assault on women.

The National Council of Senior Citizens offers the Nursing Home Information Service. You can reach it at 1331 F Street NW, Washington, D.C. 20004; telephone (202) 347-8800.

MINIMIZING THE COSTS OF DEATH

Custodial long-term care is costly enough. Long-term death is light-years worse.

Right-to-die, death with dignity, pull the plug, assisted suicide, euthanasia — the agonizing parade marches on and on. Courts despair, legislatures balk — and we pay the bills.

Put most crassly, the huge expense of high-tech medicine is no more than a gigantic transfer of wealth — from heirs to medical providers. About two-thirds of all health costs occur in *the final three months of our lives.* Money frugally saved for years to provide college educations for the grandkids, down payments for the kids, a little something extra to soften the later years of beloved friends, a bequest to save a redwood grove — all the sweet intentions derailed in the end for the joy of a nasogastric tube and the bliss of a respirator. And in the end, it's all the same: Death. A long dying instead of a shorter one. Everyone's idea of fun.

Don't blame the doctors. They are ethically and professionally bound to oblige our quest for life without end. The time-honored practice of consulting the next of kin was never strictly legal in any state. Doctors did so at their peril, and in recent years a few have paid dearly for it — including charges of murder. It isn't up to the American Medical Association to curtail all research and development of lifesaving (or death-prolonging) devices. When a patient recovers, aren't we thankful for the time the high-tech stuff bought? It isn't up to a medical society, peer-review committee, or hospital board to decide that after age eighty-five (seventy-five? sixty-five? *fifty?*) life is worthless and only pain control will be offered.

The ethical issues are thorny and stormy and real. Fortunately, in most states, you and I can bow out of the controversy and make our own decision with a properly executed medical directive.

By law you must be advised of your right to sign a medical directive on admission to any hospital (or nursing home or hospice) in the country receiving Medicare or Medicaid funds (the vast majority). But the wise person will do so much earlier. You can't sign a directive if you're comatose after a sudden stroke.

> **No facility can require that you sign one. Call your local hospital's admissions department to learn what form is legal in your state. Many attorneys include a medical directive in will and trust packages — a good idea.**

Nobody likes to think of medical directives as financial tools, but of course they are. When you and I execute one, we are directing our wealth just as surely as when we write a will. In fact, thought of in another way, the medical directive will fund the estate rather than the medical establishment.

And that brings up the most unpleasant thought of all. It is not beyond imagination (to put it politely) that some heirs sometime will see the estate as more congenial to their future plans than is Grandma. Because we women tend to die last in our families, usually it will be Grandma who will pass wealth on to the next generation — and sometimes we aren't as close to that generation as we were to our own. Grandpa usually passes it to Grandma; he has few socially acceptable alternatives. We women, then, are at the greatest risk of being shown the door a bit too hastily by eager heirs.

The distasteful interjection of finances into the sensitive area of medical directives will be resented by many, which is why I bring it up. We must make our final plans with our eyes wide open. As women, we will die differently from men. We will probably be at our husband's side when he goes; he won't be at ours. We have different considerations. We need to contemplate all the particulars when we balance our alternatives. And money, as always, is one particular. Medical directives are the best tools devised by law to move our plans from the realm of the imagination to the land of the concrete.

Don't worry that you'll change your mind later but be unable to override your written directive. Your written, oral, or *hand-signaled* instructions take precedence at all times, right up to your last breath. Your surrogate can't have the plug pulled over your objections. Even if you have been adjudicated as incompetent, your wishes will prevail however and whenever expressed. The medical directive is only for the situation in which you are unable to express any opinion at all.

Medical directives come in several forms:

- living wills
- durable powers of attorney for health (medical) decisions
- natural death acts

The principal problem is that not all states authorize these devices, and those that are authorized may be unrecognized in a sister state. If you've prudently prepared the correct form for your state, then fall ill when visiting your brother across the country, your wishes could be nullified. If you visit your relatives frequently, it is not a bad idea to execute a directive according to that state's form as well. Leave it with the one you visit.

States are, properly, very sticky about these things. After all, a life may be at stake (and maybe a fortune as well). If you've prepared a do-it-yourself directive, or filled in the blanks of one ordered through the mail, be very sure it will work in your state. Ask your lawyer or the local senior law clinic or your hospital's admission office.

If your state offers a choice of forms, the durable power of attorney for health (or medical) decisions is the surest way to secure your wishes. Natural death instruments and living wills merely put forth your wishes. Studies have shown that medical staffs are generally not guided by the document in a crisis situation — it's sitting in your medical file, and who is reading your file when your heart has just stopped?

Durable powers, however, go well beyond a mere expression of your sentiments. They name a surrogate decision maker. You designate someone you trust to make decisions when you can't. The medical team does not have the opportunity to ignore your file when your surrogate is there in person. Medical professionals are shielded from criminal and civil liability when following the instructions of a properly appointed surrogate, so their cooperation is likely to be highest with this form of medical directive. Be sure your directive goes

- into your medical record(s) (don't forget the specialists)
- to your surrogate
- to all your close relatives
- to your attorney
- to your clergy

Choice In Dying, a national nonprofit organization formed when the Society for the Right to Die merged with Concern for Dying, will send you all the information you need for your state, including the proper forms. Contact them at 200 Varick Street, New York, New York 10014; telephone (212) 366-5540.

The Well-Life Concept

Public-policy analysts have devised a new tool to measure life expectancy — one that includes quality of life in the equation. Rather than focusing only on the end of life, the well-life expectancy seeks to project the number of years the average American can expect to live free of life-altering disability or disease. For women they tell us it is sixty-three; for men, sixty.

This notion of the well life can be a very constructive tool for social planning. Will a particular policy extend the well life, or only the final life? Should priority be given to extending the former? Should our concentration on the latter be abandoned? When we push the limits of ultimate life, what do we gain in fact? Death with dignity takes on strength. The well life could be a useful concept.

Then again, what about the specter of medical rationing? Already a reality, rationing must be recognized as one of the risks in our inevitable conversion to a national health program. When dividing a limited pie, will some sectors argue that medical research directed at lengthening actual life be subordinated to projects aimed at prolonging the well life? Will life-prolonging treatments for people past their well-life expectancy be curtailed, with only pain relief available (an idea already out and about)? Will society get the idea that life isn't worth living after the well life — with concomitant marginalization of those "unfortunate" enough to have hung around too long?

One can't help noticing that we women lost some years under this projection. Our statistical advantage of eight years has been cut to three in the well-life formulary. Somebody has decided that five of those eight years aren't quality ones. Yet I wonder. I remember a friend — an athletic, fit woman all her years until breast cancer took its toll — remarking how life had surprised her with its beauty and worth even when she was at her physical worst. She actively pursued every avenue of treatment, including experimental. She was hoping for a cure, or at least an extension of time. Pain control was secondary. I can't help laughing when I imagine her reaction if some policymaker had decided that she, at seventy, should be drugged rather than cured, because her well life had ended years before. So I worry about our perceptions of what other people's lives are worth to them, and how public policy can be engineered in deeply biased ways with the very best intentions.

And I worry about women's lost five years, and whether some future policy will give women only a three-year advantage over men in treatment directed toward a cure, thus in fact reducing women's actual life expectancy to one on parity with men. I worry that male policymakers will not see this as a problem, so long as everyone has already agreed that a woman's years past sixty-three aren't worth living.

This whole end-of-life debate is desperately in need of some womanly thinking — and with Hillary Clinton's task force we're getting it. We're about to get our chance. We women have a historic opportunity to reshape American health care into our image. By the turn of the century, women will dominate the largest voting bloc in America — older Americans. The American health care system will be rewritten top to bottom, and it will be our privilege and destiny to do the writing. Whether we adopt the Canadian model of national health insurance or conjure up something uniquely American, we women will have our hands all over the outcome.

With gender awareness, we can do the job right.

CHECKING UP ON YOUR ENDGAME

1. Will your health policy move with you when you move?
2. What medical conditions does it exclude? For how long?
3. Are you paying more for your coverage because you are female?
4. Are you carrying more than one health or medigap policy? Why?
5. Has your agent switched you from policy to policy?
6. Will you remember to apply for Medicare three months before turning sixty-five?
7. Do you understand your rights under COBRA?
8. Will you have conversion rights if your coverage ends?
9. Will you have health benefits from your job after retirement?
10. Will you be eligible for free Part A Medicare?
11. Are you billed over 15 percent above the Medicare rate by your doctor?
12. Have you studied Social Security's free booklet on Medicare?
13. Have you studied the ten medigap models?
14. What is the loss ratio for your health, medigap, or long-term care policy?
15. Do you know that Medicare partially pays for mammograms and Pap tests?
16. Do you realize that the incidence of breast and cervical cancers increases as we age?
17. Are you eligible for aid in paying your Medicare premiums?
18. Does your LTC policy pay for home care?
19. Do you realize that Medicare will not pay for custodial care?
20. Do you know what nursing homes cost in your town? Today?
21. What is the dollar or time limit on your LTC policy?
22. Have you called your local hospice to learn about their services?

23. Have you found a good elder law attorney?
24. How will you finance a long home-care period or nursing-home stay?
25. Have you and your loved ones completed medical directives?
26. Have you been candid with each other about your wishes?
27. Do you know whether your directives conform to your state's law?

8
From Lonely Hearts to Pyramid Schemes
The Art of the Steal

We have covered some pretty heavy stuff so far. Let's top it off with some lighter fare — but deadly serious when it comes to keeping control of our own financial futures. The retirement stash you've planned and sacrificed years to put together can disappear in a hot minute if the wrong good old boy (or girl) comes along.

Let's face it. Women are prey. We are the special targets of special crimes, and this doesn't stop as we get older. The emphasis shifts — not away from violence (ask any eighty-year-old mugged in the elevator of her apartment building) — but as we pass through our middle years, economic crimes come to the fore.

Beware the con man, or woman, or couple. We women have their attention. Beware the shifty-eyed stranger lurking in the parking lot — and beware, too, the nice young couple who just joined your church. The one might take your purse — the other, your net worth.

In this chapter we will describe some of the hundreds of scams and swindles to which women are especially vulnerable. These generally involve trust — confidence — the confidence artist is surely the most charming person you'll ever meet. He or she will come into your life like a dream come true. Enjoy this person, while he or she sticks around, but never, *never* hand over your money.

Women are targets for several reasons.

- First, our retirement incomes are lower than men's, causing us to scramble harder just to stay even. We'll listen to the siren song.
- Second, we are accustomed to turning our affairs over to someone else — our husbands or professional advisers.
- Third, we underestimate our own ability to master basic finances — too many of us operate on leaps of faith.
- Fourth, suddenly alone, we're lonely. We welcome the stranger.
- And last, we live older longer than men — a long stretch of years to fight off the sharks.

We'll look at some of these ancient games, beginning with an old favorite.

The Pyramid Scheme

In 1919, Charles Ponzi opened an office in Boston. He promised investors that he'd pay 40 percent on money loaned to him for a mere eighty days. When he paid his first "investors" off with full interest in just fifty days, his reputation was made. More signed up for the second offer, even more for the third. And how did Ponzi do it? No problem at all. He paid off the first group with the money loaned to him by the second. The second tier was paid by the third, and so forth. Because, with the interest owed, each tier was paid back more than it loaned, the next tier had to be bigger than the last in order to provide the funds; thus the pyramid. Of course, it doesn't take a genius to realize that at some point the newest tier would have to comprise the whole world, and then the scheme would collapse, leaving the largest tier out all their money.

You remember chain letters — you were to send a dime to five people, each of them to five more, and *voilà*, you'd be a millionaire inside of a year. A Ponzi scheme. A pyramid.

Pyramid schemes are illegal today, but due to technicalities in the laws, "marketing" programs flourish everywhere that look very much like a pyramid — and can have the same woeful effect on your pocketbook.

You've seen them. They're the ones where the salesperson is more interested in selling you a 'distributorship" than the product. Why, you may ask, are they so eager to create a competitor? They get points, of course, or some sort of incentive, for bringing in the next tier — that's you. And *your* payoff, if it comes, depends on your seducing yet another tier.

Pyramids work for the first few tiers. But in the end, the collapse is inevitable. Unless you're an organizer (I hope you're nicer than that), you should always assume you will be a low-level tier. Save your money.

The Investment Letter Scam

One day the mail brings you a free stock-market newsletter. Here's the deal: You will receive four free samples, after which you can subscribe for a paltry $200 per year. Each newsletter will predict which way the market will go for the following month. If the editor predicts correctly most of the time, you think, perhaps the newsletter will be well worth the $200. And guess what? All four of your sample newsletters prove to be right on the money!

Save *your* money. Think for a minute of Doug, the promoter of the scheme. For $10,000 Doug acquired a large mailing list — say, 100,000 names — from a health magazine targeted at seniors. He spends a few thousand more on the first newsletter and bulk-mailing costs. He divides his first mailing in half. In half he predicts that the market will rise; in the other half he predicts that it will fall. The market rises. The second newsletter goes only to the half (50,000) that received the correct prediction. Again, half the letters predict a rise, half a fall. The market falls. The third mailing (25,000) goes out to the "correct" half, again split into two predictions. The fourth, now going out to 12,000, follows the same scheme. The fifth, the subscription offer, goes to 6,000 people who have each received four newsletters accurately "predicting" the market. One out of six takes the bait. Doug pockets $200,000 and leaves town. End of newsletter, and end of your $200.

Ask your local library if they know the publication before you subscribe. Also, if it is legitimate, it will be around next year. Keep the offer for a year, then subscribe.

The Bank Examiner Bamboozle

You are flattered, and a little bit intrigued. You've been selected by an important guy to help catch a criminal. The important guy is a bank examiner (or officer, or treasury agent), and you are to withdraw some money and hand it over to him. Somehow, the suspect will trip himself up, and you'll be the hero. Need I say more?

No legitimate official ever asks you to withdraw your funds to catch a crook. Not ever.

The Advance Loan Fees Hustle

You and your husband went through bankruptcy shortly before he died because of the catastrophic costs of his last illness. Now you need a loan to pay the funeral costs. You figure your credit is zip, so when ads appear promising fast loans for people with no credit, you're interested. You're asked a few easy questions, you put up a processing fee of $400 for your contemplated $5,000 loan, and that's the end of it. They stick around for a while as they pick up more victims, but during that period you're stalled when you call. Finally, they're gone, and so is your fee.

> **Don't assume your credit is bad until you've been turned down by three legitimate lenders and they tell you the reason is your credit. Then ask for a free copy of your credit report from the credit bureau. Don't go to a loan shark.**

The Respected Professional Sting

You do everything right. You're much too savvy to fall for a con; you'd never invite strangers into your home; *of course* you know all about pyramid schemes.

But you've received an inheritance, and for the first time in your life you have $75,000 to invest. You ask friends. Someone recommends an investment adviser he has done business with for over ten years. Before you make an appointment, you check her out. You call the Securities and Exchange Commission, and the state licensing board. All is okay.

But it isn't — and the licensors know it. They are investigating her for fraud, but their investigations are in the early stages, and they can't give her a negative report until conviction. She has rights, after all. So you're told her record is clean, and you proceed accordingly.

You had in mind an annuity, but she convinces you that you'll do much better in a pool of U.S. Treasury securities she's putting together. The interest rate is about 1 percent more than the going rate — not enough to set off alarm bells, but enough to spark your interest. And U.S. Treasuries — what could be safer? You turn over your $75,000. In eighteen months, you're told, she'll return to you $84,000. You're so pleased, you tell your neighbor. Her $50,000 will become $54,000 in just one year, so she buys into the "pool," too. Four weeks later, the SEC puts the broker out of business and recommends criminal proceedings to the U.S. attorney general. The government appoints a receiver, who lets you know that several million dollars have been stolen. You and your neighbor will likely recover 3 percent of your investments.

> **The SEC can't begin to monitor the nation's 17,500 registered investment advisers with its tiny staff of 150. At best, it hopes to review the smallest advisers once every decade or so. You're on your own. One precaution you can take: ask the SEC for a copy of Parts I and II of your adviser's ADV — a document that discloses credentials and the disciplinary record of the individual.**

How can things like this happen? A reputable, licensed professional for many years suddenly begins to steal. This is far more common than we like to think. Positions of trust bring the professional (lawyer, broker, CPA, banker, financial planner) into very close proximity to lots and lots of money. Over the years some begin to ''borrow'' from the funds to realize a quick opportunity. They get inside information on a particular stock, for example, and they're a little short on their own funds, so they borrow, and repay out of their profits. This is easier the second time. And the third. Then the investment goes sour. Now they have to take a greater risk in order to repay. It snowballs. Soon the professional is scrambling to pay back the investors and save her reputation. How best to do this? With a new group of investors, of course. But this group will have to part with a large sum of money, with no expectations of return for many months. The professional prays that during that time, she can turn it around. Then everything will be fine. Classic embezzlement.

You can protect yourself. Deal only with large, established brokerages or multipartner financial advisers. This doesn't guarantee honesty, but at least there may be assets left in the company to pay you back when everything comes apart. The sole practitioner is free to work a scam because he or she works alone. No one else has access to the records, the accounts, the computer. If you must deal with a loner, demand to see a bond and make sure it is current.

Never **let yourself be talked into an investment you don't completely understand. In our example above, the investor participated in something that was completely vague — a "pool of U.S. Treasuries."**

The Lincoln Fiasco

When folks walked into their trusted savings and loan to roll over their CDs, the teller was waiting with a different idea. Look, she said, why put your money in a CD when you can buy our bonds and get more interest? Retirees, living off the interest, were pleased at the prospect of a raise. These were conservative investors — they'd chosen plain vanilla CDs because of the government insurance. Even a money market mutual fund was too sexy for them. Imagine their surprise when they learned they'd bought junk bonds of the worst kind — the kind that bellies up. And belly-up Lincoln Savings and Loan did, taking the investors' life savings with them.

Always **know the strength of the underlying institution. If you feel you absolutely understand bonds, your job is only half done. Before you invest, you *must* check out the entity, whether a corporation or government agency, that issues it.**

The Solid Affiliation Rip-Off

Surprisingly, this gambit still works all the time. Someone shows up at your door selling — *anything*. Living trusts, radon inspections, earthquake-proofing, prepaid legal plan, encyclopedias — you name it. Often they suggest an affiliation with a respected senior organization, such as the American Association of Retired Persons. One successful approach has been to use a name strikingly similar to the legitimate one — American Association of (whatever — senior something, perhaps). The salesperson might flash the AARP's magazine, *Modern Maturity*, just to enhance the misimpression. Sometimes they'll take your money and run; sometimes you'll get an overpriced, shoddy product. Now and then they're legitimate. But you should assume, at least at first, that they're not. Don't let them into your home, and don't be concerned about being polite. (We women are much too worried about that; regard this person as an intruder at best, or a thief or more at worst.) If you are interested in what appears to be a good product or service, spend a few days checking it out. Shop the yellow pages — maybe the same deal is available for less. Check the Better Business Bureau (not always a reliable source, but better than nothing), state licensing boards, if applicable. Check references.

The AARP never sells its services door-to-door, and it does not phone its members unless requested to. The organization is very concerned about the misrepresentation of its good name and suggests you never let the salesperson begin his or her pitch. The AARP urges you to tell the salesperson to leave written material and a business card, and if you're interested, you'll get in touch.

The Health Insurance Scandal

Do you have a medigap policy? How about one for long-term care? And another one paying only for cancer? And accidental dismemberment? Don't you need one for your toenails? And a nice one in case you're injured on a cruise? In a plane crash?

One of the biggest scandals in recent years has been the gross overselling of dubious or overlapping health insurance policies, especially to people of Medicare age (sixty-five). In some states, regulators stepped in to some degree, and recently the federal government made overlapping sales of medigap policies illegal across the land, but policies sold before the new law went into effect are not covered, nor are nonmedigap health policies such as long-term care and accidental injury. Read the discussion on medigap and long-term-care policies in Chapter 7 for more information on some special considerations you, as a woman, should bring to your health insurance quest.

The Charity Hoax

Another door-to-door scheme. This time it is a charity. The charity may very well be the individual at the door and no one else. If you want to help an unfortunate street person, do so directly on the street. But if you want to save the Amazon rain forest, don't give your dollars at the door; look up the Sierra Club in the white pages.

This is a harsh rule, I know, but it's best *never* to give at the door. All legitimate charities have mailing addresses. You can locate them through your local United Way, the white pages, or your reference librarian.

The Obituary Deal

This one targets widows. Soon after the obituary runs, a C.O.D. package arrives addressed to your late husband. You pay for it, since you assume he ordered it before he died. It's a Bible! No way will you return it — it's like a message from the grave — so you pay *dearly* for it.

Return any C.O.D. package that arrives after your husband's death. Simply say he is deceased.

The Hot Realty Swindle

Of course you've heard of the Florida land scams of a generation ago. People remote from Florida (or California, or Arizona — somewhere sunny) received word of a very great opportunity to buy land for their retirement or investment. They'd have to act fast — opportunities like these aren't for the slow moving. After the down payment was paid, perhaps even years later, the lucky couple would see their lot — in the middle of a mangrove swamp, or the desert. Worthless.

This is just a hunch, but I think the land scam is more likely to appeal to older couples than women or men living alone. The retirement dream home is usually a couple's dream — and con artists know it. Nevertheless, there are variations that women should watch out for. Be alert for the "time-share" opportunity. A time-share works like this: you pay a certain amount for the right to use the condo or apartment for a week or so at the same time each year. The sales pitch will put forward the enticing possibility of trading your time-share rights with other time-share owners around the world. Your week at Tahoe for their week in Portofino.

Don't count on it. Although not illegal, these arrangements have a lousy track record if recovering your investment is a consideration. They most certainly are *not* what you invest in for income or growth. If you just love Tahoe in October, why not rent a condo or hotel unit every year, rather than locking up your money in something you may find very difficult to unload? Although not necessarily a scam per se, intense sales pitches target retirees with offers (complete with prizes, trips, and the like) for these and other realty ventures.

> **Be very wary of any realty scheme that comes to you over the phone or by mail — especially if it offers prizes or free trips. If you are looking for a second home, see an established real estate agent. Don't fall for the come-on. Their act is very good. Good enough to grieve thousands of unhappy investors every year.**

The 900-Number String-Along

You know that 800 (area code) phone numbers are free to you when you call. You probably also know that 900 numbers are just the reverse. You pay the phone charge, *plus* a fee levied by the business on the other end. Often the fee can be quite steep, although abuses running phone bills into the thousands have caused the regulators to step in. Still, if you can keep your phone lines ringing, and keep callers talking for ten minutes at $2 per minute, this effectively translates to $120 per hour — not bad for a no-skill, low-overhead operation. So when you get that postcard in the mail telling you you've won something wonderful — watch out! If all you need do is call the 900 number, be careful.

Here's a diabolical twist: Some shady folks, aware that some of us are getting smarter about 900 numbers, hook us into their schemes with an 800 number! After we call, we are instructed to dial another number — this time, the costly 900 one.

Perhaps you consider yourself especially skeptical. When you call, you'll know a scam when you hear it. And sure enough, the phone answerer tells you that your airfare is free, but the hotel will cost you $300 per day. All this takes a long time to explain. When you refuse the gimmick, they've already won. You weren't expected to go for the obvious boondoggle. But they kept you on the line long enough to cost you $20, and that was the real object.

A recent favorite is the letter advising lucky you that you may be a lost heir — a fortune awaits you if you're the remote kin of a dead millionaire. A variation on this notifies you that you may have unclaimed property held by the state. A 900-number phone call will open the door to these riches — for the con artists, not you.

Maybe you're too smart to fall for free giveaways. But you *are* interested in stretching your dollars — who isn't? If the investment or job opportunity comes your way with a 900 number, don't call. Legitimate investment houses offer 800 numbers, and real job opportunities will list an ordinary area code.

The 900 number is a tip-off — the business is in the business of making money on your call. Don't make their day.

The Telemarketer's Song

Bunko squads all over the country are bemoaning the burgeoning phone frauds. These are different from the 900-number schemes, in that they don't make their money off your phone call. They call you out of the blue (or because you filled out a come-on with your phone number) and try to sell you investments, or get your credit card or ATM number out of you. Telemarketing fraud accounts for $10 billion in losses annually — and 30 percent of the victims are over sixty-five.

When you get such a call, pause for a minute if you find yourself tempted. Imagine someone you respect: Eleanor Roosevelt, for example, or Mother Teresa. Imagine her receiving the phone call. Would she fall for it? Neither should you. Better you should miss one or two "golden" opportunities in your lifetime than lose what you have and feel like a chump.

The Almost-Free Vacation Racket

The irresistible travel deal targets retirees because they travel. Widows, all the better. As above, they may use a 900 number, an immediate tip-off. But even an 800 number can conceal an operation that just wants your credit card number. These scams often offer a travel package that is virtually worthless. The victims seldom complain, first because they are embarrassed, and second because their losses are in the hundreds of dollars rather than the thousands, so they'd rather bear them than admit being a sucker.

But small amounts per victim add up to real crime. One travel telemarketer prosecuted by the FTC grossed over $4 million in one year. Here's how that outfit worked its scam: The victim received a postcard announcing a guaranteed prize of a car, cash, or a vacation in the sun. When the victim called, of course, she learned she had won the vacation. But there was a $350 fee plus $100 tax and an attractive bonus for paying with a credit card. *Of course* they wouldn't debit her account until she had time to think it over — they requested her card number just for "verification." The debit was made immediately, and the sucker was stalled for sixty days (flights filled, canceled, and so on), the amount of time allowed by the bank to clear erroneous charges from the credit card statement.

Sometimes, in a variation on the theme, the sucker actually gets the half-price flight to Hawaii, but discovers the $1,500 hotel package sells for $299 every day. The profit goes to the operator.

Watch out, too, for the "frequent flyer" who will sell you his free-flight coupon to Europe at one-quarter the commercial fare because he can't use it. It is probably a phony, but even if it's real, airlines reserve the right to dishonor these coupons if they're not used by the frequent flyer or her official designee. You must call the airline and inquire about their rules before you fall for this one.

The Tourist Traps

The world is our oyster. We are healthier than men of the same age, so we have the opportunity to travel. Mature women crowd the tourist spots around the globe. And along the way we are targets of every fleecing scheme you can imagine. Some are just retailers, selling overpriced junk. Others we're steered to by our friendly "guides" who take a nice commission from everything we buy. Our purses are snatched and our pockets are picked so smoothly that we don't know it for hours. We pay for lunch by credit card — our bill is increased before we hit the border. We're distracted at the airport when someone jostles us, or squirts mustard on our clothes — their partner grabs our suitcase. The nice man on the cruise just wants our money.

Of course, we'll still travel. For many of us, it is the reward for our life's work well done. The easiest way to avoid problems is to keep as little of value with you as you can. Leave all jewelry at home. Carry no more cash than you can afford to lose. Keep copies of your passport and airline tickets separate from your purse. Leave personal photos and all credit cards at home except one major credit card that you intend to use.

Have you heard of Elderhostel? It is a reasonably priced way to see the world in the company of forty or fifty others like you (you or your spouse must be at least sixty). You stay on college campuses, take a course or two, go on field trips. Elderhostel operates in more than forty countries around the world. There is safety in numbers. The program is reputable, affordable, and well managed. If you are timid about venturing out on your own, try Elderhostel. You can reach it at P.O. Box 1959, Wakefield, Massachusetts 01880-5959.

The Mortgage Switch

These days mortgages are bought and sold with ease. Over the course of your mortgage, you may have made your payments to two or three different banks. Lately, some scammers have successfully conned homeowners into sending their mortgage payments to them by posing as the new mortgage servicer.

If the switch is legitimate, your old bank and your new one will each send a statement announcing the change. Check your account numbers, balances, and all other particulars. Then phone each bank to make sure the move is on the up-and-up.

The Lottery Ticket Racket

You're making it, but just. How you'd love to take that cruise to the South Pacific you've always dreamed about. But that's a fantasy — isn't it? When you're approached by a young woman with her tale of woe, you begin to taste the salt water and smell the plumeria. She shows you her winning lottery ticket — $10,000 — but alas, she's an illegal immigrant and can't cash it or she'll get deported. She'll sell it to you cheap. Please give her $1,000 cash. What a good idea! Believe it or not, this — as well as other lottery variations — works.

> ***Don't*, under any circumstances, give any money to strangers. Period.**

Lonely Hearts Chisel

You've heard about lonely hearts scams all your life. But the gentle, kind, thoughtful gentleman who just joined your church — the lonely widower still in mourning — is so remote from the sleazeball gigolo you've always imagined that his eventual treachery is beyond your ability to anticipate. Of course, he counts on that. If he came on to you wearing gold chains, blond toupee, and tattoos — ostentatiously picking up everyone's tab at the club — you wouldn't be interested, and he knows it. To attract a woman of means, he must fit in absolutely. It won't be long before he, somehow, is into your pocketbook, either through marriage or promise of it, or through some other scam — sob story or can't-miss investment. You may think you're an unlikely target, because your assets are modest. You're far from the rich widow of lonely hearts mythology. Don't count on it. A quick $5,000 from four or five widows a year may be all he needs to supplement his Social Security. Not all con men think big.

> ***Don't sign anything he gives you, and don't turn over your money.* Let a year — or better, two — pass while your friendship develops. If he's genuine, he'll stick around. The con man will show his hand by his immediate need. He won't be able to wait a year, much less two. The six-week whirlwind romance should put you**

on red alert, especially if it starts where widows are likely to be found: church, cruises, country clubs, and senior centers.

The Pigeon Drop

You are watching your grandchild play in the park. Two sweet-faced older women approach excitedly. They have found a bag on a park bench — it contain tens of thousands of dollars — a drug deal gone sour, no doubt. There are variations on the theme, but sooner or later you will be asked to put up some money to show "good faith," after which they will share the loot with you. Sure they will.

Ask yourself why these people want to share their good fortune with you. There is no good reason. The key to this game is the ability of the hucksters to create an emotional atmosphere that sucks you in. *You* become one of the finders — you're all in this together. *Of course* you want to show these new friends — these nice, nice people — that you are as trustworthy as they. We women are suckers for the pigeon drop. We want so much to be liked and trusted. And for this we pay dearly.

The Home Invasion Flimflam

One way or another, a couple of folks get into your home at your invitation. They tell you they're telephone or utility workers, city inspectors, or plainclothes cops. One distracts you, the other searches your home for valuables — they'll be stolen now or later.

A variation is the home-repair scam. Someone shows up who was "working in the neighborhood" and has material left over to do your roof, re-side your house, spray your trees —

it doesn't matter what. Either you will be asked for a down payment — you'll never see the guy again — or you'll pay a fair price for a job so poor it amounts to fraud.

Sometimes the Better Business Bureau has a lead on these guys, but usually they aren't around long enough to build a record. Don't do business this way. Call a licensed tradesperson or contractor.

The Lost Pet Con

With a broken heart, you advertise your lost cat. You get a few calls, you describe your cat, nothing pans out. Then someone calls who describes your kitty perfectly (of course, they had called earlier and gotten the description out of you then). You're horrified to learn that the caller knows who has your cat, and that she is being tortured by a satanic cult that means to sacrifice her horribly at the next full moon. The caller can get her back for you, but it will cost you — a lot — because of "complications." You send the money by Western Union and never see it or your cat again.

There is a cruel variation. Your animal is stolen by someone, who then "finds" it after a reward is offered.

Keep an eye on your pets. We women are amazingly attached to our pets, and everyone knows it. Some of those someones are mean people.

The Dance-Lesson Fast One

The dance-lesson or dance-club caper is an old one. Variations today include fitness and diet centers. You sign up at an "introductory" price. The introduction, however, is to as fine an array of "extras" as you can be milked for: life memberships, special deals, videos, audiotapes, food, vitamins, or diet supplements, and so on. Some of these outfits walk right on the line, others cross over to actionable fraud.

Check with the Better Business Bureau before you sign up. Unfortunately, the BBB is not as reliable as many think. It is made up of members of the business community it is supposed to watch over — a built-in conflict of interest that many local BBBs seem unable to surmount. Nevertheless, your phone call is free. If you are really suspicious, call your local district attorney's or state attorney general's consumer fraud unit.

Call the Cops

Bunko squads at police departments report that scams and swindles are vastly underreported. The victims either never realize they were taken, are too embarrassed to report it, or too afraid of reprisals. Of course, it is embarrassing to be a sucker. But to sit back and let it happen to someone else is worse. Your local district attorney is a good place to start — most have a fraud department. For any mail solicitation, call the postal inspectors. They are active and effective law enforcement officers. Your state's attorney general prosecutes consumer fraud and would be interested as well.

Flimflam artists are on the increase, police report, especially targeting the elderly, who are increasing in number and affluence. Since the majority of people over sixty are women, scams and swindles are a women's issue of first import. Put scams on the agenda at your next club meeting. Have someone from the bunko squad talk to you. Read up. Share stories. Get smart. If your local police department does not target this type of crime, put pressure on. New York City cops work with the Department of Aging to provide social services to victims and organize prevention programs. Get your senior center excited about it. Perhaps your local community college could sponsor seminars. Economic crimes against older women are rising steeply, and you can be part of the solution.

CHECK YOUR VULNERABILITY TO SCAMS AND SWINDLES

1. Are you afraid to break the chain in a chain letter?
2. Do you readily give your credit card number over the phone?
3. Do you pull the carbons from credit card receipts at the store?
4. Have you bought a product in a pyramidlike scheme?
5. Would you pay $100 for an insider's tip to the stock market?
6. Would you let strangers into your home if they have a good story?
7. Are you desperate for credit?
8. Are you looking at every angle to keep your head above water?
9. Have you ever made an investment you didn't fully understand?
10. Have you checked out advisers with their licensing bureau?
11. Do you do financial business with sole practitioners?
12. Do you trust people when they identify themselves?
13. Do you give to charities at your door?
14. Do you respond to personals advertisements?
15. Have you loaned money to recent acquaintances "on faith"?
16. Are you anxious to remarry?
17. Do you find lotteries and sweepstakes irresistible?
18. Do you ever respond to obvious come-ons "just to see"?
19. Are you always on the lookout for the oddball travel deal?

Epilogue
Staying in Control

We Americans make a big deal out of independence, individuality, and freedom. We cherish privacy, respect distinctiveness, honor uniqueness — and prize *self*.

And one word covers all of these: control. Control of self, control of opportunities, control of choice.

As women, we're acquainted with control. We're familiar with all three of its functions. We have

- exercised it
- delegated it
- abdicated it

We've *exercised* it in raising our children, conducting our households, doing our jobs. We've *delegated* it to those we supervise, our children's teachers, the babysitter. And, much too often, we've *abdicated* control — to the banker, the lawyer, the doctor, the landlord, the accountant, and the financial adviser, and to husbands and even friends.

We get into trouble when we confuse abdication with delegation. Consulting with professionals, friends, relatives, and experts is *not* abdication — indeed, it is a useful means of exercising control. But the relinquishment of our choices to others is debilitating, and debilitation strikes at the heart of what this book is about.

In these last pages, we'll slay the procrastination dragon. What follows is a summary of tasks to get you started as the power-person in your life. We round up some of the resources in earlier chapters and present them here without the intervening text, to simplify your job in getting a hold on your financial life.

Do each task listed, and check them off as you do them. The 800 numbers are toll-free; those beginning with 202 are in Washington, D.C.; 212 is New York City.

- Write this number in your phone file: **(800) 555-1212**. This is the 800 information operator and will plug you into any financial institution in the country.
- Call the Mutual Fund Education Alliance (sponsored by the no-load mutual fund companies) for their educational materials: **(816) 471-1454** (Kansas City).
- Locate all your life insurance policies. Line them up. Are they whole life, or term? Annuities? Are they worth the premiums?
- Phone **(908) 439-2200** (A. M. Best; they charge a small fee); **(212) 553-0377** (Moody's); and **(212) 208-1527** (Standard & Poor's) to get their ratings on each insurer.
- Subtract your age from 104. Many experts recommend you commit that percentage of your investments to equities. How does your portfolio stack up?
- Find the current inflation rate (call your reference librarian or look in the financial pages of your newspaper). List it here: _____ .
- Line up all your credit cards, including those for stores and gas. Get rid of all but one VISA and one MasterCard. Keep the ones with the lowest interest and the lowest annual fees. If your credit line is more than $5,000 on each card, consider writing the bank and declining the surplus.

- Write for the free *Consumer Information Catalog*: **Consumer Information Center — Dept. 92, Pueblo, Colorado 81009**. This lists scads of free or low-cost government pamphlets.
- Find the credit-reporting agencies in your yellow pages. Call and ask each one for your report — but ask first what the fee (if any) will be.
- Call the National Committee to Preserve Social Security and Medicare for a list of their informative materials: **(202) 822-9459**.
- Write this all-purpose Social Security and Medicare toll-free phone number in your file: **(800) 772-1213**. If you are not yet drawing benefits, call and ask for a Personal Employment and Benefits Statement.
- Call the Pension Rights Center for a list of its helpful publications: **(202) 296-3776**.
- Write the American Association of Retired Persons (AARP) for information on its Medicare/Medicaid Assistance Program if you are over sixty-five: **(202) 434-2277**.
- Like to travel with like-minded folks on a budget? Write Elderhostel: **P.O. Box 1959, Wakefield, Massachusetts 01880-5959**.
- Look at your monthly mortgage statement. How much of your payment is going to principal? Can you afford to add to that in order to pay off earlier?
- Write these numbers for the IRS in your phone file: **(800) TAX-1040** (for questions); **(800) TAX-FORM** (for forms). If you are self-employed or employed with no pension, call the forms number and ask for forms to set up a SEP-IRA.
- If you own, or hope to own, your own business, call **(800) 827-5722** for the Small Business Administration's list of publications.
- Pull out your and your husband's wills and/or trusts. Is everything still as you want it?
- If household financial records are kept in a computer, make a printout and file a new one monthly.

- If you are widowed, call the AARP's Widowed Persons Service for information: **(202) 434-2277**.
- Call NOLO Press for a list of their splendid do-it-yourself law books: **(800) 992-NOLO**.
- Determine the type of ownership for each account you cosign. Tenants-in-common? Or joint tenancy? Ask the bank, see the deed.
- Calculate your net worth — add your assets, including the equity in your house, and subtract from them your debts, including your mortgage. If your net worth approaches $600,000 (in early 1993), make an appointment with a probate lawyer to discuss estate tax planning.
- Call three nursing homes in your area and ask what the basic monthly charges are. Use this information in planning/insuring for long-term care.
- Do you like your attorney? If not, use the test in Chapter 5 to find one you can work with.
- If you are near or over sixty-five, order medigap policies A through J from five health insurers in the yellow pages. Compare the prices and services offered — the benefits will be the same.
- Pull out all your health policies — group, individual, Medicare, medigap, indemnity, and long-term care — and compare them benefit for benefit. Are you paying for overlapping coverage? Are there gaps?
- Call the Older Women's League (OWL) for a list of its publications and membership information: **(202) 783-6686**.
- Call the National Council of Senior Citizens for membership and publication information: **(202) 347-8800**. Ask about its Nursing-Home Information Service.
- Call Choice In Dying for information on medical directives (right-to-die or death-with-dignity instruments) for your state, including the proper forms: **(212) 366-5540**.

Information is always the doorway to control — and when you've completed this task list, you'll have at your fingertips some of the top information available, mostly low cost or free. Don't let it pile up when it comes — *read every word*. Be diligent in making further inquiries where appropriate. Consider this: College tuition today can cost several hundred dollars per credit — or nearly $70,000 for four years. Information is very expensive. Take full advantage of the low-cost education available to you through these recommended materials. You'll find others in time — check out their reputation, then *use them*. They are dollars in the bank.

Set up a two-hour time block once a week to go over material, adjust your portfolio, compare your returns. Consider this time period as close to inviolate as you can make it. Don't make appointments that conflict with your "control time," say, every Monday morning from ten o'clock until noon. Within a few months, you'll begin to feel very comfortable with your collection of investments and you'll surprise yourself by having fun.

So there you have it: your financial declaration of independence. By understanding the basics that drive the financial world, and understanding how you fit into those basics, you will control your own life. The wise judgments you've always made through the years will broaden to include new horizons — and those new horizons you'll call your own.

You are a new breed of woman — the first to define maturity for the twenty-first century.

Go for it.

Resources

American Association of Retired Persons
601 E Street NW
Washington, D.C. 20049
(202) 434-2277

Choice In Dying
200 Varick Street
New York, NY 10014
(212) 366-5540

Consumer Information Catalog
Consumer Information Center
Dept. 92
Pueblo, CO 81009

Displaced Homemakers Network
1625 K Street NW, Suite 300
Washington, D.C. 20006

Elderhostel
P.O. Box 1959
Wakefield, MA 01880

Gray Panthers
2025 Pennsylvania Avenue NW, Suite 821
Washington, D.C. 20006
(202) 466-3132

Internal Revenue Service (IRS)
(800) TAX-1040 (for questions)
(800) TAX-FORM (for forms)

Mutual Fund Education Alliance
1900 Erie Street, Suite 120
Kansas City, MO 64116
(816) 471-1454

National Academy of Elder Law Attorneys, Inc.
655 North Alvernon Way, Suite 108
Tucson, AZ 85711

National Committee to Preserve Social Security and Medicare
2000 K Street NW, Suite 800
Washington, D.C. 20006
(202) 822-9459

National Council of Senior Citizens
1331 F Street NW
Washington, D.C. 20004
(202) 347-8800

National Employment Lawyers Association
535 Pacific Avenue
San Francisco, CA 94133

National Organization for Women (NOW)
1000 16th Street, NW #700
Washington, D.C. 20036
(202) 331-0066

NOLO Press
950 Parker Street
Berkeley, CA 94710
(800) 992-NOLO

Older Women's League (OWL)
666 11th Street NW #700
Washington, D.C. 20001
(202) 783-6686

Pension Rights Center
918 16th Street NW, Suite 704
Washington, D.C. 20006
(202) 296-3776

Small Business Administration
1825 Connecticut Avenue NW
Washington, D.C. 20009
(800) 827-5722

Social Security
(800) 772-1213

U.S. Department of Labor
Office of Pension and Welfare Benefit Programs
200 Constitution Avenue NW
Washington, D.C. 20210

Widowed Persons Service
c/o AARP
601 E Street NW
Washington, D.C. 20049
(202) 434-2277

Index